Sea Dog

A.M. PETERSON

The Adventures of Yacht Boy

"Sea Dog" The Adventures of Yacht Boy - Book 2
By Anne Marie Peterson
Copyright ©2022 Anne Marie Peterson.
All Rights Reserved.

All rights reserved. No part of this publication may be reproduced, distributed, or transmitted in any form or by any means, including photocopying, recording, or other electronic or mechanical methods, without the prior written permission of the publisher, except in the case of brief quotations embodied in critical reviews and certain other noncommercial uses permitted by copyright law.

ISBN: 978-1-956986-03-7 (paperback)
ISBN: 978-1-956986-04-4 (hardback)
ISBN: 978-1-956986-05-1 (eBook)

Any references to historical events, real people, or real places are used fictitiously. Names, characters, and places are products of the author's imagination and/or created to ensure privacy for the individuals who are used as examples.

Book design created by Anne Marie Peterson
Cover artwork and illustrations by Jon Tocchini
Editing by Liza Gershman of Gershman Creative Agency
Interior Design, Hardback Cover and Prepress by Kailash Black
Printed and distributed by Amazon, in the United States of America.
First paperback, hardback, and eBook editions released on 2/8/2023.

Publisher Contact Info:
Young Navigator Books LLC
For permission requests, write to the publisher via email:
Attention: Permissions Relationships Manager
Email: publisher@youngnavigatorbooks.com
www.YoungNavigatorBooks.com

Fiction
DRA Guided Reading Level: 40-70
Scholastic Guided Reading Level: M-Z
Lexile®Levels: 740-1070L
Word Count: 74,000
Grade: 8-12 (ages 12-18)

Contents

To my dear and loving Irish Mother...

You have always been
an incredible source of encouragement
and could replace an army of cheerleaders.

You stewarded and resourced me in many ways for which I am always grateful.
You always showed loving support and attention while I was exploring my creativity.

XOX

Author's Note

My mother came to America in 1959, straight from the middle of Ireland, at a time when women did not elect to "go it alone." Many who know and love her would agree with me that she is a very strong-minded and interesting character worthy of multiple biographies, but she would not like this idea. She loves to communicate ideas with people, and she does this through simple conversations full of smiles and laughter, informal speaking, and writing.

My mom grew up without television and read books. To this very day, she keeps reading material handy in every room of her house, handbag, and car. Her ability to converse with anyone is surreal. She is a master conversationalist, with a tremendous sense of humor and loads of charm. My mom is not afraid to talk to anyone, as she has a genuine love of people and connects to them through both her words and the energies behind the words she chooses. She could, as they say, "charm the birds out of the bushes."

My mom raised five children and read bedtime stories to all of us, every night. Our father did, too, but this dedication is to my mom and what she brought into our lives. She would sing, invent animations for the characters in both songs and books, and bring all our favorite stories alive.

She could tell us stories from memory, invite us into the stories to tell parts of the story, and got us reading independently before we entered kindergarten.

Books became a currency of magic and escapism in our house. This was especially true because she got rid of two televisions when she saw we were becoming hypnotized by them in our early childhood.

The more you are exposed to the writings of others, the more you develop a collection of systems and structures for communicating your ideas to specific audiences, a.k.a. your readers. Yes, your readers, because you are a writer, a communicator of ideas, even if you are not published anywhere (yet), because you write in text, emails, homework assignments and even proposals, presentations and more when in discussion of ideas with others.

My dear reader, I invite you to consider every opportunity you have to read, whether it is the nutrition info on a label, an article in a magazine, a blog online, newspaper or book, and ask yourself, "what did the author share with me?" And consider it from many perspectives:

- Did I have physical experiences reading? –did I freeze, cringe, scowl, hold my breath or laugh?

- What did my mind think about what the author shared? –was it illogical? –did it make sense? –am I still thinking about their ideas in the book hours and days after reading it?

- What emotions did I experience? –did I feel moved to tears or anger? –did I perceive someone lacked integrity and feel righteous anger bubble up inside me? –did I have compassion or empathy for a victim?

- How did the author's message affect me spiritually? –do I want to be a better person? –is there something in me that could support the person with the conflict in the story? –do I feel separate from some quality I admire in others? –did I go into judgment of a character because of their lack of integrity, courage, or stupidity?

Beloved readers, I encourage you to read something every day. Everything you read is valuable. Your wonderous brain will pick up information --even about the type of font used, the spacing, the font size, and even the use of color selected to capture your attention. Your brain will begin to notice how to write with a minimum of words to communicate with efficiency. Then one day, when you must write something, whether it is an essay for a homework assignment, to create a party invitation or a letter of appeal to a group of people in your community, you will consciously choose a font typeface that matches your communication, a font color and size and all of it will come from some part of you that connects with "how to design your communication" because you will have a hidden database inside you.

Take time to notice what you read, where you read it, and how you receive the author's words. Read out loud to hear the author's words. Is there a rhythm? Ernest Hemmingway reportedly wrote his words to the flow of Bach's music. How do the words of the author resonate with you or your environment when you read them out loud? What feeling do you attribute to the words? –silly, serious, important, or simple rhetoric? (Rhetoric is a good word to look up, by the way.)

My mom always asked my dad (he was our resident word expert in our home because he studied Latin and Greek) or opened a dictionary to look up a word she didn't know. She continued to grow her vocabulary, and at this writing she is eighty-nine years old, and continues her love of reading words to connect with the consciousness (thoughts) of authors. I hope my mother's love of knowledge and other people's perspectives will tell you how interesting this world is and can be explored through books.

Did you ever fully appreciate that when you write something, whether it is in a greeting or thank you card, an article for a blog, school magazine or newspaper --and maybe a few of you have published your first book ... that you are sharing your consciousness with others? It's true! Your thoughts and emotions (consciousness) go into the world and others connect with it when you present your words for others to read. And they add to it, just like you add your consciousness to this book and all its ideas.

Your true nature is and always will be Love. The next time you sit down and write something, I invite you to write from your true nature of love (and with non-judgment for what you write, or for the reader of your words), as you consider what you have created with words from your consciousness. I think you will be pleasantly surprised with your outcomes!

Smooth sailing always,

Anne Marie Peterson

Los Angeles, CA USA

November 12, 2022

Quotes

"Now then, Pooh," said Christopher Robin, "where's your boat?"

"I ought to say," explained Pooh as they walked down to the shore of the island, "that it isn't just an ordinary sort of boat. Sometimes it's a Boat, and sometimes it's more of an Accident. It all depends."

"Depends on what?"

"On whether I'm on the top of it or underneath it."

— A.A. Milne, Winnie-the-Pooh

IRISH PROVERB

There are good ships
and wood ships,
ships that sail the sea,
but the best ships
are friendships,
may they always be.

Chapter 1
Say Cheese

English Harbour
Antigua, West Indies
Caribbean Sea

Aboard the 66m Motor Yacht *Arabella*, Captain Gunnar Johnson stood before his entire crew on the main deck at 0700 just days into the new year. The captain held a clipboard under his arm and a cup of steaming hot coffee in his right hand. The bright Antiguan sun was climbing steadily in the sky and tropical temperatures were climbing. Sitting on the loungers, many of the crew held coffee mugs or glasses of fruit smoothies and listened attentively to their leader.

Adrian Abercrombie, the young teenage son of the yacht owners, sat cross-legged on the vast white sun lounger, surrounded by a sea of pale blue uniform t-shirts imprinted with the name *M/Y Arabella* on their upper left chest. His serious hazel eyes focused with intent on the captain.

"Today we are going to head south to Guadeloupe, a French Overseas Department island. We will berth in the superyacht marina in Grande-Terre. By my estimation, if we leave at 1000 hours, we will cover the roughly forty-seven nautical miles in about four hours and arrive around 1400 hours.

"Who here speaks fluent French besides our French-born sous-chef Jean-Marie?"

Roberto, Raffa and Francesco, the three Italian crew members all raised their hands and said in chorus, *"Moi, capitaine!"*

"Of course, you do," the captain smiled as the laughter died down. "I forgot that you three spent considerable time in Nice and Cannes before joining our yacht. Good."

The captain looked directly at Adrian when he spoke his next words. "When we arrive in Guadeloupe, we are technically arriving in the country of France. The people on this Caribbean island are French citizens and predominantly speak French. It is advisable to have one of our French speakers with you and your family at all times. I know your father speaks some French but confesses to being rusty since he doesn't use it. Therefore, we are going to temporarily assign our four French experts to you and your family while in port."

Raffa twisted around to wink at Adrian, *"Je ne comprends pas toujours les femmes...*so perhaps you need Jean-Marie more than me, no?"

Seeing the confused look on Adrian's face, Francesco gave his cousin a slight push of reprimand that knocked Raffa off the sofa to the teak decking while laughing aloud. "Adrian, he is saying he doesn't always understand women and no truer words were spoken!"

The crew was grinning from ear to ear, but Adrian wasn't fully getting the joke. "Okay," he drawled with enough tone in his response to imply knowledge of the inside joke, but inside he wondered if Raffa was insinuating something he wasn't picking up on. He would have to ask Jimmy, his Jamaican steward and Chief Officer of the yacht, later. Raffa was a deckhand who occasionally would transition to being a steward when there were guests on board. He and his two cousins performed a variety of maintenance duties daily to keep the superyacht in top-top condition .

"*Aucun problème, Capitaine!* No problem. I will assist my good friend Adrian here with all the things these island girls want to share with him. I will help him successfully make new friends." Jean-Marie reached around Gabriella to pat him on the shoulder. "I will look out for him. We don't want our beloved Raffa getting Adrian hit on the head with a purse or anything else."

Now Adrian was grinning openly, "*Merci,* Jean-Marie! I appreciate you looking out for my best interests." He high-fived her behind Gabriella's back. *Now I get it*, feeling a tad sheepish.

Continuing with a list of minor repairs, engine and water systems checks the captain continued the meeting taking input from his crew and Chief Engineer Pete Robinson, whose t-shirt stretched across his arms and chest revealing the body of a super middle-weight wrestler. He always stood at ease with his hands clasped behind his back, typically to the right of the captain, whenever space allowed. His broad face sported a heavy sprinkling of brown freckles, and his auburn hair glinted red in direct sun. Although he cracked lots of jokes and smiled frequently, his eyes were always dead serious. Adrian liked him, but also found him a bit hard to figure out. Pete was the master at deadpan humor, and it could be confusing. The only thing he got loud and clear was that when Pete spoke in a soft tone of voice, he meant business.

"Captain, both MTU engines are operating smoothly since haul out. The oil is clean and we're burning at predicted rates. Now that the shakedown cruise has proven that we're functional in the water on all mechanical levels, I do want to work out a new schedule for short- and long-term maintenance and upload it to the computer so we can all work off the same program management software."

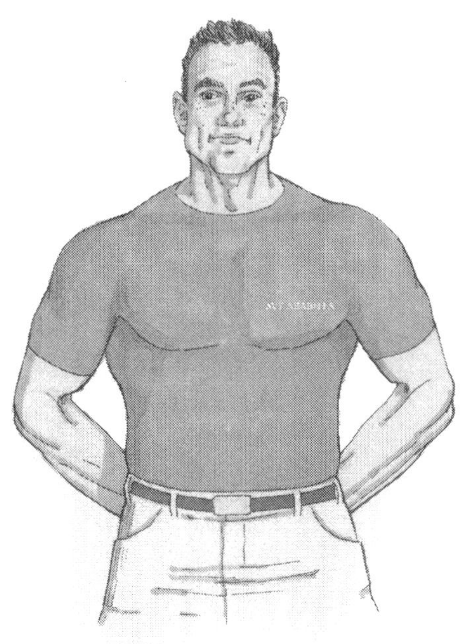

"Thanks, Pete, I'd appreciate that." The captain wrote a few notes on his clipboard and tucked it back under his arm. Reaching beside him to the nearby table, he picked up his coffee mug and took a sip. "Anyone else?"

"*Oui,*" Chef Zak announced in French, then continued, "I know you and I spoke about this trip to Guadeloupe, Captain, but I want to let everyone know that it was me that requested we stop in at the island." All faces turned to Zak. Adrian was surprised by this, as he thought his parents had requested the stop on the itinerary.

"Guadeloupe has some important culinary items that I wish to procure for our journey. This island grows coffee, cocoa, medicinal plants and vanilla beans, among other things like cheese. I want my young galley apprentice, Adrian, to see firsthand a high-altitude coffee plantation." He smiled in Adrian's direction. "Wait until you see where we're going. It's quite the adventure. I hope you have the, uh," he coughed suggestively before adding, "intestinal fortitude, for the journey up the mountain."

"Sounds awesome!" Adrian responded with excitement. "I can't wait!"

"OK, if there is nothing else…" the captain looked around at his crew as many stood up to disappear below decks, "back to our usual programming."

"Captain?" Adrian queried, as he leapt to his feet and took two steps to stand before the commander of the superyacht, "do you need anything from yacht services office before we go? I'm expecting an overnight package and heading over there now."

"Yes. You can drop off some letters for me. Follow me and I'll get them now for you." The captain turned and strode towards the port staircase to head up two flights to his cabin on the bridge deck of the yacht with Adrian on his heels. The captain was a tall and very fit man in his early forties and Adrian was impressed that he always took the steps two at a time and never got winded. He often wondered when the captain had time to work out to stay in shape as he never saw him in the gym or on deck exercising, like he did the crew. *For an old guy*, Adrian smiled in admiration, *he sure can move!*

Half an hour later, Adrian slipped his boat shoes on his bare feet after walking down the passerelle from the back of the yacht to the quay. No shoes were allowed on the boat to protect the smooth teak decks and also for health reasons. He loved being barefoot and loved this aspect of cruising.

Walking through English Harbour for what might be the last time, he waved to some of the vendors he had met during his stay. Everyone was so friendly, and he enjoyed their accented voices as they called out to him when he passed.

Once out of sight of the harbor, he glanced through the captain's mail with some curiosity. His strong slanted cursive handwriting in blue on the crisp white envelope made him smile. His own handwriting was messy and he knew he needed to keep practicing because the last time he wrote a postcard to his friends Brody and Braden, his hand ached and he didn't write that much.

One of the letters was addressed to a Mr. and Mrs. H. Wright on the island of St. Lucia south of their present location. *Maybe he's letting them know we are coming their way,* Adrian mused. The envelope was pretty thick. *Maybe he had a lot of catching up to do with them. I'm pretty sure the captain's hand must've hurt from all that writing!*

Within a few minutes, he reached yacht services where crew and owners could receive mail and packages or messages. After dropping the captain's mail in the outgoing mailbox, he waited for the woman behind the desk to look for his package. When she returned, he was surprised by the size of the box that was addressed to him from his uncle back in the States. After signing for the box, she looked at him then the box and said, "Hold on a moment and I'll help you with the door." Coming around the counter, she walked before him and held the glass door open so he could slide through. Laughing a throaty laugh because it looked like a box with skinny legs, she asked him, "ya got that now?"

"Yeah," he laughed because he could not see over the top of the box, "I think so. Bye, and thanks!"

During his walk back to the yacht, he shifted the box different ways so he could see around it and, at one time, even tried walking with it on his head. He was tempted to open it and ditch the packaging, but he would do that once he knew he didn't have to return it.

At the quay, he set the box down on the concrete walkway parallel to the stern of the Arabella and studied the box. It was covered in neon red fragile stickers. Wiping sweat from his brow, he reached into his back pocket and pulled a pocket knife out and flicked the utility blade open.

"Whoa! Hold up!"

Adrian looked up to see his sister Grace with her cellphone out, skipping lightly down the passerelle. "Uncle Mike wants me to film your face when you open the box. I thought I missed you and was freaking out!"

"Oh," Adrian smiled. "Good thing you found me in time. Ready?"

Grace aimed the camera at him, and he held up the large blade menacingly next to his face. "Behold!" he cried with deep drama before plunging the knife into the side edge of the boxtop to slice open the tape binding. When the tape was cut and the lids opened, he straightened up and looked at the camera with a look of repugnance. "Seriously, Uncle Mike?!" With a deep sigh, he folded his knife and said, "I'll be right back."

Grace paused to consider what was inside the box and laughed. "Of course, he over-packed it with Styrofoam peanuts! That is sooo Uncle Mike!"

A couple minutes later, Adrian was back with a kitchen garbage bag in hand, waving it in the breeze to open it fully. Grace resumed filming while Adrian pulled handfuls of packing material out of the box and nearly filled the bag. Soon his hands encountered a box covered in shrink wrap, which he pulled out and gasped with huge delight.

"Oh my gosh, Uncle Mike this is incredible! Thank you! I can't wait to play with it." Adrian gushed and enthused before the camera which caught his reaction to receiving a remote-controlled sailboat.

Diving back into the box, he came up with another big squeal of excitement and declared, "Grace, there's two of them. We can race together! Oh, my gosh, I can't believe it! This is so amazing!" Turning full on to the camera he exclaimed, "Best gift ever, Uncle Mike! I love them!"

He continued to fill the sack with peanuts and then tied it off when it was bursting at the seams. He didn't want them blowing about the harbor or getting into the water. He removed all the additional wrapping from the smaller boxes that held the boats and controllers and sliced the shipping box further, to collapse it all for proper disposal.

"Hey, Grace, can you take these up to the lounge outside our cabins? I want to dispose of the trash." He waited while she moved the first one onto the boat and looked at the image and notes on the side of the box. It was an incredible toy. He passed the box to Grace for her second trip up the passerelle and bent to pick up the cardboard and garbage bag.

After recycling the cardboard in the appropriate dumpster for the yachts to use, he went to the giftshop and stuck his head in the door.

"Morning," the woman greeted him.

"Hi, I was wondering if you could use a bag of clean packing peanuts for shipping merchandise. I just received a gift, and the box was full of them." He smiled and held up the bag, "I would love to see someone recycle them."

"Mmm," she nodded, walking towards him with a hand outstretched, "Yes. I can use those. Thank you, young man."

Adrian shrugged. "You're welcome. I'm glad you can use them." He passed her the bag and turned to leave her store. As he pushed open the door, he looked back and said, "Bye! Have a nice day!"

He ran the short distance to the yacht and, hopping on one foot, ripped off a deck shoe and then the other. He dropped his shoes at the top of the passerelle on the main deck since the boat was close to leaving and raced towards the TV lounge on the starboard side past the main lounge.

Grace was on her knees holding a bright red hull of a racing sailboat the length of her arm in her hand. She held it up to pass it to her brother, "The other color is royal blue. What do you think they are made of? They don't feel like plastic."

Adrian scanned the packaging information. He'd never seen anything like this before. "Ah! Here it is...they're carbon fiber. No wonder they are so lightweight." He hefted the hull in the palm of his hand as if it was light as a feather. He rolled it over in his hand, exposing a slot. "Where is the keel and ballast? It should have come with one."

Pushing aside plastic wrappers and paper wrapping that protected the parts during shipping, she found a torpedo-shaped weight to attach to a long dagger-shaped blade about the length of a ruler that formed the keel. "Here."

Together they assembled the two boats on the rug outside their cabins forward of the main deck. A slight elevation in the rumble coming from the engine room below their deck alerted Adrian to the time and he jumped to his feet. "Oh, shoot! I lost track of time. I need my headset and radio. The captain should be moving us out any minute. I'll be right back."

Racing into his cabin a few feet away, he opened a drawer and took out his earbud and clipped his walkie-talkie to his belt on the back of his cotton cargo shorts. Tuning into the ongoing conversations of the crew and captain, he walked out of his cabin and headed for the stern of the yacht to assist with leaving the quay. He waited for a break in the talking before announcing his presence on the line. "Adrian here; on standby. I'm on the stern with Raffa and Francesco. Over."

Jimmy, the Chief Officer, answered him. "Prepare to deflate the fenders when we clear the other yachts and bring them aboard."

"Roger that. Wilco." Adrian replied, knowing he had to be as brief as possible when using the radio. Turning to leave the guys who were working to free the stern lines from the quay where the yacht was backed up against the concrete seawall, he made his way forward along the port side deck towards the bow.

Enormous inflatable fenders, almost as tall as him, hung over the sides of the yacht to act as bumpers between the neighboring yacht tied up beside them. All the yachts that were stern tied to the quay had ground lines off the bow to anchors down in the waters of the harbor. Prior to coming into the harbor after the new year celebration in Dickerson Bay, Adrian had helped fill the fenders with a small portable air compressor and move them into position.

Although Adrian knew he didn't have to work aboard the superyacht because his parents owned it, he loved joining the crew to work different deckhand jobs. Technically, he was supposed to be traveling the world for one year while being homeschooled by his parents, but he was starting to realize that perhaps being an active member of the crew was where he was getting his education.

With great care not to rush the process of leaving the quay to prevent injury or damage to the superyacht, the captain inched all two-hundred and sixteen feet forward with all-hands on deck participating in the activity. Adrian monitored the port side, poised and alert to report potential problems. On the magnificent yacht next to him, a cautious deckhand stood on the starboard deck doing the same. They exchanged a curt but friendly nod to each other as the two yachts moved nicely past each other. Adrian watched as the stationary yacht's deckhand got farther and farther away.

The moment the stern of the *M/Y Arabella* cleared the bow of the neighboring yacht, he knew it was safe to untie the fender's yacht braid from the bulwark cleat and haul it up over the railing.

With nimble fingers, he unscrewed the air valve cap in the neck of the air bladder and gave a quarter turn to the plastic valve that prevented the air from escaping and deflated the entire fender. Grabbing the bottom end, he rolled it up like a sleeping bag to push out the air and prepare it for storage. Then he walked aft to the next fender and repeated the process. Raffa was working from the stern towards him. Together they picked up an armload of deflated fenders and moved them to storage.

"Grazie mille," Raffa said in appreciation before he pressed his radio button and reported portside fenders and stern lines stowed.

More excited about his radio-controlled sailboat than being a deckhand at the moment, he reported to the captain and crew over his personal radio, "Adrian here; on standby. I'll be building a radio-controlled sailboat outside my cabin."

"Roger dat." Adrian smiled, hearing the Jamaican accent over the earbuds. Jimmy had been by his side from the moment he stepped into the parking lot of the marina where they boarded their yacht in Ft. Lauderdale for the first time back in November. The first officer had acted as his steward, which was most unusual, but since Jimmy appeared to be tasked with his education, he appeared to be more of a mentor, and he helped him navigate his resistance to embracing a life at sea.

He recalled how Jimmy had been quick to change his perceptions of his parents and show him opportunities and potentials aboard the yacht for expressing his intelligence, innate skills, and abilities. He sensed Jimmy had been creating more openings for his curiosity to be engaged than he could point to, which kept him busy. *I have nothing but respect for that guy,* he mused, as he slid to his knees like a base runner onto the soft carpet where parts and pieces of his radio-controlled sailboats lay scattered with instruction manuals and wrappers; *I just wish all my teachers at school were as cool as him.*

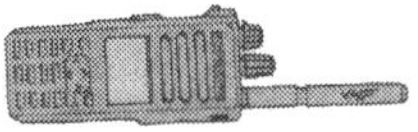

French Overseas Department of Guadeloupe
Leeward Islands
Caribbean Sea

As the butterfly-shaped island came into breathtaking view, the captain called Adrian over the crew walkie-talkies. "Adrian, report to the bridge please."

"Roger, Captain. One minute, please." Adrian finished gathering all the garbage from his project and stuffed it into a plastic bag to discard. He moved the two racing boats into his cabin and laid them on his bed. He placed the radio controllers in a drawer along with the instruction manuals and other product info he didn't have time to read.

Leaving his cabin behind, he raced up the nearby staircase two flights to the navigation deck. He announced his presence a few yards before he entered the high-tech bridge that controlled the superyacht by calling out in a sing-song voice, "You rang, Capitan?"

Without turning, the captain pointed out deep emerald-green islands of Guadeloupe off the port bow. From his vantage point, tens of feet up over the sea, Adrian had the perfect view. He reached for the high-powered binoculars to scan the island. He aimed them at the coastline and then aimed at the top of the highest peak. Finding a spot of contrast between white clouds and ridgeline, he touched the sensitive controls for adjusting the lenses to his eyes.

In the first weeks aboard the yacht, Jimmy had shown him how to use marine binoculars, which were waterproof but individual focus rather than center focus, which are a more common type of binoculars with a central adjuster between the two lenses. Every time he went to use the binoculars, he had to focus them for his eyes. But once focused, Adrian could look out to middle and far distances and see everything he looked at with focus and clarity. He especially loved these lenses since they picked up objects at sea in low-light situations. One thing he didn't like was that near objects tended to get out of focus, and they weren't ideal when he had his sunglasses on. Best of all, he had the widest field of view at sea with individual focus, which he appreciated the most after comparing the two types.

Jimmy had explained that all waterproof binoculars have dry nitrogen gas in them at a pressure higher than normal atmospheric pressure and it keeps moisture out of the binocular body. He explained that nitrogen gas cannot hold moisture, which meant that the marine environment could not get inside the binoculars. Adrian thought that was pretty cool technology.

He moved the lenses to focus on the shoreline and took in the compass reading superimposed over the image in his eyes: southeast. He ignored the built-in infrared laser readings for distance, height, angles, and speed since they were moving, and they were a distraction. Adrian had trained his brain to ignore these while looking through the lenses except when it mattered, like in an emergency situation.

Sticking his head back inside the bridge for a brief moment, he asked, "Hey, Captain, you got a second?"

"Sure. What is it?" Captain Gunnar turned from the wheel to look at Adrian, who stood outside on the deck with his head just inside the door with the binoculars in his right hand.

"Well, Jimmy once told me that anything over seven times magnification causes seasickness. Any idea why that is?"

"I suppose it has to do with magnification. Not just objects get magnified; motion does, too." He stroked his goatee with his right hand. "The real answer might be between your ears. Your brain might have a conflict with the movement signals your eyes are feeding them when your inner ear and position-sensing nerves aren't detecting movement."

"Oh! That makes so much sense to me!" Adrian exclaimed. "My mom cannot watch me play video games as it makes her nauseous. Yet, she never gets seasick. I bet her eyes and ears are disagreeing!"

"Could very well be." Gunnar turned back to his instrument panel when a slight beep went off and he began talking to the crew while Adrian returned to taking in the island. When land he had never seen before was to come into sight, he asked that the captain notify him so he could take it in from a distance. There was something he liked about seeing the approach to land from out at sea.

Because he had looked it up on the internet earlier in the day, Adrian knew that Guadeloupe's highest peak was 1,467 meters or 4,813 feet high and all of it was on the western side of the island. He thought the name of the volcano, *La Grande Soufrière* or big sulfur outlet, was kind of a funny name, but it sure sounded deluxe in French but very common in English.

His gaze found the top of the crater. *It looks like the typical conical volcano, the sides are steep, and the peak is pointy just like how I imagined it. I wonder when it last went off...?*

He continued to scan the hills and coastline, noting the red rooftops and clusters of buildings that denoted villages that were spread along the beaches and narrowed as they gained elevation and filled the canyons like ribbons a few hundred feet above sea level. Beyond that, the hillsides looked too steep for buildings.

Raising the binoculars, he saw dense tropical forest growing along the sides of the volcano. *I think I am looking at a nature reserve.*

"Adrian," the captain's voice came in over his earpiece, "we're approaching Jacques Cousteau's underwater bio reserve. Do you know who I am referring to?"

"I think he's a famous marine biologist from France. I saw some documentaries in school that showed him diving on shipwrecks. Where do I look?" Adrian released the walkie-talkie button and refocused his binoculars on the beach and sea on the western side of the mountain.

"Between those small island rocks and the beach. That entire area is a reserve. It's a dive site with corals, sea turtles and fish." A hint of laughter entered the captain's speech, "I would also expect there are some interesting objects, like shipwrecks to dive on. I heard a rumor that there is a statue of him underwater...somewhere around here. We can look it up if you like."

"Huh." Adrian said thoughtfully. "Are we going to have a chance to explore his reserve? It sounds interesting. I'd like to see that, if possible."

The Arabella began to head east around the southernmost point of Basse-Terre, which was the western half of the two large islands that formed a butterfly shape in the Lesser Antilles. From what Adrian could see, Basse-Terre was more populated along the west and south coasts than the north. The area began to become more industrial, harbors appeared, and the shipping traffic increased significantly. He moved the binoculars upward just as the engines began to reduce speed for entering the bay. His heart skipped a beat when he noticed a thin, dark stripe on the green mountain with a white line coming down it far in the distance.

"Captain!" he shouted through the bridge door, "I think I see a waterfall!"

Captain Gunnar grinned, "Back in 1493 Christopher Columbus may have seen the exact same thing."

"What do you mean?"

"Well, his ship's log reports that he saw a waterfall from the ship, and it caused him to make a decision to anchor and go ashore to find fresh water to stock up." The captain turned his eyes back on his instruments and signaled for Adrian to come inside.

Adrian placed the binoculars back on the rack where they belonged when not in use. "You need me?"

"If you like. One moment," he made a quick reach for the ship's radio when he heard customs and immigration call twice for *Motor Yacht Arabella*. The captain quickly discussed the email reservation he had made to berth the superyacht at a marina based in Grande Terre, the largest island of the Guadeloupe Islands and confirmed with the port authority assorted details pertaining to size, draft, and utility needs. The moment he put down the phone, he called the crew on the walkie-talkie and brought everyone up to speed and assigned roles.

"Adrian, would you like to work the stern lines with Francesco and Roberto? I think you've seen it enough, yes?" The captain raised his right eyebrow a fraction and Adrian nodded.

"On it, Captain!" He turned to walk at a fast clip down the passageway from the bridge to the staircase and took the steps three at a time. Down on the main deck he walked aft and lightly skipped down the final steps to the stern platform everyone called the beach deck. He found Francesco waiting for him with a pile of neatly flaked lines at his bare feet that would flow free when the mooring line was pulled ashore without tangling or getting caught on anything.

"*Ciao, Adriano, come stai?*" His lean, angular olive-skinned face topped with black curls smiled in a friendly fashion as he handed Adrian a coiled line with a weighted ball, sometimes called a monkey's fist, at the end.

"*Ciao*, Francesco, I'm good, *grazie*. But I've already forgotten how to say that in *Italiano*!" Adrian grinned at his admission of forgetting his basic Italian greetings. "Is it *sto bene*?"

"*Si!* You do remember! Now, let's see if you remember how to throw a heaving line. Show me how." He stood back and let Adrian untie the coil of soft three-strand twisted polypropylene. The small diameter rope had a weighted three-inch rubber ball dangling at one end. The other end, or the bitter-end, was whipped in a waxed thread and the fibers melted into a solid flat plane of hard plastic by a hot knife.

Francesco had already tucked the robust mooring line through the stainless-steel eyes built into the bulwark and pulled several yards across the top of the railing. With the bitter end in his right hand, he tied a clove hitch to a bent loop of fat mooring line that would hold the stern of the yacht to the berth they would soon occupy. Whoever caught the heaving line on shore would drag all of it to themselves and eventually pull the 48mm thick line to the shore to be wrapped around a bollard and returned to the yacht for securing.

Next, Adrian placed the end of the line with the ball on the end in his right hand and created his first loop. He stretched out the line to make sure it was not kinked anywhere and with his left hand gently rolled the line across this palm so that it did not twist into a figure eight. His next loop he placed close to the first one in parallel without crossing it over the previous one. One after the other, with care not to kink or twist the line he coiled until he reached the end of the standing part where it was tied to the mooring line. Looking up he caught Francesco's watchful eye. The deckhand nodded but didn't say anything or move.

Shifting several loops to his left hand and careful not to cross any of the parallel lines, he kept the majority in his right hand. The weighted ball was hanging just below the first loop and would not get entangled in the coils. He felt confident that his practice throws on the quay in Antigua over the last week made him an accurate heaving line thrower. Pretty confident that he was good to go, he asked, *"va bene?"*

"You're good!" Francesco pushed a button on his walkie-talkie clipped to his right hip on his white uniform braided belt. *"OK, capitano, Adriano lui e pronto.* We are ready!" He repeated for Adrian, *"Siamo pronti!"*

Roberto showed up with an armful of stainless-steel stanchions that would be inserted into the passerelle, which would form the handrail, when the yacht was secured. He laid them down with care, so they did not clank, get scratched or injure the teak deck. Then he joined Adrian and picked up the port heaving line he had prepared earlier.

While Francesco called his perceptions of the lineup of the yacht to the dock adding in decreasing distances and suggested speeds to the bridge over the walkie-talkie, the captain, with extreme care, backed the two-hundred-and-sixteen-foot yacht into the berth inch-by-inch. The two men standing on the dock beckoned to Adrian and Roberto to throw over their heaving lines.

Adrian nodded and took a steadying breath and spread his feet shoulder's width apart, with his right foot slightly behind him. He took three practice swings to find his throwing rhythm and when it felt right he released the coil of rope in the man's direction, letting the weighted ball fly out over the water and it sailed over the shoulder of his target. His left hand he had kept flat open to allow the balance of the line to fly free on its own accord and the line was caught with ease by the fellow on shore. Roberto and his counterpart on shore had success, too.

"Perfetto!" Adrian cheered for himself and the men who were pulling the heavier mooring lines to shore now that he had pulled in all the heaving line and was wrapping the stern line in figure eights around a substantial shiny stainless-steel bollard. Francesco reported the port and starboard mooring lines were ashore and to pause the engines.

Francesco and Adrian, with the stern lines tied off ashore, wrapped their end of the mooring lines around a winch and began pulling the stern closer to the dock. Some adjustments were called for as the starboard line needed more slack, so the stern was more parallel to the dock.

Next, to prevent the stern from moving side to side, springlines were rigged as diagonal lines that crisscrossed across from the port- and starboard-stern quarters to bollards on the dock.

Over the walkie-talkie, Adrian heard Pete, the chief engineer, call to the captain that both engines and steering columns were both off; bow thrusters were off; and stabilizers off. The captain acknowledged that with a simple "Roger."

Roberto had resumed extending the long teak and stainless-steel passerelle gangplank that would make disembarking easy for passengers and crew. The hydraulics moved the telescoping planks out from the stern deck and moved them towards shore. Francesco began adding the stanchions with rope handrail on both sides of the planks and called over the radio a fresh progress report.

The whole operation took less than twelve minutes. Francesco called over to Roberto to get the shore power plugs attached as he moved to hook up freshwater hoses. The finishing touch was a custom carpet with the name Arabella on it for people to step out of their shoes before stepping aboard.

Chef Zak was the first to appear with Jean-Marie, each with two garbage bags in hand. The garbage from the galley was disposed of ashore every chance they got to move it out of cold storage.

"Good job on the heaving lines, Adrian," Zak praised him. "You got a good throwing arm."

"*Oui!*" Jean-Marie beamed at him, "*Bien fait!* Well, done, team!"

Adrian grinned at the praise. "I was nervous that the line wouldn't make it to the shore and that it would land short in the water."

"But it didn't!" Francesco clapped him on the shoulder. "When I take holiday, you are my replacement."

"I'm up for that." Adrian said with confidence. "I have watched you guys do this enough times, I think I could get the hang of it."

"*Naturellement!*" Jean-Marie gushed and tousled his short brown hair as she walked towards the galley. "Our Adrian is a natural!" As she walked away she waved to everyone behind her and said, "*À bientôt!*"

"See you soon," Zak agreed. He stretched his arms up high over his head and let out a groan. "Whoa! I feel out of shape. I need to get out and walk more." Turning to Adrian he asked, "Are you ready to explore the local area of *Pointe-à-Pitre*? Part of provisioning this yacht is about shopping for the finest ingredients. If you want to join me at some local markets, I'm going to pick up farmer's market items, wine and cheeses. And I promise you, it won't be boring!"

"OK," Adrian agreed as he and the deck crew and chef looked up at Gabrielle clipping the yellow Q flag to the halyard hanging from the varnished mast mounted above the main deck. Until the captain and port authority cleared the vessel and all listed passengers and crew, everyone had to stay on board. Together they walked inside the yacht via the main deck, "I'll meet you here after we clear quarantine status with the port."

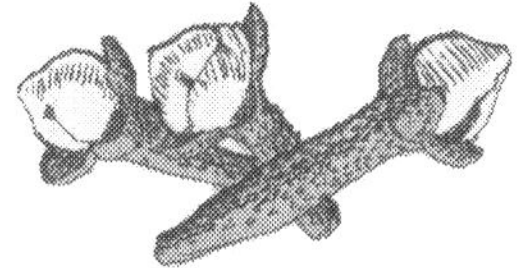

Pointe-à-Pitre
Grande Terre Island
French Overseas Department of Guadeloupe

The city's sights and smells somewhat reminded Adrian of St. John's in Antigua, but there was something rather different about Pointe-à-Pitre. He paused to tilt his head and listen while his eyes scanned the street busy with people and cars. It was drumming. Straightening up he turned to Zak and asked, "Is that drumming I hear?"

"Yes. Locals often gather around a favorite neighborhood spot and play their drums together and hang out." He smiled as he asked, "Think you could jump into the circle of drums and dance to that?"

Adrian pulled back in horror and shook his head to say no. His eyes said it all, but he added for dramatic emphasis, "Are you kidding me?!"

Chuckling he said, "Come on. We have some major shopping to do."

Walking alongside Adrian in the open-air market, he pointed out the various specialties of the island. They walked past dark-skinned local women in colorful head scarves sitting astride crates and stools with tables and boxes of fruits, vegetables, herbs, and spices. They chatted in what sounded to Adrian like Creole. Zak stopped to inquire about the spices a woman had in clear plastic bags on her table. She opened the bag in question and offered it to Zak to smell.

"Adrian!" His face showed every earmark of pleasure as he handed the bag to his young apprentice. "Smell!" He commanded.

Adrian saw hundreds of short stubby little brown sticks half an inch long topped by four spikes and a tiny spherical lollipop not bigger than a small bead. He put his nose to the bag and took a deep breath. The heady smell went up his nostrils and he recoiled in sensory shock. "Hey! I know this smell! Wait..." he held up a finger and dove back into the smell this time with questions and associations in his mind. "It smells like Christmas. And gingerbread. And apple pie." He looked with curiosity at Zak. "It's not cinnamon. I know it's not ginger..."

"Cloves. It's a dried flower bud" Zak supplied. "Crush one between your fingers and taste it."

Picking one out, Adrian could feel the energy of the tree in his finger and thumb. The sample looked like a small medieval torch. He used his opposite hand to crush the round ball since the stem was too hard. He took a small whiff of the powder on his fingers then put it in his mouth. Instantly, a stinging, burning and oddly numbing sensation hit him. "Uhh..."

Zak and the lady roared laughing at Adrian's mixture of surprise and awe at the potency of one fresh clove. "I'll take the bag." Zak said to her, "And some fresh nutmeg with the mace, and cinnamon bark."

The lady picked up the nutmeg which still had the red lacy outer covering known to the culinary world as mace. Ground up, it was used in pumpkin pie and other dishes. The curly bark of the cinnamon tree was a soft reddish brown and bundled neatly in plastic to protect it from moisture, like all the other spices.

"My mouth is feeling kind of numb. Is that normal?" Adrian asked.

"Don't worry. It'll go away soon. Or your brain will stop noticing it in eleven minutes."

"Why eleven minutes?" Adrian asked with much curiosity.

"I read somewhere that our brains will pay attention to something like a bad odor or odd sensation in the body for eleven minutes on average and then it will automatically tune it out if it is not life threatening."

"Interesting." Adrian opened his backpack to place the spice purchase inside. "But why is it numbing my tongue?"

"Eugenol." Zak shared. "It's used in medicine as an anesthetic among other things. Sometimes it is mixed with other herbs or spices to make a pain salve or to improve circulatory response in the muscles, like to warm them up. Athletes use it. It's even in some toothpaste for people with sensitive gums or teeth."

"How come you know so much about the medicinal uses?" Adrian asked him with genuine interest.

"Once upon a time, I took a medicine class in herbs and spices to get certified." Zak shrugged as if it was no big deal, "It seemed to me a natural fit with my culinary classes. Food is medicine to me. And by medicine, I mean energy medicine. Didn't you notice the energy of the cloves immediately?" Adrian nodded in agreement. "There's some very potent energy stored in such a tiny dried up flower bud, which is why we only need a tiny amount when we use it. A flavor like clove would dominate one's cooking, it is so full of..." Zak made a fist and punched the air.

"I get it." Adrian said. "What else is on the list?"

"Merci beaucoup, madame," Zak thanked the seller and moved to the next stall. "Check this out, Adrian! These are vanilla beans also known as the Spice Queen."

Adrian looked down at the table where Zak pointed. Funky dark brown beans about six to eight inches long were bundled and tied together with the kind of colorful ribbon used on helium balloons. Their leathery skins had long brown and black striations from stem to tip. In fascination, he picked up a bundle and smelled it. As expected, the tantalizing fragrance he had known since childhood entered his olfactory system and he grinned from ear to ear with pleasure. "Wow. That really is amazing. How does vanilla extract get made from these?"

"Well, I'll take about twenty of these beans and cut them open lengthwise and put them in a large jar and pour about two or three cups of vodka over them and let them sit for about two months. You do have to shake the bottle once a week to stimulate the release of the vanilla molecule from the bean into the alcohol, which preserves it. I keep it in the pantry in the galley away from light. Look for it next time you are in the galley."

"That's it?" Adrian asked in surprise. "Wow, I can make my own vanilla extract! Who knew?" He straightened up and decided to tease his chef a bit. "OK, dude, what is the molecule in vanilla that creates its value?

"Vanillin." Zak didn't skip a beat. "You testin' me?"

Adrian laughed, "Yep! So, is all vanilla the same?"

"Good question and no, there are probably a good dozen or so types of beans from different tropical regions in the world. I've used Madagascar, Mexican, Tahitian, Indonesian, and Bourbon."

"Which ones are these? Are they grown here in Guadeloupe?"

"The bean that is native to this island is called banana vanilla or Vanilla Pompona but sadly it is disappearing since it is not commercially cultivated. It's difficult to find. Hang on." Zak got the attention of the vanilla vendor and he asked in halting French if he sold banana vanilla. The man shook his head no but pointed to a woman a few tables over and suggested they ask her.

Before moving on Zak passed a rust colored eight-pointed star shaped dried flower pod to Adrian. "Star anise." A faint smell of licorice and vanilla wafted up through his nose and he smiled.

"I like it. What do you use this in?"

"Chinese five spice, for one, but also I add it to curries and desserts. It has a very distinctive smell and taste, so I use it lightly."

Approaching the vendor that was pointed out to them they learned that she had some of the rare banana vanilla, which Zak bought with great joy. "Adrian, this is like the find of the century for me! This stuff is so hard to come by."

"What will you use it for? And does it taste like bananas?" he asked the chef while smelling it. There was zero hint of banana entering his awareness.

"No, but that would make for an interesting vanilla flavor, wouldn't it?" Zak said with appreciation. "It's the shape of the bean and how it grows. I will use this in fruit salad dressing, perhaps custards or macaroons. Now this may sound strange, but it can be used when slow roasting meats.

"Just like wine or chocolate," Zak continued while shoving his fingernail into one of the short stubby beans, "Vanilla has notes. Smell it again. What are the notes of this bean?"

Adrian inhaled deeply of the rare beans in his hand. *What the heck is that?* He tried again and then shrugged his shoulders in defeat. "I get a hint of licorice and maybe something buttery and flowers, but I can't place the other smell. I don't know what that could be."

"It could be a tobacco leaf smell. Ever smelled a cigar before it was lit?"

"No, and why would you think I would have smelled one before?" Adrian was a bit shocked that Zak would think he would know that info at his age. "I don't smoke and don't plan to."

Zak laughed. "I was thinking of your dad and your uncles that you've been around that perhaps enjoy a cigar every once in a while."

"Oh. I wouldn't have, because I'm not interested, but now you have me curious." He blushed, "Not that I want to smoke or any-thing, just to know another note, you know."

"Of course!" Zak smiled, "Hey, buddy, I'm not here to give you grief or suggest you smoke cigars, just learn the smell when you get a chance because it shows up in lots of things as a smokey hint."

"Give me an idea of where it shows up," Adrian invited. "BBQ?"

"Not like that kind of smoke, which is mostly from mesquite or hickory wood. This is a more subtle flavor that you might notice in chocolate, a cup of coffee, tea...depending on the leaf," he paused while he searched his memory, "sometimes prunes can have that distinct flavor."

Zak paid for the banana vanilla, and they headed off once more. The drumming sound was much closer, and the crowds were increasing. A lively hustle and bustle surrounded them as they wove in and around people, outdoor dining areas and cars. Stepping on and off high curbs that channeled large volumes of rainwater towards the sea, they made their way to the drummers.

Men of all ages sat around in a casual circle beating a vari-ety of drums. Some pounded out complementary rhythms with their eyes closed, others were keeping time with each other and keeping eye contact as they moved to the beat. Young children were dancing and moving to the rhythm all around. No one was standing still. Everybody in sight was moving to the not-so-subtle command of the drums and the sound woke up something festive even inside himself. I can't believe I'm swaying to this music. His head started jutting forward in time to the beat and Zak clapped him on the back. "I knew you wouldn't be able to resist!"

Adrian laughed a bit sheepishly. "It is kind of irresistible. Is there a special occasion today?"

"Probably not. I always see a group playing somewhere in the market. It's all a part of their history. Everything you see comes from the time of slavery. The drums, the clothing...see all the gold jewelry?"

"Yeah. What does that mean?"

"Their ancestors had both English and French slave masters and they saw the wealthy plantation women, in particular, wearing gold jewelry to express their wealth. Slaves were not allowed to have any wealth so they would be kept powerless. When they were finally liberated, one of the things the people did was wear a symbol of their freedom, which was gold jewelry."

"What about the drums? How were those symbols of slavery?"

"Drums are a call to war in most cultures. Humans can be aroused by drums into different states of being. Soldiers march with courage and strength from the beat. Dancers sway to sooth and tell stories, people can be summoned by a commanding sound of urgency, and more. The slave owners knew that if the people had drums they would be more powerful, so they were forbidden. Again, once they were free, they could drum like their ancestors, mostly from Africa, where they were stolen from." He paused while they looked at the variety of drums the men held between their knees or sat on top of with the face of the drum just in front of their legs.

The cacophony of sound was mesmerizing, and it seemed like a random, improvised percussion, but the more Adrian trained his ear to listen the more he found a central theme that the men played.

A friendly English-speaking male tourist turned around to talk with them. "They're quite something aren't they?"

"Yeah, they sure are!" Adrian said in a raised voice.

"I just learned from this guy on my right that it's called *Gwo ka*. It's their folk music and the drums are also Gwo ka drums."

"Oh, good to know." Zak replied in a friendly fashion. "Did he share anything else?"

"He said there are seven different rhythms, the big drum

makes the foundation sound, and the small drum interacts with the audience, like those kids over there."

"Do you know if this is the same music they play during Carnival?"

"Yes, it is, according to that guy." The tourist's wife dragged him away and they waved goodbye.

"Well, that is interesting." Adrian mused. "I never did get past a few months of piano lessons, so I don't know much about music. This is very hypnotic music, though."

"Come on, let's go." Zak broke the spell of the drums by pushing him through the throng of bright shirts, yards of traditional plaid ruffled blouses, dress skirts, and headscarves back into the markets. "We're on a mission. We have some shopping to do, and I must get back to the galley."

At a liquor store, Zak bought a vast selection of French wines and paid to have them delivered to the yacht. There were over a dozen cases of wine, many of which would be used in the galley for cooking, poaching, flambéing and more. The rest were for the guests.

Next they entered a small cheese market that Zak knew from experience. Adrian had never seen such an incredible array of cheese in all his life. "Holy Sheep's Milk, Chef, this is incredible!" He walked in and turned a slow circle taking it all in. The clerk smiled a big happy smile, *"Bienvenue! Bonne après-midi."*

"Good afternoon," the guys replied in English. The store clerk switched to English for them.

"May I help you find something?" he asked in a lilting Guadeloupe accent that was both French and Creole and Caribbean all at once. Adrian couldn't help but smile. He loved hearing how people spoke in the different islands. "My name is *Louis.*" He pronounced it Louie.

"Thanks, Louis, I am provisioning a yacht. Here is my list." Zak handed him a paper he had printed earlier in the day on ship stationery with his contact info and stuffed into his leather planner that he carried in his backpack.

"Let me help you with most of these, Chef Zak. I will get boxes and a cart." He offered, "Please, look around while I help you."

"Merci," said Chef, and bought two very large boxes of assorted cheeses. "This store is fantastic. The French make some of the most incredible cheese on the planet. I encourage you to start a

notebook in the galley and track what you like, the smells, flavors and more. It is easy to have a love affair with cheese."

"It's addictive, you know."

"No, I didn't know, but I would have guessed." Zak responded. "How is it addictive?"

"Caseomorphins in the milk work on opioid receptors in our brains. I did a science fair experiment in seventh grade on it."

"Really!" Zak looked interested, "Go on."

"Well," he began with confidence in his subject, "Most of the casein, which is the protein in cow's milk, turns into a morphine-like opioid protein fragment or by-product in our intestines because we don't digest them as humans. That fragment attaches to morphine receptors and can either make us sedated, sleepy, feel good, etcetera. The problem is that it is addictive. And you know what else?"

"I'll bite." Zak said with good humor. "What?"

Adrian grinned, "Pizza is the most addictive food on the planet according to my assessment of my school who took the survey. Do you know why?"

"The cheese is made from milk?"

"Well, there's that. But the crust is made with wheat flour which has gluten in it which turns into gluteomorphins in our guts and that is also an opiate-like molecule. It's double-trouble!"

"Ahh!" Zak nodded with appreciation for the lesson. "So, pizza has to be the world's most addictive food?"

Laughing, Adrian shared, "Well, that's what I thought. I made a radical conclusion and an assumption about that, which my science teacher didn't share, and I got downgraded. He also thought I should have been disqualified for providing samples to the judges of the best pizza in town. He called it a form of bribery."

"Clever."

"I thought so. I ended up getting a special mention by the judges." He grinned as he recalled his success. "As it turns out, the vast majority of kids in my school admitted to loving pizza and it's their first choice of food. And a part of me wished I never researched it at all because I learned that the foods we are most addicted to are the ones that are often hurting our bodies the most."

"How do they hurt the body? You just told me they make you feel good."

"Oh, because both milk and wheat cause inflammation in many people's gut. They just don't feel any pain when they are eating it because the proteins are producing morphine like by-products making them feel happy in the moment."

"So, let me get this straight: pizza is off the menu on the yacht." Zak said somberly, then added, "And mac-n-cheese, bagels and cream cheese, and..."

"No!" Adrian laughed but his face registered a slight touch of alarm. "I didn't say that!"

"Gotcha!" Zak laughed hard that he was able to fake out his young shipmate. He punched Adrian's upper arm with affection. "Dude, it was the perfect set-up."

"Argh, I should have known..." Adrian shook his head with a tight smirk on his lips. "Just for that, you have to make pizza twice this week." Zak just grinned in response and went back to perusing the fromage.

They wandered down the store reading labels of cheeses and noticing the different milks used in the cheese-making process. Everything from cow, buffalo, sheep, and goat to nut milks like almond and cashew for the vegan or dairy intolerant market. Adrian spotted cheese that had herbs, spices, dried fruits, nuts and even smoke added to it.

Louis approached them with two cheeses sliced on a small plate. "Here is your chance to be a cheesemonger."

"A what?" Adrian asked, not sure he heard the words correctly.

"A cheesemonger," Zak repeated with a wink to Louis, "it means a professional cheese taster who gets paid to eat cheese."

"*Oui s'il vous plait.*" Adrian reached for the slice of the first cheese. His mom had been making him say a few phrases in French for days, helping him be a polite visitor in Guadeloupe and this was a perfect moment to say yes, please.

He saw Zak smell it and look at the color and feel the texture. He noticed the strong odor, dry texture and how it didn't leave his fingers messy, the light-yellow color inside the gold and white rind, and the rather salty and nutty flavor.

"Hmmm," Zak savored the sample before guessing, "*Vieux Comté*?"

"Correct. Now try this one, which is much older." Louis extended the plate with the other sample.

Zak and Adrian looked at each other and Adrian cracked a smile first. In a strained voice he commented, "It's, uh, rather strong." Backing away from the plate to make a personal statement about that sample, he shared, "No offense, but that is not for me."

The men laughed and agreed that it was strong, but it was a delicacy that can trace its history back to the middle ages.

"Yeah, well, they should have left that cheese back in medieval times. It smells and tastes like it's been aging too long in my opinion."

"I'll take the first one. Thank you." Zak continued bending over the case of cheese next to him and exploring the labels and details of the different round, square and triangular shapes.

After Zak paid the bill and Louis agreed to deliver it to the superyacht harbor dock, they all shook hands and wished each other end of the day greetings.

"*Bonsoir*," Zak and Adrian said in unison, as the sun was just about set over the western sky behind the volcano.

"*Bon Voyage*," Louis said as he wished them a good trip and held the shop door for them to pass through. "*À bientôt!*"

"Yes, we will see you again!"

Adrian entered his cabin and threw his empty backpack on the floor next to his desk. Zak had taken all the spices and assorted things he bought in town back to the galley leaving his pack smelling like apple pie and vanilla ice cream. He freshened up in the head with a quick shower to get the sweat and grime of the day off his body. The tropical heat made itself known to every one of his senses, just by stepping off the air-conditioned yacht. In a fresh pair of shorts and a shirt, he picked up the manual to the radio-controlled sailboat and headed to his parent's private deck above the main deck for happy hour.

Happy hour was a fun family event and most often occurred around the dining table on the private owner's deck outside his parent's cabin. The crew had a well-stocked bar of fruit juices, sodas, and sparkling waters for the underage drinkers, namely himself and his older sister Grace. They loved to come up with unusual drinks and invent new soda flavors with the help of Jean-Marie the sous-chef and Roberto the deckhand who was a formally trained mixologist from Italy and occasionally stepped up to the bar when there was a party or a happy hour in need of a bartender. The rest of the bar was for the parents and special guests.

Tonight was special, and the captain joined his parents, Zak and Jean-Marie for a wine and cheese tasting before dinner.

"Hello, Adrian, I heard you had quite the experience in town today," the captain greeted him. He was holding a wine glass and talking with his dad while standing next to the dining table that was laid with multiple plates of cheese, crackers, smoked delicacies from the sea, *pâté*, and fruit. In baskets were slices of baguettes and crackers to accompany the cheese. He saw dried figs and apricots tucked around the cheese platters with assorted cheese knives.

"It was amazing, Captain! You wouldn't believe all the cheese we found in one store!" Adrian enthused as he reached for a slice of bread and glided a small, rounded knife through a soft triangle of brie. "I am now considering being a cheesemonger."

"A what?" Grace asked with disbelief before stuffing a hunk of orange cheese into her mouth.

"A professional cheese taster!" Adrian knew he would get a warning glance from his mom for talking with his mouth full, so he briefly covered his mouth while he answered. "Isn't that the most perfect career? Getting paid to eat cheese all day?"

"If you want to be a curd nerd, be my guest, but it's not for me," Grace declined as she tucked her hair behind her ear and leaned across the table to reach for more cheese, "I'm pretty sure my face would break out if that was my line of work."

Adrian kept his mouth shut rather than instigate something on the heels of that comment. His sister was concerned about three things in life, from his perspective: Her skin, getting a driver's license, which was ridiculous while out at sea, and getting a boyfriend. *Be nice,* he reminded himself, then took a breath and let go of the judgment that his sister was self-absorbed. He was shocked to learn of late that she wanted to be a marine biologist, but it made sense since the last couple of months at sea had opened his family's eyes to life underwater in big ways and to the impact humans and industry have on the oceans.

"How did building the sailboats go this morning?" The captain looked at both teenagers and raised an eyebrow. "Are you close to taking them to the water?"

"Well, I thought we would learn how to use them in the swimming pool first, you know, before we take them to open water." Adrian looked at his sister and shared, "Grace was a big help in reading the instructions, sorting the parts, and tracking where we were at with both models. We got them built in record time, I think."

"Thanks, Yacht Boy, that means a lot." She smiled in his direction, "You're not so bad yourself."

Grinning, Adrian turned to his dad and asked, "Did you and mom ever have a nickname for Grace that I don't know about? It only seems fair that she gets called something, too."

"No, not that I recall," his dad returned with a negative shake of his head. "I think Gracie is the most that we changed her name to."

"Give it time," the captain encouraged, "Her nickname will reveal itself in good time when we least expect it."

His mom, who had been talking with Jean-Marie and Zak wandered over and turned around to beckon to the chefs. "Come. Please share with them what you just told me. It's fascinating!"

Zak came around the side of the captain where he could address everyone. "I was just telling Mrs. Abercrombie that there are almost four-hundred known types of cheese in France and because of assorted animal and nut milks, there are over a thousand varieties."

"No, no," his mom interrupted him with a laugh and a dismissive wave of her hand. "Tell them the part about the ancient history of cheese making."

"Ah." Zak bowed his head while gathering his thoughts then smiled. "Well…

"No one really knows when cheese was first discovered or how long humans have been making cheese. It is presumed to be a food we have been consuming for over eight thousand years. We know this because they have hieroglyphics in Egypt that sequentially show animals being milked, the milk being placed into animal skins and bladders, and people riding on animals with the skins full of milk. There are suggestive images showing what happened to that same milk. Historians speculate that the milk turned into cheese from bacteria or yeast, heat, and due to constant disturbances of the skins from the motion of travel and people loading and unloading…voila! Cheese!

"It makes sense that curdling would occur," he concluded and glanced at his audience in rapt attention before continuing. "What I am most curious about is what went on with the monks in monasteries in France."

"Ah, yes." His dad interrupted to share, "I once knew a professor of chemistry who swore to me that monks would bathe their feet before collecting a certain bacteria called B. Linens from between their toes to add to raw milk to make cheese." His dad laughed with the other adults who knew which cheese he was probably referring to.

"I suppose it is possible," Zak concurred, "however, nowadays, they buy their *Brevibacterium linens* that creates the unique properties in the cheese." He grinned at Mr. Abercrombie, "Stinky feet, stinky cheese."

"Which one is the stinky feet cheese? Because I am not going to eat that one!" Grace looked horrified.

"Limburger!" All the adults answered at once and laughed together.

"Ugh." An involuntary shudder ran down Grace's spine at the thought of what that cheese might be like. "I can't imagine the smell and taste of Adrian's sweaty socks in my mouth. No thanks."

"Grace, love," her mother began, "you don't have to worry tonight, we're tasting French *fromages*, not German ones."

Adrian grinned at the thought of daring his friends to try Limburger. He knew he would be up for the challenge. Then he had an idea, "Hey, Zak, have you ever made cheese? And could we do that?"

"Yes, but not Limburger!" he cracked. "I've often made fresh mozzarella, ricotta and mascarpone, which are all very easy to make and we can do that one day." He nodded his head at that idea as it developed in his mind, "Maybe when we get to Italy, we can meet in the galley and do as the monks do."

"You mean scrape our feet and make cheese?" Adrian asked and laughed his head off.

"Very funny, Curd Nerd," his sister scowled.

Jean-Marie who was sitting at the table quietly spoke in her south of France accent, "You know, in France there is a cheese that is so smelly, they forbid people from riding the bus with it. It's called Vieux Boulogne and it is so stinky it made the Guinness World Records."

The captain wrinkled his nose and shook his head no. "I think I am with Grace on this one. No reason to punish your senses and create a memory that might haunt oneself." He winked at her to show support for her position. Continuing he added, "I seem to recall that cheese was made by monks to eat on religious days when they could not eat flesh like meat or fish, and it provided protein. They also sold cheese to pay for goods and services they couldn't make for themselves. In fact, Jean-Marie, isn't monk's head cheese how they paid their taxes to the landowner?"

"Oui, capitane." Jean-Marie nodded in agreement. "Monk's head cheese is very special." Holding her hands apart to illustrate the size of a coconut, she said, "It's this big around and you place it on a round wooden board and place a tool in the top center, which goes down through the semi-hard cheese. You see, this is cheese that you shave!" She pantomimed turning a crank around the top of the cheese. "There is a flat steel blade that takes the top layer off into thin flakey ruffles of cheese that you can place on soup, salads or just eat it. It is *très délicieux!*"

"Jean-Marie, perhaps you can answer this question," his mom invited the sous-chef, "would you know if the cheese is regional like the wine growing regions? Are the wines and cheese in France paired together or differently?"

"Oui, madame. The land or terroir creates its own unique flavors. Bacteria and yeast are regional. Those organisms feed on different ingredients in nature in the north than the south. Most people will pair the same region as they are complimentary notes. There are people who spend their whole career studying wine and cheese." She laughed and pointed to herself and Zak.

"Speaking of cheese," began the captain, "did you know that Christopher Columbus was the son of a cheese maker in Genoa, Italy. His ships, the Niña and Pinta, not only listed cheese in their inventory, but they carried goats for milk and possibly for making cheese. "

Adrian noticed his father smiled and looked deep into his wine glass as if this was amusing. His mom turned to Roberto who was offering her a new wine glass. Grace was looking at the captain with disbelief. "Are you kidding me?"

The captain held up his hands as if to say he was innocent and rocked back on his heels. "It's all true! I'm not making this stuff up. Allegedly, his father was a wool merchant and weaver, primarily, but where does wool come from?"

"Sheep, I think," said Grace.

"What is cheese made from?" asked the captain.

"Milk," said Grace.

"Could all those sheep that Columbus' father owned possibly have been milked and the milk turned into cheese?" Adrian asked hesitantly.

"Correct," the captain nodded. "Not too long-ago most families made a variety of products based on their livestock. They also could sell services based on their livestock, too. For instance, goats could eat acres of plants to clear the land for planting, provide milk, which in turn could make cheese, and later on, when they no longer were producing milk, they could be slaughtered and cooked or fed to pigs, which will eat just about anything. Sheep are no different: wool, milk, slaughter, eat."

"Eww," shared Grace, her nose upturned in disgust.

"Ewe?" asked Adrian, bent over in laughter, slapping his leg. "Wouldn't ewe know it! Grace making a pun. Ewe are one in a million sis. Ewe all herd that, right?"

"Adrian," his dad warned him with a twinkle in his eye, "Don't ram the point home. We get it."

The captain laughed and put down his empty wine glass, grinned and delivered his parting shot, "Well, I think it's time for me to abandon sheep."

Everyone groaned aloud and Grace threw a crumpled cocktail napkin at her brother. "Look what you started."

"Hey, that was a sheep shot."

"Mom, make him stop. He's so annoying!" she complained.

"I think it's time we plan our day for tomorrow's trip to the coffee and cocoa plantation," she responded in an attempt to stop the terrible punning.

"Well," said his dad in a somber tone, "all's wool that end's wool."

This time it was his mom that threw the spent napkin at his dad.

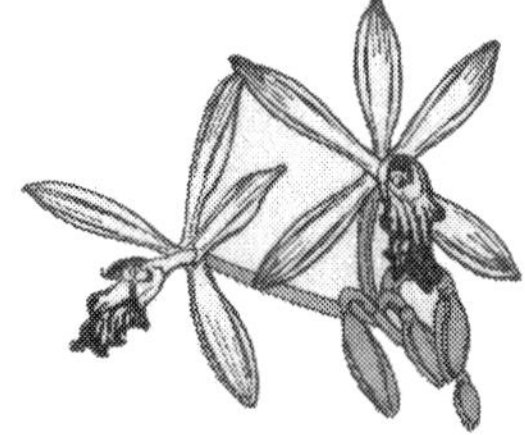

Chapter 2
Rocky Road

Habitation La Grivelière
Basse Terre
Guadeloupe Island

Chef Zak hitched his backpack over his shoulder and looked his group in the eyes. "Everyone ready? Covered in bug spray?" Heads nodded and he continued, "Our crazy Italian crew members are going to do the driving today because what you are about to experience will be hair raising. This trip is not for the faint of heart! The last time I drove the road up to *Habitation La Grivelière* my hands gripped the wheel so hard, it took an hour before they relaxed."

Adrian exchanged an excited look with his sister Grace. His eyes were glinting with anticipation, but his grin revealed a clenched jaw. Grace responded with raised eyebrows and a super-fake grimace that showed all her teeth. He knew she was mocking him somewhat...or the chef. They both loved scary rides in amusement parks and dangerous thrills, but a part of them knew that Zak was not exaggerating. He had shared that the single lane road going up the mountainside was rife with blind curves, steep hilltops that prevented a driver from seeing over the crest even when the frontend of the car's wheels were already pointed downhill. Some cars bottomed out at the top of some hills and had to wait for someone to push them over them. A shiver ran down Adrian's spine.

The sky was bright, but clouds were moving in with the morning breeze. Francesco was at the wheel of one of the three rented four-wheel drive Jeeps. Earlier in the morning, he was laughing with Raffa and Roberto in the parking lot of the marina when he instructed them to "only rent the worst looking Jeep" on the lot. His reasoning was that the road was so bad there was a chance that their car rentals would get more scratches, so it was better that they get abused vehicles, so they were not charged for damage to a new vehicle.

His parents, Jean-Marie and Raffa, were in one Jeep. Zak and Roberto were in the second Jeep and signaling Francesco to move out with Grace and Adrian. As one small convoy from the marina, they left the parking lot and headed to *Domaine de l'Habitation la Grivelière* –or "field of semi-detached housing" on the west side of the island.

The coastal village road was pleasant at first, then it began to get bumpy in places as it climbed in elevation. The trees and tropical vegetation got denser, and birds rushed out of trees across their path, as they rumbled close. The sun was somewhat behind the mountain, and they drove in the shadow of the dormant volcano on their way up.

The coffee plantation rested six-hundred and sixty feet above sea level on the steep hillsides of Basse Terre Island's western shore. Thick, lush greenery surrounded and scraped the jeep's sides as they hugged the hillside. Grace and Adrian were gripping their door handles to stay seated. On one deep pothole that

Roberto didn't clear in time, they landed hard on their backsides, and everyone let out an "ooof!" The road was full of switchbacks and hairpin turns, steep climbs and downhill runs as the road engineers of long ago had determined the path of least resistance up the mountain. The mountains appeared to be fighting them and forward progress was tedious and slow.

Francesco, it turned out, was a great driver. He appeared to be loving every minute of the trip. He was singing in Italian but every time they hit a bump, his voice stopped working and they would all giggle. Francesco had an easy-going nature, and nothing seemed to bother him. He laughed when he made mistakes, he encouraged others when things were difficult, and the teens enjoyed being around him.

The rains from the night before and early morning had left the road wet. Trees and vines dripped rain on the jeep and occasionally Francesco turned the wipers on to clear his view of the road. Several times he slowed to drive through streams of runoff that poured off the boulders along the side of the narrow road. Short concrete walls bordered the sides of the road where there was a steep drop off. Even though it was early morning, several cars were coming down from the plantation and everyone held their breath when they passed each other with inches to spare.

Each time they rounded a corner or came to a blind spot, Francesco tooted his horn to alert oncoming drivers of his presence. Just then, a pickup truck appeared in front of them, and Francesco slowed to a stop along the mountain, pressing the jeep up to the rocky wall.

"Uhh," Adrian said with deep anxiety in his voice, "I don't think he can pass us. He would roll off the edge." All eyes were on the truck. There wasn't enough space.

Looking back over his shoulder he could see the jeeps staying back. Thinking quickly, he used his cellphone to call his dad to alert him to their situation. "Dad, there's no room to pass. Please tell Raffa not to proceed, but maybe back up. The road is super narrow here between us and your jeeps. There doesn't seem to be space to pass. Tell Roberto."

The opposing driver inched closer to the jeep and proceeded forward with caution. He stopped and rolled his window down and folded in his side mirror to make his truck slimmer. Suddenly, his front right tire slipped just enough off the edge and his truck tilted towards the cliff. It was not safe to proceed. The whites of the driver's eyes showed his alarm. He indicated that Francesco should back up. He did the same. He managed to back up down the road several yards until he was near a patch of grassy road that the jeep could pull off. The truck driver beckoned with his hand through his window that Francesco should drive towards him.

Francesco guided the jeep into the ferns, vines and bushes and the noise of branches and gravel scratching the fenders and doors made the teens cringe. No one spoke a word.

Adrian took a deep breath and released his clenched jaw and flexed his hand that was holding the door handle. This road was nerve-wracking. He glanced at Grace, and she looked like he felt. Her right hand gripped the bar meant to stabilize passengers and her left hand had coiled around the extra seat belt like a rodeo rider on a mean bronc. "Breathe, Grace. Breathe."

"Oh, man, I hate this." She took a deep breath. "It's like watching a train wreck. I don't want to watch, but I can't take my eyes off it." She let out her shaky breath and tried to smile at her weak joke. "I kept seeing the front of his car tipping towards the edge and it looked like he was going to die. Did you see the look of shock and fear in his eyes, Adrian? And he's a local!"

"I know." Adrian comforted her. "I'm sure he's OK, just a little shaken. He probably drives on these roads all the time. The rain may have made things a bit loose and slippery."

The truck inched past them and waved as he got past the previous tricky spot. "OK, *Andiamo*!" Francesco laughed, putting the jeep in drive. "That was some excitement, no?" He moved forward and Adrian craned his neck to look to see how the others were faring back up the road. Soon they were out of sight, and he turned around.

"Wow." He caught Francesco's eye and smiled, "Dang. That was a close call."

"*Si.*" Francesco nodded. "My heart is pumping. It makes me think of a song." He started singing again and the siblings laughed at their loveable crewmate. One more pothole over a large crack in the road and they saw the stretch of land with some cars parked along the hillside. Francesco maneuvered the jeep in a three-point turn to face downhill and parked. Taking a deep breath, he turned off the jeep, double checked to make sure the emergency brake was on and announced, *"Siamo qui!* We made it! *Andiamo."*

Leaping down from the four-wheel drive jeep, they stretched and shook off the tension created by the road. The other two jeeps were rolling into the parking area and soon they were reunited as a group. While his dad went inside to pay admissions, they all wandered and took pictures with their phones.

They walked down a slight incline of stairs paved with small rocks that prevented walking in mud. Cascading down the mountain on terraces were wooden sheds, a millhouse or roasting house with chimneys and a handful of small identical houses that were nestled in the steep valley. The sun was much higher in the sky and steam was filling the air from evaporating moisture brought on by the rain. Adrian loved to see evaporation and condensation in action and thought water molecules were fascinating. Further down beyond the buildings he could hear the rushing of water. They had seen the grand river, as it was called, through some peek-a-boo spots along the road, where the trees had thinned, and the river was close to the hillside. He looked for a rainbow in the mist of steam but couldn't find one.

Rain runoff or perhaps a local spring was redirected to a water wheel attached to the main processing shed of the coffee plantation. The wheel deposited the water into a culver that led under the walkway and down the mountainside to join the river below. Butterflies of all colors and sizes danced in the air. He turned around to see what attracted them and began noticing all kinds of plants with flowers.

Jean-Marie called him and the others to gather around her. "OK, here is the plan. I will translate the tour guide information for you as we go. This lovely madame is going to help us learn all about *l'histoire* and I hear she is very enthusiastic about this place and gives the best tour. This way *s'il te plait*."

Zak hung back with Adrian and trailed the group. They chatted about the old buildings that were weathered by the tropical weather and over a hundred years old. The tour guide took them to the side of a building. Where they stood in the shade of a calabasa tree, looking up they saw large round bright green gourds clustered tight to the branches under the leaves in pairs. Nearby were palm-like trees overflowing with green banana branches. A donkey was tethered nearby munching grass. Workers were already moving about the property with tools to garden and sharp steel machetes to clean plant overgrowth. A warm but refreshing breeze stirred the trees and everyone lifted their faces to look up to the cloudless blue sky.

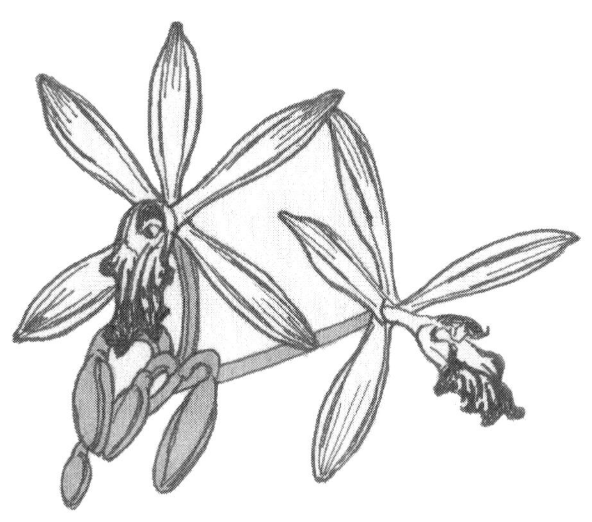

Walking along the trail through lush and verdant trees, they stopped to inspect a vanilla vine growing up a tree trunk. The vine was as thick as Adrian's thumb and the branch with the flower was much thinner than his pinky finger. A green orchid flower had opened and was being pollinated by hand as a demonstration. Several buds that had not opened yet were in line to open just behind it. Jean-Marie explained that there is a team of people that must hand pollinate the vanilla flowers daily to assure the beans, which contain the seeds, matured properly. Without pollination, there would be no vanilla bean harvest. Before she turned back to the tour guide she added, "And the only bees that pollinate vanilla flowers live in Mexico."

Without warning, Grace let out a bloodcurdling scream and jumped backwards into the group from the tree she had been standing under. Adrian knew that sound from the last time she had seen a spider. Adrian rushed over to get a closer look while his sister stood trembling in the safety of her mom's arms with her dad next to her for comfort. She pointed to a branch about face height off the ground.

The tour guide lifted her small machete and poked the tree's leaves, revealing a six-inch-long neon-yellow and black-ringed caterpillar with orange legs and a cherry tomato face with black micro freckles.

"It's a frangipani worm or Rasta caterpillar," Jean-Marie translated. "They are all over. When they gather on a frangipani tree, they can eat all the leaves in one to two days." She snapped her fingers to demonstrate how fast they could eat. "They are hungry caterpillars, no?"

Adrian asked Jean-Marie to ask the guide if he could hold it. The guide nodded, yes. He grinned and picked it off the leaf and laid it across his hand. As the guide spoke to Jean-Marie, Adrian allowed the worm to crawl over his palm. It stretched the entire length of his hand from tip to wrist.

"Our guide said that it will turn into a Hawk Moth that is brown and six inches in wingspan." Jean-Marie looked at the colorful Rasta worm and shook her head. "Where does all that color go?

"She said you have to be careful at night because they will fly into your face and scare you senseless." She shuddered at the thought and looked at Grace, holding her hand up to say stop as she turned away and walked into an area that was free of vegetation and sunlight.

"Anyone want to hold this fat fella?" He had no takers, so he carefully placed the worm back on the leaf and waited as the caterpillar carefully grabbed the leaf edge with his mouth, forelegs and grabbed on with his back legs and inched along. Very cool!

His dad, who had been taking pictures of him with the worm in his hand and returning to the tree, asked him what he thought of the experience.

"It's beautiful, but it is a beast." He said thoughtfully. "That's a ton of destruction these guys inflict on a tree."

"I have a hard time imagining just how many caterpillars it takes to eat a mature tree in one to two days," he shared, shaking his head in disbelief. "I suppose it all grows back fairly rapidly in the tropics with rich volcanic soil, tropical rains and sunlight."

"Good point." Adrian conceded. "I just assumed it meant the tree died."

Catching up with Jean-Marie, he asked her a question for the guide to answer. She returned with an answer, "The Rasta caterpillar is poisonous because the leaves they eat are toxic to animals and humans. The bright colors warn the animals to stay away."

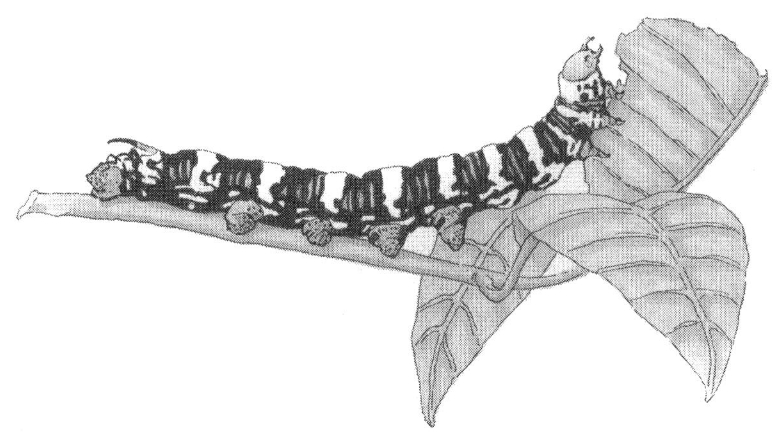

The guide talked about the time in the late nineteenth century when they had coffee leaf miners burrow into the leaves and suck them dry of nutrients and Guadeloupe nearly lost their crop. She looked for a leaf on the tree next to her and pointed to a leaf with a brown squiggle on the leaf. The small worms threaten every coffee tree on the 'bean belt' around the globe, since they have ten generations per year. The nearly invisible larva turns into a moth and lays eggs before the plants have a chance to recover. Because of this serious coffee crisis, the plantation owner invested in roucou, also known as annatto or achiote tree that produces an edible red colored paste for flavoring and coloring food, to compensate for the financial losses.

As they walked around between the trees and assorted buildings, it was revealed that, since the end of the eighteenth century, Guadeloupe's agricultural speculations in cocoa, coffee and roucou, which have made it famous, rendering the ninety hectares plantation a historic monument.

The guide paused beside a compact coffee tree with waxy green leaves that were elongated and growing in pairs. Jean-Marie waited for the guide to finish, then shared, "I did not know this, but coffee is from the berry family! Oo-la-la!" She raised her eyebrows to the group in surprise. "Wow wee! The beans are called cherries." She laughed a throaty laugh and swirled her hand in the air for lost logic emphasis. "Beans, berries, cherries..." And everyone chuckled with her.

"OK," she gained her composure and continued, "A young plant grows for three to four years and then produces small but fragrant flowers similar to a jasmine flower. Sounds so nice, no?

"Young people, cover your ears," she teased, "the plant's sex cells are what help the plant reproduce over time. Maybe six weeks later, *voilà!* A baby coffee cherry appears! And..." her voice turned singsong as she smiled broadly, "Just like a mama, it takes nine months from flower to harvest."

Everyone was grinning at Jean-Marie's colorful talk. The guide said something to her, and she laughed and admitted to the group, "I just got offered a job as a tour guide!" The Abercrombies cheered and her Italian crewmates whistled and clapped *"Brava! Brava!"*

"Eventually, the cherries will turn red, orange, yellow, and pinkish, as you can see here." She nodded to the guide who lifted a branch and allowed everyone to see the berries clinging to the branch by the dozens. "She says one tree can live eighty years. They keep them pruned to allow workers to reach the berries, so no more than five to seven feet tall."

The guide talked rapidly for a few minutes and Jean-Marie counted off the facts on her hands so she could remember them. "Remember like wine and cheese, the land and climate flavors the produce. Same for coffee. She says that a good harvester can pick one to two hundred pounds of coffee cherries daily. That results in twenty to forty pounds of coffee beans that can be consumed." She opened a third finger and began again, "Not all berries, I mean cherries!" She laughed, "I can't keep it straight! Let me try again. The cherries do not all ripen at once, so a harvester must return to the same tree to pick the future beans when they are at peak ripeness."

She opened a fourth finger and looked amazed, "You won't believe this, but the honeybees love the coffee flower nectar and sip the same caffeine that we do! No wonder they are busy!" Turning to the guide and touching her forearm, she said a dramatic, *"c'est incroyable sur les abeilles!"*

"Seriously," Adrian grinned to his family and Zak, "a bee with a coffee buzz?"

Grinning back, his dad said, "Keep up the dad jokes and I won't have to make them!"

Grace elbowed her brother, "Do you remember what the bee said to his girlfriend?" He looked at her funny, and raised a worrisome eyebrow. She continued, "I can't help pollen in love with you."

Giving her the gratuitous groan, he asked her, "What did the bee girlfriend say in return?" This time Grace shook her head and shrugged. "Hive never felt this way bee-fore."

She cooed and said, "Oh, Adrian, that was way too cute. I actually give you points for that one."

The guide brought them to a curious building with long metal railings coming out from the bottom. She indicated Grace and Adrian, and their parents pull on the drawer handles and gave a tiny demonstration before stepping back. She named them *"boucans à drawers."* To their amazement, ten-foot-long trays six inches in depth and perhaps five feet wide rolled out from under the building to stretch out in the sun for drying coffee beans. There were millions of small pale yellow beige beans in each drawer. A man with a rake came out and began raking the beans, pushing them around to circulate the air around them.

"They use what is called the wet-method to husk the cherries and remove the peel and pulp to get to the beans" Jean-Marie continued as they walked, "They use water to wash the skin and pulp. Then they place them in a big vat of water to separate out the floaters, which are the bad or less dense beans. What is left is a sweet sticky gelatinous viscous secretion called mucilage. But here we have a problem!" She hoisted her index finger up into the air over her head. "*Mes amies*, it is not water soluble! What to do? One moment!" Turning to consult with the guide, she said a few ahs, and *ouis*.

"We ferment it, *mes amies!* Like a fine wine, the beans stay in the vat of water and the enzymes in the coffee cherry eat away the mucilage, converting the sugars into acids, gasses and sometimes alcohol.

"Then it goes to the spa for a luxury bath and massage?" Adrian's mom asked with a hopeful sigh, brushing at the flies and the sweat on her brow.

Jean-Marie smiled, "Good guess, madame. They are rinsed with clean water, then they get to sunbathe for ten days before going to the mill after the holiday. Now, we go to the roastery for one of the best coffees in the world."

"Will we get to taste the coffee, Jean-Marie?" his dad asked. A chorus of people echoed the request.

"*Oui*, when we finish the tour. We are about to learn about the world's most popular food..." she informed them enthusiastically and ended with an excited, "*Chocolat!*"

Adrian thought for a moment that it sounded so much more inviting in French the way she said it. *Chock-oh-lot*. He practiced under his breath. *Chockolot. Chocolat*. Biting his lower lip at how good he thought he sounded, he grinned and said in his best French accent, "*Chocolat*, people, let's go!" And led the group forward behind their guide.

After a few words to the guide, they headed out a side door and down a lush path. Stopping by a woody plant with oblong leathery leaves and red-purple and yellow-orange fruits protruding from it like stiff Christmas ornaments, she touched one carefully in her hand.

"This is the cacao plant where we get chocolate!" Jean-Marie translated.

Grace and Adrian reached out to touch the gourd-looking fruit with long grooves. It was warm to the touch. It was firmly affixed to the tree branch. The guide took a knife and cut off both and handed one to each teen. They sniffed it and passed it around. "It doesn't smell like chocolate," Grace observed. "If anything, I think it smells a bit like citrus."

"Are cacao beans legumes?" Adrian asked.

"No, they are from the mallow family. At least, that is their classification" Zak inserted, "Formally, it is called Theobroma Cacao, which translates to food of the gods in Greek."

"Mallows?" Adrian asked with extreme interest, "Like marshmallows?"

Laughing, Zak said, "No, buddy, sorry to disappoint you. More like cotton, okra and hibiscus. If memory serves me, balsa wood, too."

The guide chatted with Jean-Marie for a bit, who resumed translating, "Our wonderful guide shared that the flowers are so complicated and there are these small flies and midges that pollinate the flowers, so we have this fruit of which there are about twenty species.

"She says each tree grows up to seventy fruits per year. They take less than six months to ripen. Oh, and a pod can hold twenty to sixty beans." She gleaned more information and added, "One person can harvest about six-hundred and fifty pods per day. They use a knife to make sure they don't hurt the tree because where the cacao pod comes off is where more flowers will emerge."

The guide took the end of her machete and hammered the fruit a few times in the palm of her hand. It cracked open to reveal a whitish pulp, from which she took a small piece and tasted. Passing the fruit around, everyone took a taste. "Oh, it's like lemonade!" Grace exclaimed. "That is so weird, right?"

Everyone was confused. The guide pulled out the cacao beans in their slimy lavender-white coating and held them in her hand and, in French, explained the next steps. Jean-Marie shared that the pulp is juiced and used for desserts and sorbets.

"These have to go into a tank for six days and the temperature has to be no more than 50 degrees Celsius or 122 Fahrenheit while they ferment. The fermentation process turns them brown. Then the beans go on the rack of drawers, just like the coffee beans.

"Next, the beans are roasted for about a quarter of an hour, then the beans are shelled by hand. Once the skins are removed, the beans can be crushed or milled by hand into a fatty paste. Remember, these beans are rich in cocoa butter. From this paste, they roll it into a *kako* stick by hand. This dries and forms a skin and then it is packaged."

"Oh, *attendez,*" Jean-Marie spun around and waved her hands in front of everyone, "*Avertissement,* the kako stick is not sweet! There is no sugar in it. No expectations of a beautiful Belgian truffle, okay? This is produced from the beautiful cacao tree and a very powerful *chocolat.* Let's see the plantation manor, then go to the gift shop."

The three Italian crewmates had been hanging out by themselves at the back of the group, joined up with the others and went inside the manor turned museum. Italian, French, English and Creole voices could be heard in the room as everyone was talking and observing household items from French history on the island.

At the gift shop they made purchases and tried both the café and the hot kako, as they called it. Adrian's mom and Zak were busy calculating purchases for projects in the galley. By the looks of it, Zak was getting pounds of everything, especially the Arabica coffee. His mom was selecting liquors in glass bottles made from tropical fruits. Raffa and Roberto hauled the produce to the jeeps.

"Adrian," his dad quietly approached him to ask, "Would you like to thank and tip the tour guide or shall I?"

"I'll do it, Dad," he offered and put out his hand for some Euros. He stuffed a tip inside the jar of the gift shop for the workers to share and walked over to get Jean-Marie. "Will you join me for a moment to translate? Although, this probably doesn't need translating." His eyes twinkled across the space to the yacht's sous-chef and she winked at him.

"Please tell her we all enjoyed her tour, it was very informative, and we all learned very much." He watched Jean-Marie repeat his words and when their tour guide smiled at him, he shook her hand and passed the cash in a folded wad over to her. *"Merci!"*

"Merci beaucoup," she returned with a big, enormous Guadeloupean smile. "Thank you! *Bon voyage!*"

The trip downhill was equally harrowing, but they were soon on the road and headed to the coast for a quick lunch of Creole and French cooking.

The humidity was high due to the rain of the night before and everyone was feeling the heat. It was agreed they would go back to the yacht to regroup. Adrian's mom and dad wanted to relax and take a nap. He and Grace wanted to hit the water somewhere but not where they were moored, since it was heavy with traffic from shipping and recreational or fishing vessels. He wanted to consult with Jimmy about their options. He was thinking it was time to put the tender in the water and find a white sandy beach or go snorkeling.

Tossing their grubby shoes on the mat, the teens raced ahead of the crew and their parents to seek out the first officer. Jimmy was ashore with Pete but would be returning within the hour, according to Jane, and the captain was in his office and did not wish to be disturbed for the next hour.

Adrian and his sister headed to their cabins and agreed to touch base within the hour. Since he didn't have an opportunity last night to read his owner's manual for the sailboat, he threw himself on his bed and opened the operating instructions. *I can't believe I can't keep my eyes open.* He let the booklet fall to his chest and fell fast asleep.

Chapter 3
Kings and Queens

Grace knocking on his door woke him up. She stuck her head in when he invited her in.

"Ha! You fell asleep, too!" she laughed and added a bit sheepishly, "I just got up. It's been over ninety minutes. Jimmy's back but he and Pete look busy with engine room stuff. Want to call him on your radio?"

Rolling over on his side, he reached for the drawer in the nightstand and pulled it open. He lifted out the earpiece and walkie-talkie with care. "Adrian to Jimmy, over."

Instantly, Jimmy was in his ear inviting him to talk.

"Any chance we can drop the tender today and find a beach? Grace and I were hoping to go for a swim and continue exploring."

"No chance today, Adrian, we're making a checklist for the tender and replacing a navigation light on the stern. Tomorrow works. Over."

"Roger that. We'll talk later. Thanks, Jimmy. Out."

Turning to his sister, he reported, "Well, not today, but tomorrow works." He rolled onto his back. "How about a swim in our pool? Although, I gotta say, I love the air conditioning in my room."

Sitting on the edge of the bottom bunk bed next to him, she toyed with the idea. "Um, we could."

"We should hike the volcano tomorrow," Adrian announced,

sitting up. "I want to see it before we go. There will always be sandy beaches, but that would be very cool. We've never seen one, Grace. This could be our only chance!"

"Do you have Fear of Missing Out?" Grace grinned, then added with some haste and assurance, "Not to sound like mom or anything, but you sound like it's going to be your only chance in a lifetime."

"OK, I let go my FOMO, and you're right, there will be other volcanoes." He grinned, "You do sound like mom sometimes, but it's a good thing."

Grace smiled back. "Don't you remember that I used to get FOMO so bad, I'd stop thinking like a normal person and go into this panicked gotta-have-it mode? Mom got me to see there were multiple fears behind FOMO controlling me." She stood up and stretched. "Remember when Lizzie said that the end of the school year dance tickets were limited and expected to sell out by noon? I was pushing people out of my way trying to get to the line outside the library, not sure I had enough money on me that day, scared that they would sell out and I wouldn't get mine, and no one could tell me if there were still tickets? Well, I was almost crying in line, praying that I could get them or my Sophomore year was going to be ruined.

"Are you serious?" He didn't try to hide his disbelief and amusement, "You were in tears because you feared you couldn't get tickets to a crummy dance?"

"Yeah, yeah, laugh all you want." She stuck her tongue out at her brother and gave a self-deprecating laugh, "Turns out, it was a hoax that there were limited tickets. The guys thought it would be fun to spread fear with the girls. And we all fell for it."

"First, let's find out who wants to go tomorrow, then ask Gabriella to find us a guide. Let's go find mom and dad."

Together they rushed up the port side stairs to their parent's apartment above the main deck, but they were not there. Rushing up the next staircase to the bridge deck, they found the captain, Bryce and Pete in conversation on the bridge.

"Whoa! Slow down there! Where's the fire?" Pete asked with a trace of laughter.

Grace and Adrian started at once, "We're looking for mom and dad."

"Whoa!" the captain echoed with a twinkle in his eye, "What's the problem?"

"Oh," Adrian said with a smile, "No problem, Captain. We're just looking for them so we can plan a trip to the volcano tomorrow and we want to get it organized and see who wants to join us. Do you know where we can find them?"

"They're not on board," Bryce informed them. "I helped them ashore about an hour ago. They wanted to walk over to the museum of the Nobel Prize winner Saint-John Perse."

"Boring," Grace uttered in response with an exaggerated roll of her head. "It figures. That's totally something only parents would do."

"Actually, it's not," the captain injected. "School children on this island study his poetry so they can take the perspective of a poet. These students go on field trips to the museum to learn from his many letters and poems, and take his point of view on politics, and consider his colorful expressions of life through his words. He was also a fine sailor." He ended by saying, "There is nothing boring about him, Miss Grace."

"Well, you know what I mean," Grace said in response, "And I guess we'll hear all about it at dinner tonight, sparing us a trip to his museum."

The men laughed with knowingness. Meals were a time when

everyone discussed their adventures in great detail and plans for new excursions were initiated. One thing that this family was noted for was a theme of heart-centered consensus. They seemed to choose to participate in something everyone wanted to experience, and no one was left out. The captain and crew noticed that if one person was against it, they negotiated with each other until all members of the family were happy with the choice of activity. They accommodated each other so that happy solutions were created, and no one was forced to participate or left out.

"Well, I guess we can get ourselves organized for tomorrow and just include them if they want to go hiking," Adrian concluded.

"A fine idea, since I think your father expressed an interest in seeing it," the Captain agreed, "since *La Grande Soufrière* is considered an active stratovolcano."

"A stratovolcano?" Adrian asked for clarification. "Meaning layers?"

"Yes," the captain confirmed, "The volcano is built up from hardened layers of ash and lava over time. They are identified by the classic conical shape." He arched his fingers backwards and placed the tips together. "They have steep sides and have the characteristic blown top and crater at the summit. And because they are periodically active, they have explosive eruptions that are quite effusive."

"Is this one active now?" Grace asked with concern and hesitation, "We're not putting our lives in danger hiking to the top of the crater, are we?"

"No, not at all." Pete assured her with his hands on his hips. "All governments around the world monitor their active volcanoes and move people out of danger if there are signs of life-threatening activity. Earthquakes are the main signs of activity. And trust me, this volcano, like all others, is under constant surveillance by volcanologists eager to be first to the eruption party."

"What do you think we will see there?" Grace inquired. "Would we even feel an earthquake if there was one?"

Bryce chuckled, "Grace, you have nothing to worry about. It is rare to feel an earthquake. They are more noticeable when you are stationary, like indoors with a reference point for what is stable. When your chandelier starts swinging from the ceiling, and your glassware is clattering in your cupboards, you know the earth is shaking. Outside, all you might notice is that all the birds go quiet and fly off. Of course, by a swimming pool, you might see the water slosh over the edge."

"Yes, Grace, you have nothing to worry about! I think, in all likelihood," began the Captain as he walked towards the chart table and pointed to the western tip of Basse-Terre, "You will have a difficult time seeing the top of the volcano as it is high up in the clouds. I noticed on this nautical chart that the summit is at four thousand and fifty feet above sea level, which is 1,467 meters high. That is a very steep hike, in case you wondered. The good news is that the drive to the parking lot will get you a good part of the way there." He pulled out a tourist map from a notebook off to the side of the chart table.

"Look here." He spread the brochure on the table and pointed to a marker near the southwest of the summit. "You start the trail here at parking *des Baïnes-Juanes*. A *baïne* is a pool of water near a shoreline. Never having been up to this place, I surmise that this is a bathing pool. Volcanoes produce thermal springs and mineral-rich water that is healthy to bathe in. *Juanes* must be a proper name."

Grace had stepped closer to the table to see the map better. "Captain, what does the island do when the volcano looks like it's about to blow? Does everyone have to leave?" Grace asked with genuine concern. "And what about the animals?"

The captain put a reassuring hand on her shoulder, "The scientists in charge of monitoring the volcano alert the local governments who have emergency plans in place to evacuate the citizens, so they are safe. As for animals, I would imagine that family pets are given priority over livestock."

Grace cringed upon hearing that pronouncement. "I get it. People are the priority. It must be hard enough to get the people off the island without risking people's lives by sending rescue workers back to the island to save animals. Although," she looked thoughtful for a moment, "at best, the livestock here must consist of horses, cows, goats and chickens, right?"

The captain nodded. "I think I see where you are going with this."

"Yeah," she added, "The number of animals can't be that great. As an American, I think I'm guilty of thinking in terms of entire ranches with thousands of heads of cattle, but here it wouldn't be the same. Maybe a local would know."

"I'm certain many locals would know and have an answer for you."

Adrian was studying the map and surmising distances with a silver toned metal divider, a navigation tool for estimating distances on a chart. He had spread the delicate tool that resembled a compass, to the unit of one kilometer annotated on the chart, then tightened the screw between the legs so that the sharp tips could walk the distances he wanted to measure. "Captain, it says here there are three sections of the hike. I think if we could get to the second parking lot, we'd shave off some time."

"Not possible," the captain replied, "The last eruption incident destroyed it in 2004."

"OK, we have a vertical climb tomorrow," Adrian announced

with some seriousness. "That is quite strenuous. Grace, are you up for that?"

Tossing her hair over her shoulder and lifting her chin, "I can do it. Can you?" She challenged her brother.

"Oh, easy-peasy," he scoffed, "I just never see you at the gym or running laps on the deck or taking the stairs."

"I do, too!" She reacted hotly. "We'll see who gets to the top first tomorrow."

"You're on!"

The men simply looked at each other and shrugged. They knew the mountain was quite steep and, to make it more challenging, it was wet and muddy since the trails were under the canopy of a rainforest for part of the trip and in the clouds at high altitude. There was an excellent chance of rain tomorrow that the teens were unaware of.

"Bring a wind breaker for the top of the summit." Pete added, "The winds will be quite strong."

"And smelly," Bryce offered. "I hope you don't mind the rotten hardboiled egg smell."

"Don't bother with a hat," the captain suggested, "I've heard they blow off at the top."

"Roger that. Anything else?" Adrian asked.

"Might want to have a couple liters of water each." Pete suggested, "One to go up, one to come down." The captain pointed to Pete and nodded yes. "And don't count on any bathrooms along the trail. Just remember to relieve yourself facing downhill," his normally deadpan face grinned at Grace's horror that he was talking about potty breaks out in nature with her. "Otherwise, it will run down onto your shoes. And ideally, relieve yourself with the wind blowing at your back."

"Uh," Grace stuttered, unsure how to react to such candid

advice about using the bathroom on the trail. "OK...I think." She turned to her brother and asked, "Ready to go?"

"Yeah." Adrian was still studying the map but put down the dividers he had been spinning on the map in place. "Thanks for your advice."

"Bye guys," Grace said as they inched their way to the central passageway that led to the elevator and formal staircase. Backing down the bridge deck hallway, she called out in a loud voice to her brother, "Race ya!"

Adrian bolted for the portside staircase to jump down the teak steps two at a time to the owner's deck. He dashed to the next stairs and nearly crashed into Jane on her way up with a tray in her hands to collect galley ware. "Ooops! Sorry, Jane!" He pressed his body against the handrail so she could squeeze past and as she laughed, he jumped the rest of the flight to the deck and yelled, "Touchdown!"

"Yeah, but I beat you little bro!" Grace said as she entered the middle of the main deck dining area and met her brother. Both were flushed and smiling.

"No fair," he protested, "I ran into Jane in the middle of the staircase!"

"You know the odds," she reminded him, "it could have happened to me just as easily."

He walked past her and lightly high-fived her in acknowledgment of her win. "Want a bottle of cold water?"

"Yeah," she said, wiping her forehead with the back of her hand. Leaning on the bar, she watched her brother squat down and open a refrigerator under the counter and pull out two bottles. Handing one up to her, she leaned across the counter and grabbed it. "Thanks!" He fished around for paper napkins and grabbed some bags of chips and threw them on the top of the bar.

Cracking the bottle and lifting it to his lips, he took a long swig. Gasping for breath, he set the bottle down and looked Grace in the eye, "We better hydrate really well for the hike." Pulling open a bag of potato chips, he took a few out and popped them in his mouth. He tipped the open bag over to her and offered her some.

"Hydrating is a good idea," she agreed, reaching into the bag. While munching a couple of chips, she rolled the cold bottle over her hot forehead to counter the tropical heat. "While you're back there, why don't you put on some music."

Turning around, he opened a cabinet door and turned on the digital sound system and the entire deck was pumping Caribbean night club music. Picking up his bottle of water and a chip bag, he wandered to the port railing to look out over the water towards the bow. There was no one berthed next to them, but further down the quay were a couple of colorful tugboats painted in red, green, black, and yellow. Leaning over the railing, he munched away until the bag was empty, then he balled it up and shoved it in his pocket to dispose of later.

"You lookin' so thoughtful, my friend."

Adrian turned to smile at the source of the Jamaican accent he had looked forward to hearing every day since meeting the first officer. "Jimmy!" He gave him a manly high five and half hug. "Dude. I feel like I haven't talked to you in forever."

"I know." Jimmy smiled back. "Da captain has me busy, mon. Pete and Bryce are changing a few things in the engineering office, and den we had some maintenance on de tender." He shrugged. "You remember dat I work here, right?" He laughed a deep rich sound that enticed Grace to slide off the bar stool and walk over to join them.

"Hey, Jimmy, what's up?" Grace smiled in his direction. "How's the tender? Ready for a spin, I hope?"

"Yeah, 'bout dat," he began, "by tomorrow afternoon, I promise."

"Good timing," Adrian assured him, "we should be back from hiking the volcano. Maybe we can take her for a test drive around the eastside of Grand-Terre?"

"Yeah, maybe. But you may have rubber legs after the hike." He did a funny little rubbery-leg duckwalk a few feet away from the teens and turned to come back looking just as funny with his face tight with supposed pain. The teens laughed out loud and denied that was their future fate. "Oh, yeah, just you wait and see. I'm in good shape but I don't climb volcanoes every day, so you know…" he wobbled his legs again like he was quaking in his boots, getting another laugh from the teens.

"Yoo-hoo" his mom called in her singsong manner, as she walked up the passerelle. She was all smiles. His dad was right behind her. "Adrian, love, can you get me one of those waters, please?"

"I'll get it," Jimmy said and moved with haste to reach around the bar to open the fridge. Setting two bottles on the bar, he stood back respectfully. He grabbed his walkie-talkie and clicked the button to state in a quiet voice, "Gabriella and Jane, Mr. and Mrs. A are on the main deck." He released the button and listened for a response. Satisfied, he stopped speaking with the stewardesses. Moments later, Jane came through a door that led to the galley. She smiled and asked if she could make them a drink.

"Why don't we all go upstairs to the owner's deck to hang out and plan our day tomorrow and have a drink up there?" his dad suggested.

"Dad, we've been thinking that we could hike the volcano tomorrow!" Grace excitedly shared with her dad.

"Sounds great," he concurred, "but I need a shower before we continue this conversation. How about we meet upstairs in fifteen minutes?"

The Abercrombies arranged themselves around a dining table on the owner's deck under an air-conditioned ceiling and prepared their hike. Gabriella made some calls but was unable to find a dedicated tour guide. She suggested they show up and follow other hikers on the trail. All the companies she called said the trail was well marked and there would be groups leaving from the parking lot on the hour.

Jane and Gabrielle brought over rum drinks for the adults and mixed tropical fruit slushies with coconut cream for the teens to enjoy. A large charcuterie board was brought up from the galley with local cheese, cured meats, fresh and dried fruits, and nuts for the family to snack on. A basket of French baguette slices with a variety of seeds on the crust accompanied the board.

"What do you say we get an early start, so we have the afternoon free?" his mom asked. "I always prefer strenuous activity in the early part of the day. I'd rather go up when it is ten degrees cooler and descend the mountain when it is the hottest."

"Sounds great," his dad agreed. "I've been looking forward to this for months."

"Really?" Adrian was shocked. "You never mentioned it."

"Well, when we thought about traveling in the Caribbean, I thought it would be neat to visit a volcano, since I've never been on an active one."

"Have you been on a dormant one?" Grace asked.

"All of us have," he responded with a bit of surprise, "Don't you remember hiking Crater Lake in Oregon? Or Mount Shasta and Mount Lassen in northern California? We did a camping trip with your cousins two summers ago and the rangers told you all about the volcanoes in the region."

"I must have tuned it all out," she confessed. "I'm not really into volcanoes. And besides, I was probably taking photos."

"When I was your age," his mom started, "I went to Yellowstone National Park, which has volcanic activity all over the place. The part I can't handle very well is the smell of sulfur. Ugh. I just gag."

"Well, sweetheart," his dad began, "This one is named sulfur mine for a reason and you may not want to get too close to the steam vents."

His mom waved a hand under her nose at the thought of smelling sulfur again. "I'll try to breathe through my mouth. And stay upwind of the smell."

Just then, Chef Zak, followed by the captain, came onto the deck with a small platter. "Hello! Hello! I brought up some pineapple for you to taste the difference between the fruits of two neighboring islands. This one," he pointed to the fruit on the left side of the platter, "is Black Pineapple from Antigua. It is considered the sweetest pineapple in the world.

"On the right, this is Gwada meaning it's local, which I suggest you start with since it may not taste as sweet following the Antiguan one." He stood back and waited while everyone reached for the local version of the tropical fruit. He had cut the fruit into small triangles and left the skin on. The captain also helped himself to a sample.

"The same year that Columbus arrived here in Guadeloupe, he ate pineapple. He, quite possibly, was the first European to ever eat pineapple and he brought pineapples back to Europe. The pineapples held up very well on the trip back, which led to increased production in tropical regions because everyone loved them." The captain took a bite and nodded with appreciation. "I do believe the King of Fruits is my favorite. ”

"Is it really the King of Fruits?" Adrian asked the captain, noting his dad was back to grinning at the captain's words. What the heck? What was funny about the captain's words? Turning back to the captain, he said, "What makes it the king?"

"The crown!" Zak declared before the captain could speak. "But let's be clear: different parts of the world have their own ideas about who the king and queen are based on their local fruits, and they may have different fruits for different seasons. Like pears are the queen in the fall with westerners."

"Who's the queen?" Grace rushed to ask. "Wait! Let me guess..." She paused to consider her choices. "Does it have to be a tropical fruit?"

"In this case, I would say yes." Zak reasoned.

"Umm..." With all eyes on Grace, she gave it some serious thought while people reached for the Black Pineapple and began to munch it. "How about the star fruit?"

"That would be a good guess, but no. In tropical regions, mostly Asian, Mangosteen is the Queen of Fruits."

"Never seen it or tasted it." Grace informed him. "How could I have known that?! Mango- what?"

"Steen. Mangosteen. And it is quite beautiful." Zak shared. "It begins as a beautiful rose-pink and pale green orchid-like flower with red back petals, then a small sphere of fruit grows with a five-petaled flower-shape on the bottom and a crown of red petals at the top. When it ripens, it is a deep dark purple tone, and when you cut around the middle about a quarter inch, and twist off the top half, it reveals a delicate white pulp-crown inside that is sweet."

"What does it taste like," Adrian asked with curiosity. "Is it similar to mangoes?"

"No, not mango. I would share that the tasting notes are along the lines of citrus, with a hint of banana with peach and lychee flavors all in the mix. They are super sweet with just a hint of tartness. You would definitely like them, Adrian, since you love sweet and sour. However, these fruits are not sour."

"How come I've never seen one?" Graced demanded, "We have just about every fruit in the stores back home, but not mangosteen. I'm sure I would have tried it if it were there."

"Correct, Grace. It is the hardest fruit to grow on Earth. They thrive in a hot area in wet —but not too wet soil. They like a sea-level climate but not near salt air. They cannot tolerate any cold air."

"Wow, I think I would have called them the prima donna of fruit, not the queen." Her parents and the captain all raised their glasses to her in acknowledgement of her comment.

"Takes one to know one," Adrian laughed. Grace stuck her tongue out at her brother in rebuttal. "OK, Chef, so where did you taste one?"

"Malaysia. In Asia they eat durian with mangosteen, probably because they are harvested at about the same time." He picked up a slice of Black Pineapple. Before taking a bite, he added with a hint of a smile, "You know, in Malaysia, the law prohibits people from bringing those two fruits into a hotel room. In Singapore they say durian tastes like heaven and smells like hell. To me," he touched his chest, "It smells like rotten sewage with a hint of turpentine. And the mangosteen permanently stains everything it touches, so it is forbidden in hotels because it can stain not just the linens, but furniture, walls, and any other stuff people touch their fingers on."

"Oh!" his mom lamented, "That is a mother's nightmare!"

"Dang. That's a lot of power if the stain is permanent." Grace was impressed with the fruit's description. "I wonder if they use it for dying clothing."

"Maybe," Zak replied. "Many plants are used for dye, Grace. For example, Japan and Bali use indigo to make fabrics blue."

"If you'll humor me, I'd like to get back to the topic of mangosteen for a moment," the captain redirected them, "I recall a story from one of my friends who is a naval historian. There was some debate about this, and no one knows for sure, but long ago in the United Kingdom, Queen Victoria promised knighthood to the sailor who could bring her back a mangosteen from Asia. Given the journey and the fragility of the fruit, I don't think anyone was knighted and the queen probably died never tasting the exotic fruit from the east."

"That's quite the quest for the late nineteenth century," his mom commented. "Returning home after a long voyage around the world and being knighted would have been quite rewarding."

"So! What do you think of the pineapples?" Zak inquired of the family before him, shifting the attention back to the reason he joined them. "Do you have a favorite?"

The vote was split half and half and they thanked him for

the opportunity to learn about the pineapple. "Before you go, Zak," Adrian started, "Why do they call it Black Pineapple when it is not black?"

"The dark green skin color between the spines appears black, but it is not. When you see the black, it means it's ripe," the chef explained. "The other variety you sampled is the Smooth Cayenne variety and may have come from South America or Martinique for cultivation, which is why it is more of an orange-red color. It's also more tart, which I like. But in the galley, just as you use the right tool for the job, you also use the right fruit for the recipe."

"Thank you, Zak," his father said, "I think we all enjoyed the experience."

Zak reached for the empty platter, sticky with juice and removed it from the table. "My pleasure."

"What's for dinner tonight?" Grace asked as she placed the pineapple rind on her plate and wiped her fingers on a napkin.

"Traditional Guadeloupe seafood in curry, which means Creole food with a French influence. And a coconut sorbet for dessert with vanilla and chocolate French butter cookies made with love by Jean-Marie." He smiled and took a step back to incline his head towards the group. "Now, if you will excuse me, the galley calls."

"Oh, wow! I can't wait!" his parents exclaimed together. "Why don't you both get cleaned up and meet us here for dinner."

"And if you have time," his mom added, "get your clothes and backpacks ready for tomorrow. I think you may want to wear your cross-country running shoes tomorrow. And be prepared for getting very dirty. I read that the trails can be very muddy in places."

"Roger. Wilco." Adrian saluted his folks and turned to leave. "See you at 1900 hours."

"Ditto," said Grace, who pushed in their chairs at the table and turned to leave. "Mom, if you brought them onboard, pack your carbon fiber walking sticks. I may want to use one."

"Hey, Dad," Adrian said from the doorway, "Can you bring the drone camera? It might be nice to get some pics from the top when we are clear of the trees."

"Roger that," his dad agreed with a thumbs up as the teens left the owner's deck.

La Soufrière Volcano
Parc Nationale de la Guadeloupe
Saint-Claude, Bassa-Terre

Wow, this road is possibly more twisty than the one to the coffee plantation!" his father exclaimed after a particularly tight hairpin turn around a sharp rocky outcrop of land. He was hanging onto the dashboard with both hands and sitting next to the driver of the minivan taxi.

The taxi driver laughed. And took another curve close to the mountain. Adrian's dad had asked the driver questions on Grace's behalf on the way to Saint-Claude from Point-de-Pitre which was relatively flat and easy driving. Once they got onto the slopes of the volcano, he stopped talking so the driver could concentrate.

The driver, who spoke some English, told them that the last

time the mountain spewed considerable magma was in the mid-sixteenth century. Now all that the volcano shares is steam, sulfuric mud, ash and hot water, which brought Grace relief.

They entered a parking lot with people getting out of cars, milling around, and stretching. At the foot of the hills covered in lush, dense foliage and trees were three square unpainted wooden buildings with peaked roofs and a road off to the left covered in signage and blocked by a chain-link fence.

The driver gave Adrian's dad a phone number of someone to come pick them up in Saint-Claude and drove off.

They noticed a group that had entered the trailhead and followed them. "Here's to reaching the top," Adrian said to no one in particular, "and a good day hiking." He walked ahead of his family and took in the landscape.

Every shade of green was present on all sides of him. A heavy canopy of strong trees and vines dripped the occasional water droplet down, but it seemed to be condensation, not rain. Leaves covered the ground and low plants. The national park had done a good job of laying stones in the ground to help hikers. In places, stones and logs were inserted into the hillside to form natural staircases with short stretches between them. At times the trail became single-file, and the path was cut between the mountain and rock to create a passageway. Plants grew towards the trail and at times he had to push them aside to get through. Within minutes, sweat trickled down his temples and his backpack was hot against his shoulder blades. He turned to look over his shoulder and his family was evenly spaced behind him and keeping up. His mom was at the back.

At first, the hike appeared easy and the pace steady, but as they gained altitude, the trees grew thin from wind and altitude, and the hike began to get more challenging. *Wow. This is a tough uphill climb.* He placed his hand on a log and climbed over it. It was damp, and the ground around it was a bit muddy. He spied a tiny spring that showed up on the other side of the hill oozing out from the rocks and dirt. The moisture was everywhere. Adrian lost track of how many small springs and trickles of water were traveling across the trail or down the mountain. The rainforest was alive and well.

Everyone they passed exchanged a pleasant greeting, *"Bonjour... bonjour"* Adrian smiled to himself. *If I didn't know better, I'd think that saying good morning or hello was a requirement up here. I guess it's polite and nice to acknowledge people on the trail. I guess it is the same in the States,* he reflected. *We always say Hey or Hi. Humans really are friendly.*

The sky showed through in places, but it was gray with clouds. *I hope it doesn't rain.* When the plants and trees gave way to a small view, he took a moment to look out over the valley and take it all in. Grace caught up with him. "How long do you think it will take to get to the top?"

"A few people said an hour and a quarter if you are in fantastic shape and don't meet anyone else on the trail. Otherwise, it takes an hour and forty-five minutes if you are in decent physical fitness, and several hours if you are out of shape. Some people never make it up, and I can see why. The ground is not easy to navigate." He turned to move up the trail and Grace followed. "You know it is nearly four and a half miles round trip?"

"Yep!"

As they ascended, the path became strewn with small to medium sized boulders and they had to step with care or risk an ankle injury. The breeze picked up as they climbed in elevation. Some of the clouds were moving off the mountain and the blue sky played peek-a-boo with the hikers.

Ferns and grasses grew out of the rocks and dripped with moisture. They saw centipedes and butterflies and heard a woodpecker.

An old parking lot that had closed provided a welcome break from the steady climbing. Coming out from the canopy of trees into an open space with a clear view of the mountain was startling to him. The landscape drastically changed from rainforest to low shrubs and groundcover filling the fissures and crevasses of the mountains that were etched like deep grooves and scars in the steep hillsides.

Catching up to Adrian, Grace confessed, "I'm afraid to drink my water," as they stopped on the edge of the parking lot to look up the green mountainside. Clouds swirled around the summit, obliterating the view. They had no idea how far they had come or how much further they had to climb.

"Drink up." Adrian advised with an encouraging sound, "you're sweating out pints of water and need to replace it. You may be too dehydrated to even need to use the bathroom until we get down the mountain."

"You think?" She took off her backpack and lifted out the bottle of water from the side pocket. Taking a long swig of refreshing water, she sighed and closed the cap. "Oh, my gosh, I so needed that."

"This climb isn't too hard, is it?" she asked her brother as he took pictures with his cellphone camera.

"It's pretty much climbing a steep staircase to the top from here. I'm impressed with some of the people who passed us on the way down. They must be as old as our grandparents. I hope I'm in good physical shape when I'm their age!"

"I know," she concurred, "and everyone we pass is being so friendly."

Soon, their parents joined them for a quick water break and together they climbed the most difficult part of the trail. Every step of the way they had to choose where to place their feet. More people were coming down and offering encouraging words that they were close to the top. Irregular and knobby boulders wet and muddy from footprints demanded sharp eyes, careful foot placement, and balance. Water oozed from all sides. Within a quarter of an hour, the teens reached a place where they could walk across a relatively flat uphill spot and knew they were close.

The greenery had become so sparse, and the terrain was mostly rock formed from an intense geothermal phreatic eruption of steam, magma and ash layers covered in pale yellow-green lichen.

Strong gusts of wind were whipping everyone's clothing and hair.

"Isn't this great!" Adrian shouted into the wind at his sister with his arms outstretched like an airplane. "I feel like I could fly!"

They were both sweating and breathing hard. A mild smell of sulfur infused the air, but the wind carried it off in haste. They slowed to a stop to consider their next direction. They could see the top of the summit, which was mottled in brown and gray colors of old ash and lava rock.

"I think we are inside a cloud," Adrian mused aloud. Swirling around them, evaporating, and wisping up towards the sky appeared to be white fog and mist. "Wow. It's surreal up here." They could see simple fencing protecting hikers from the edge of the crater, which was huge. People were trying to get selfies in the fog. While it wasn't Mount Everest by any stretch of the imagination, the sense of accomplishment was significant. "Come here, Grace. Let's get a selfie over here." He took out his cellphone and prepped it for their photo by attaching it to a telescoping and gimballed stick.

"How about we stand on this rock and get some of the fencing in the backdrop? It's the only thing that would suggest we were here, since there will be nothing that screams volcano in the photo."

"Yep. I'm with you!" They positioned themselves and took a few pics. "Here comes mom and dad. Let's get some pics with them, too."

After family pictures, they decided to walk around the summit and try to read the signage with diagrams explaining the volcano and its timeline.

"Let's go!" Grace said with impatience. "I want to see Hell's Gate then go. I'm cold and it's damp."

"Well, put your windbreaker on," Adrian urged. "No need to suffer."

"Sweetheart," his dad said to his mom, "that vent in the distance is going to smell like sulfur. You might want to wait here since the wind is blowing in this direction."

"I didn't come all this way to not see the vents!" his mom declared, and marched forward with Grace taking the left fork in the summit trail loop.

"Suit yourself." His dad lamented and followed the ladies.

They continued around the summit trail in silence, taking pictures with their cellphones here and there. There were several vents, the first one being *Dent de l'Est*. As they approached the fenced off vent called *Gouffre Dupuy*, people surrounded the area with the signage and took selfies.

Not too far away, Adrian spotted another steam vent. "Hey, Dad! I think that is the *Gouffre de Tarissan!*" Steam escaped the ground and rose into the sky above them and disappeared. The ground looked as if a giant had plunged an axe into it and by pulling it out, left a deep wedge-shaped hole in the ground. The sides of the vent were gray and rocky with hearty plants trailing down into the hot opening below.

"I think you are correct." His dad walked up the trail and paused to look across the summit to another active steam vent spewing a constant flow of moisture and gas into the air. For the safety of the hikers, no one was allowed near the vents as toxic gasses could cause injury or even death. Carbon dioxide often kills people near volcanoes due to the lack of oxygen. "Wow. That is just amazing. We're walking on an active volcano. Isn't it interesting that the ground doesn't feel hot? One would think it would be."

"Well," Adrian began, "Maybe it is in places."

Continuing, they saw massive boulders of lava, jagged and thrown helter-skelter across the summit. The smell of rotten eggs was much stronger. All of them were slightly gagging on the smell in areas where the wind did not dilute the smell. They passed plants with long stems and red flowers like spearheads growing along the trail. Grace stopped to take some photos.

"I would imagine it is a difficult area for plants to grow here and they must be very hearty to survive these conditions," she commented to her dad and Adrian.

"Yes, and I would add," her dad began, "Volcanic ash is an excellent source of minerals and plants do very well with it. There is plenty of water up here, but the rocky soil, wind, extreme sun, and altitude with noxious gasses has to add to the struggle. It's impressive what can thrive in these conditions."

With the sun rising higher in the sky, and the wind blowing the clouds off, they soon could see the azure Caribbean Sea and islands in the distance. People were taking pictures as fast as possible, knowing the clouds could rush in and hide the view once more.

"This is so beautiful!" Grace exclaimed. "It was so worth the hike."

"Dad," Adrian cut in, "How old is this volcano? Do you know?"

"I believe I read it is estimated to be two-hundred thousand years old." He chuckled and added, "Don't think for one moment that an age of a hundred-thousand-years is old, because it is considered quite young by volcanologists."

"Oh. So, does that mean that the height and growth of the island is a result of magma growth?" Adrian asked, attempting to comprehend the age of the mountain he was standing on. "Like, how many years does it take for a volcano to become forty-eight hundred feet tall?"

"The history I looked at on the web suggested that it was a fountain of lava for a hundred thousand or half its life. They figure it reached a height of seventeen hundred feet at that point based on the type of rock and from studying other young volcanoes."

"Wait. You mean they think it was..." he did some quick math in his head, "seven-hundred and sixty-four feet higher than it is today?"

"Yes. The scientists who have studied this volcano posted that forty-two thousand years ago it had a notable event."

"Wow." Adrian let out a low whistle. "What happened?"

"How do they even know this?" his dad continued, shaking his head in disbelief, "I have no idea, but they estimated that during this massive eruption, Soufrière blew a plume of volcanic ash thirty-five kilometers into the atmosphere." He pulled out his phone and opened the calculator app. "Rounded up, that is twenty-two miles up into the sky." He paused and said, "Adrian, let's put that into perspective. Consider that airplanes fly at thirty-thousand feet," he did some quick math to convert miles to feet and shared the results, "That's around a hundred and fifteen thousand feet up."

"Holy smokes!" Adrian was impressed by the sheer force that shot a plume of fiery ash high into the atmosphere.

"Exactly." His dad grinned at Adrian's exclamation. "So, just imagine that all the guts of the volcano go up into the sky leaving it empty, right? What do you think happened next?"

"The top and sides collapsed into the belly of the volcano, leaving this big sweeping summit?" Adrian asked excitedly. "Hey! Just like that chocolate lava cake dessert. The top crumbles into the crater when the molten chocolate oozes out the side. I get it!"

"You got it! It went one kilometer into the ground and formed a three-kilometer caldera. There were more eruptions of significance, and from what I understand, it eventually settled into this current form many thousands of years ago."

"I saw that it went off in 1976-1977. Was it as dramatic as those other events?"

"No, but it did create some large cracks on the western side, and it is labeled as having structural instability. That parking lot we passed suffered from the instability. Those phreatic eruptions were devoid of magma, meaning it was steam and ash."

"What does instability mean to the island?" Adrian liked to consider the future and look ahead to future outcomes. This didn't sound like it was an optimal situation for the people living below the volcano. "Is the volcano going to erupt again soon?"

"First," his dad stated as he navigated a single-file group of hikers coming their way on a narrow section of trail, "that western side could slide down into the sea and cause everyone in its way to lose their home or life if they aren't alerted to move out. This could potentially cause a tsunami if a sizable chunk of the island hits the water.

"Second," he waved at the last hiker and resumed walking up

the rocky trail. "Those cracks mean magma is building up again and pushing against the inner walls of the caldera. Like a baby growing in the womb, eventually it will want to come out. And when it does, that will be spectacular, but also create havoc worldwide."

"You mean transporting all the island's people for miles around?"

"Think thousands of miles." His dad negotiated a tight corner around a tall boulder and caught up with Grace who was waiting for them. "The enormity of the tsunami is mind boggling. It could potentially wipe out every island in the Caribbean. I don't like to think about it."

"Hey, Dad!" Grace beamed at him. "I think we have come as far as we can on this trail. I suspect mom is waiting for us by now. And," she pointed to something.

"Ah-ha! *Porte de l'enfer!* Now this is what I came for!" his dad announced with some barely concealed excitement. "Wow. It's a stinky one for sure! Whew!"

Directly behind the crater, inside the cone was a lovely green sunken area. Surrounded by steep rock walls covered with grasses, many lichens, and mosses, it was a miniature valley void of volcanic activity. After a complete examination of the area, they were ready to leave the crater.

"Going down may be fast and dangerous in spots and very crowded." Adrian's dad continued, "We ought to all go together and help each other if necessary."

"Good idea!" His mom agreed and they set off single file down the volcano. Along the way, they encouraged hikers on their way to the top that they were almost there. At about the halfway point, Adrian's dad chuckled and suggested they stop announcing to hikers that they're almost to the top. Laughing, they returned to just greeting folks with a friendly hello.

Upon arrival back at the yacht, Jimmy announced that they would be departing Guadeloupe and arriving in St. Lucia in the morning. Grace and Adrian looked at each other and shrugged. It made no difference to them where they went, since they were having the time of their lives.

"Wanna try out the sailboats?" Grace asked as she pushed Adrian's cabin door open and stuck her head inside.

He swung his legs over the bed and sat facing her within two seconds. "Great idea! I guess we don't need to read the manual, do we?" Grinning, he picked up the radio controller for one and handed it to her. "Let's just mess around with one of them and see what is possible. I'll carry the beast."

"Wait! I need to get my swimsuit on. Give me five minutes." She was gone in a flash. Adrian rushed to change as well. He was lifting the nearly five-foot-tall sailboat and testing the awkwardness of carrying it when his sister opened the door. "Hold the door, Grace, I'm coming through.

"You need to grab the controller, though." He walked sideways through the door with the ridiculous boat that was nearly as tall as he was into the lounge area outside his cabin. He padded across the main deck to the stern where a large swimming pool stretched across the main deck. Laying the boat on its side next to the pool, he turned back to talk with his sister. "On second thought, I think I'm going to need..." his voice trailed off as she shoved the booklet of operations into his hand. To his surprise, she had the other boat in her hands and controllers under both armpits.

"This?" Laughing, she said, "I figured you might need to know how to hook up the battery or switch it on or make a connection with the radio controller. After we learn those things, we can probably toss it."

"You rock, Grace!" he praised her with a smile. *Sometimes Grace just sees what we need before we know we need it.* Turning to the table of contents, he scanned the titles to find the one 'on getting started.' He opened that page and skimmed through the set-up and troubleshooting.

"Well," he announced, setting the booklet down on a nearby lounger covered in pillows, "This should be easy." Minutes later, both boats were in the water and they each held a radio controller in their hands.

"Here goes nothing," Grace announced as she used her thumb and index finger to move the control on the main sheet that controlled the biggest sail on the mast. She squealed when the boat started to heel over and ram the side of the pool. "Ack!" And frantically moved buttons and control sticks to get it to move in the opposite direction. Her voice rose in frustration as she talked to the boat hoping it would help. "No, no, no, don't go there." She leaned her body to one side as if the boat could be influenced by her body's modeling of how she wanted it to move. "No, stop. Don't do that!"

"Um, Grace?" Adrian was silently laughing at her and didn't know where to begin to help her. "The boat is powered by the wind, not the controller, your mind or your body."

"Don't talk to me, Adrian! I'm learning how to sail." She was leaning so far over to her left trying to get the boat to fall away from the swimming pool edge and catch the breeze, Adrian walked over to her and took the controller out of her hands.

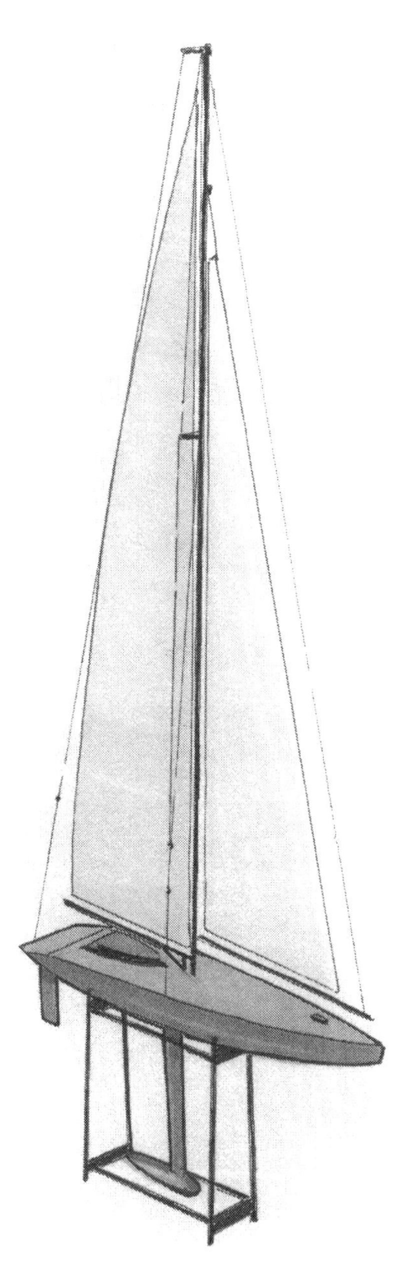

"Grace."

"What?!" she demanded, placing her hands on her hips. "Why is it so hard?!"

"Wet your finger," Adrian instructed, and she looked at him curiously.

"What does that have to do with anything?" she countered with suspicion.

"Just wet your finger and hold it up over your head."

She put her right index finger in her mouth up to her second knuckle and then raised it up. "Why am I doing this?"

"Where is the wind coming from?"

"Oh." Her eyes darted around as she sensed her damp finger. Then with clarity, she spun around and pointed to the stern of the boat. "There."

"Good job, Grace." He smiled and nodded. "Remember flying kites with dad? We always pulled our kites up into the wind. He taught me that trick, but your hair will tell you the same info if you know what I mean."

"Right. Gotcha." She nodded her understanding. "So, are you saying that we have to drive the boats into the wind? I thought they could go in any direction we steered them in."

"Almost." He walked over to his boat and carried it to the stern where there was nothing to obstruct the breeze coming off the water. "Watch how the wind hits the sail. And don't forget where the wind is coming from, okay?"

"Okay."

Adrian held the boat by the long keel attached to the underside of the hull. He slowly held the boat with the bow directly into the wind. Wind blew on both sides of the sail and it luffed around but it never filled and formed the shape of an airplane wing. "Now watch, Grace! Watch what happens when I move it 45-degrees to the direction the wind is coming from." He angled the boat off the wind and suddenly the wind hit the sail and filled, forming a graceful, curved shape.

"Oh! I get it!" She bent down to get her controller which Adrian had placed at her feet.

"Wait, Grace!" Adrian ordered. "You need to see what happens when the boat is perpendicular to the wind and going with the wind." He turned his body and the boat 90-degrees to the wind, so the wind filled the sails. "This is where you want to let out some of the sail so it dumps the excess wind, or the boat will heel over sharply. Like this." He angled the sailboat on its ear, and she grimaced, imagining the railing underwater.

Using the controller to release some of the lines holding the miniature sails on board, he held the boat until the wind came from behind his back and it filled the sails, blowing them forward. "Get it?"

"I think so." She adjusted the sail controller, so the lines holding them in were slack and the sail filled a bit more and the boat floated off the edge of the pool. Now it was bobbing tentatively along the glass retaining wall. "Why is it so slow? The breeze is strong enough, right?"

"Try bringing in the sails just a bit. The wind is spilling off the sails and it's depowering your boat."

Grace fiddled with the controls until the boat picked up speed and she gasped, "Oh, no!" just as the bow crashed into the corner of the pool. Adrian laughed and walked to the stern stairsteps that were near the corner of the pool and gently nudged the boat around. "Try again. Maybe ease the sails and go downwind?"

Adjusting the controls, Grace got the sails to ease out and she formed butterfly-like wings and the boat accelerated down the pool. "Oh, no, it's going to crash again! What do I do?!" Her voice registered panic and she walked to the edge to prevent the bow from hitting the opposite side.

"You have to pick a direction you want the boat to travel in and bring the sails to one side of the boat or the other. If you bring the small sail in the front onto the same side of the main sail, you can round up the boat into the wind to reach across the wind or head up into the wind by pulling both sails in tight. Your other choice is to jibe the mainsail boom across the deck and then round up into the wind."

"How do you know so much? We don't even have a sailboat!"

"Laser sailing at Boy Scout Camp last year, remember?" Adrian placed his boat in the stern end of the pool and walked over to his radio controller. "It wasn't easy at first, but you know, after a while you figure it out. I fell overboard many times, flipped the boat over at least a hundred times, lost my rudder, broke a tiller, crashed into other boats and docks, but it was fun."

"How did I not know that about you?" Grace asked with some puzzlement. "I never knew you learned how to sail."

Adrian shrugged with indifference. "I dunno. Maybe because I don't have photos of me on a Laser?"

"Maybe," she said, holding down a sail trim button as she watched her boat's sails move inboard as far as they could, and the boat heeled over and began moving towards the side of the pool where she was standing.

"Well, Grace, if it is any comfort to you, I have no clue what you were doing last summer either." He shared without taking his eyes off the blue racing hull. The sails were close-hauled and the boat was sailing as close to the wind as possible making its way to the stern wall of the pool. "What were you doing while I was in scout camp?"

"I was riding horses, falling off them occasionally, knocking training jump poles and rails to the ground, and kicking over floral bush boxes by accident. Yep. The same thing you were doing."

"Ha!" He barked with a trace of self-mockery, "So basically, we were both falling off our mounts and crashing into things! And no photos to show for it."

"For which I am doubly glad," Grace added with a tinge of horror. "I'd hate for something like that to get out on social media. Ugh."

"You know what we need?" He put his controller down, left his boat bobbing along the side of the pool and snapped his fingers with excitement. "Sail racing buoys! I'll be right back!" And with that, he ditched Grace and ran to the galley.

Bursting into the galley, he found Zak and Jean-Marie working on the evening preparations with rapid but confident movements. "Not a good time, buddy." Zak warned in a casual tone. "Make it quick."

"Yep," Adrian agreed. "Sorry to bother you, but can you please think about what kitchen items I can use to make tiny racing buoys for the swimming pool. Maybe corks and twine with a weight at the bottom? Or maybe a small plastic squeeze bottle I can float at the top of an anchor line? I'll also talk to Pete and Jimmy."

"Roger that, wilco." Zak never broke his pace with his workplace goals but did look up to heaven for patience after the door closed behind Adrian. "Darn it!" Zak exclaimed with a touch of irritation to the ceiling, "I added salt twice to the sauce." The chef turned to his sous-chef and sighed, "I swear he can be the King of Distraction and Interruption some days."

"Oui, Chef," Jean-Marie agreed as she wiped her brow with the back of her forearm, "He is a good boy, but he is full of disruptive energies. I don't think he knows how much he is breaking people's concentration when he interrupts their work."

"He's a great kid, don't get me wrong, but sometimes he just blows through the galley door like a gale force wind, and it feels like…" Zak took a deep breath and carried the heavy saucepan to the sink to pitch half of it out. "I will talk to him." Walking to the fridge, he opened the heavy door and said to no one in particular, "Now, to fix my sauce…"

Adrian found Pete in the soundproofed engine room working at his computer desk. "Hey, man, can I talk to you?"

"If you make it quick. What's up?" Pete had pushed his chair back and swiveled around to face Adrian. His broad freckled face was serious, and Adrian knew he was interrupting something. He took a deep breath and described his problem.

"Grace and I are playing with radio-controlled sailboats in the pool. I wondered if you had any materials I could use to make tiny buoys I could anchor in the pool for us to sail around." Adrian was leaning against the glass door he had entered a moment before. Pete's small office was air conditioned, and the hum of the generators could be heard throughout. Floor to ceiling banks of engine monitoring equipment were stacked and labeled neatly with plastic imprinted plaques. He waited while Pete searched his memory for available materials the young teens could use.

"I can't solve this now. Let me think about it and get back to you," he began as he straightened up in his chair. "As a first thought, you may be able to tie something around the neck of a bottle or something. Maybe an empty wine bottle with a cork in it? And duct tape an anchor line to the bottom of the bottle."

It sounded a bit big to Adrian's ears and he dismissed the idea as viable. "Not bad. Not bad." He commented with some hesitancy. "It's a bit big and I don't like the idea of glass in the pool. Maybe a plastic jug…"

"A juice jug with a rope tied to the handle sounds perfect," Pete leaned forward and placed his hands on the armrests of his office chair, indicating he was ready to pull himself back to work. "If you can find a string, I've got a load of stainless-steel washers you could tie together to make a weight at the bottom. Let me know what you decide."

"I like that idea!" Adrian beamed at him. "I'll keep you posted. Thanks, man."

Pete was already pulling himself back to his monitor before Adrian opened the door.

Tempted to return to the galley but knowing the dinner prep was well underway, he headed to the main deck where he found Grace still playing with the controls.

"Find anything?" she asked without looking over at him.

"Not yet, but I have an idea and Pete's offered us anchor weights for whatever we decide to float." He picked up his controller. Studying the pool, he assessed their racing buoy needs. "I think we only need two floats, given its size. We can do upwind and downwind racing and change the buoy rounding to mix it up."

"What do you mean?" Grace asked, a bit confused.

"Oh, sorry," he replied, "I mean we can make the rules for going around the buoys and agree to keep the buoys on the port or starboard side of our boats, but we have to agree to which way we are going to go -either we round both the buoys to port, or we round them both to starboard…or we round some combination of that."

"Ah." Grace had been getting the hang of how to maneuver the sailboat in the pool and was making smoother tacks and jibes. "Check this out!"

She steered the boat downwind along the starboard side of the pool and then pulled the sails in and rounded the boat 90-degrees to the wind to sail along the next edge of the pool. When she got to the corner, she tacked the boat and sailed it from the port edge to the middle of the starboard edge before she tacked once more and headed back to the port side of the pool. On one more short tack she would have the boat back at the stern wall of the pool.

"Wow! Not bad, sis!" Adrian was very impressed that she had figured it out so fast. Not to be outdone, he moved into position and began chasing her boat around the pool. Soon he caught up to her and forced her to tack away from his boat to get clear air.

"Hey!" She complained, "You blocked my air. That's not fair."

"You know what they say," he grinned, "All is fair in love and war, and racing."

"Dey do not say dat, mon," Jimmy had quietly come down the port stairs behind them and walked over to them without a sound in his bare feet. Both the teens jumped and started to laugh.

"Jimmy! You scared me for a second," Grace laughed. "Don't sneak up on me like that."

Jimmy laughed. "Let me try dis for a minute." He extended his hand out to Grace, who placed the controller in his hand. "Now let me see…" He fiddled with the buttons and fussed over his first attempts and just as Grace was about to reach in and point out to him what to do, he arched away from her and raised the controller up out of reach on the side away from her. "I got dis. I can figure it out. Mama didn't raise no fool." Grace shook her head with a laugh as she took a step back and waved her open hand in front of her feet, indicating that he had the floor.

He looked at Adrian who was watching him with a barely concealed grin. "What you smilin' for, young man?" Turning to Grace he said, "Grace, why don' you move both boats to de forward part of de pool. An' den Master Adrian and I will play touch 'n go. De first one to touch de stern pool wall on de third time is de winnah."

"Touch the forward and aft walls of the pool for three racing legs total?" Adrian clarified. Jimmy nodded with a serious face.

Adrian grinned. "No problem, mon. I got this."

Grace held both boats by their sterns at the forward edge of the pool. She kept them almost three feet apart with their bows headed directly into the wind. The sails luffed. "On your mark, get set, go!" She let go and jumped back to watch the race.

Adrian hadn't quite figured out the controller as much as Grace and he was feeling awkward with the steering joysticks for the sails and rudder. Without warning, the red sailboat operated by Jimmy was sailing along in parallel, inching up from his stern. Nearing the port wall of the pool he declared, "Tacking!" And both he and Jimmy rolled their boats across the wind towards the opposite side of the pool. Thinking he could stay clear of Jimmy's dead wind off his main sail, he tacked without warning and headed back to his side of the pool. The red boat kept going.

Jimmy headed toward the long edge of the pool at a 45-degree angle and Adrian tacked quickly to zigzag towards the port stern wall. Jimmy shouted "One!" as the bow of his boat banged into the thick tempered glass wall and he spun the rudder to turn the boat and ease the sails to go dead downwind towards the opposite wall.

"One!" Adrian called and followed Jimmy but at a distance and just a few seconds behind. "Hey!" he voice expressed reproach, "You were pretending to not know how to work the RC."

"All is fair in love and war and racing..." Jimmy laughed, and the sound was a deep rumble in his broad chest. "In The Art of War you let your opponent think you are weak when you are strong and strong when you are weak. So, yeah, I got dis." He touched the bow to the pool wall and declared, "Two. Better catch up, mon."

"Arrrgh." Adrian ground out in frustration, "Two." He spun his blue sailboat around and began the task of heading upwind for the wall. He was half a boat length behind Jimmy when the first officer called "Three! And I'm de winnah!"

Grace was grinning at Jimmy and high-fived him for beating her brother. Taking back the RC black box, she began trimming the sails while her brother pouted at losing.

"No fair. Why do I feel like I've been conned?" Adrian laughed a hollow laugh. His eyes did not reflect his laugh.

"'Cause me got you gud, mon. You so confident, you didn' see me comin'," Jimmy chuckled. "See you around. I got to get back to de captain. I'm sure he's watchin' on de cameras and havin' a good chuckle."

Adrian turned to look in the direction of one of the high-definition security cameras on the main deck mounted discretely near the pool. He waved at the camera hoping the captain was watching.

"Ringer!" Adrian hollered at Jimmy's back as he walked away. Jimmy roared laughing and raised his right fist to the ceiling in triumph and shouted back, "I'm de king!"

"I think I'm done messin' around with the boats for today. You?" Grace asked him with the lift of an eyebrow. "I want to go talk to mom."

"Yeah. Can you bring the controllers back to my cabin and I'll carry the boats?" He asked her. "And get the door for me?"

Grace took the box out of his hand, picked up the manual of operations and waited until she saw that her brother had both boats firmly in hand. "I think I better carry one of those. You probably shouldn't carry it by the keel. And look, the masts are getting crossed."

Adrian looked up and sighed. Grace met him and tucked one

of the boxes under her arm and used her free hand to accept the model boat from him. "Why are we trying to bring everything in one trip?" She laughed and put down the controller and marched off to his cabin and opened the door. Stepping inside, she used her body to hold open the heavy wooden door and waited until her brother entered and placed the boat in its cradle. She passed him the other one. "We need to practice and then have a rematch with Jimmy."

"No kidding!" He adjusted the boats, so they were not touching. "Thanks. I'll get the boxes and manual. See you at dinner?"

"Yep!" Grace left and Adrian walked back to the stern to clean up and found Francesco picking up the remaining pieces of their activity.

"*Ciao, Francesco!*" He received the two boxes the deckhand passed to him. He picked up the booklet and tucked it under his arm.

"*Ciao, Adriano! Come stai?*"the deckhand asked him in his usual friendly fashion. "We all heard Jimmy did a little match racing with you."

Adrian sighed, feeling uncomfortable in the spotlight. "I guess everyone knows he has experience, and I don't?"

"*Si, amico. Va bene*" He put a comforting arm around his young friend. "You'll get him next time."

"Count on it!" Adrian did knuckles with Francesco and took the two RC boxes and manual to his room and set them in a drawer, then changed for dinner.

Chapter 4
Liberty

Saint Lucia
British Commonwealth
West Indies, Caribbean Sea

During the night, the captain and crew moved the boat just over 125nm to the southwestern coast of the island of Saint Lucia. The Abercrombies woke up to the magnificent site of the famous Pitons, two volcanic plugs covered in dark green vegetation against a blue sky off the stern deck. The clear aqua-bluegreen waters sparkled in the early morning sun. A fringe of palm trees lined the coastline and white sand beaches curved along the island's edge. Pastel colored buildings with assorted roof colors crowded each other and dotted the landscape from the beach front back up the mountainsides. There was no wind and sea birds floated on the water under the hot sun. It looked like a tropical postcard. Inviting.

On the main deck, Chief Stewardess Gabrielle from South Africa, placed a glass jug of cold orange juice on the bar. She picked up a basket of chocolate croissants and placed it in front of Adrian and his dad with a grin. "Your daily bread, Adrian." He grinned at her as she used silver-toned tongs and placed one on his plate and one on his dad's plate. "Coffee this morning, young man?"

"No, thank you. I'm trying to cut back." His eyes twinkled and he leaned back in his deck chair. "I don't want to ruin my chances of growing to my full height."

"Aww, I'm disappointed," she teased. "You bought into the myth." She moved around the table to the bar and made him a vanilla latte and placed it in front of him. With a friendly wink she said, "In case you change your mind."

His dad laughed and said, "Gabrielle, don't encourage him!"

Adrian's mom took a sip of fresh orange juice and set her glass down. "Adrian, friends of the captain are coming aboard after breakfast. I think you will want to meet them."

"Why's that, Mom?" He asked as he tore another bite of the flakey croissant off with his fingers and stuffed it into his mouth.

"Oh, you'll find out soon enough." She picked up her fork and took a bite of juicy red grapefruit. Her secret smile meant that she wasn't going to divulge a single detail and he would have to wait.

"Are we going ashore today?" Grace asked as she toyed with her linen napkin. "Or staying at anchor?"

"Oh, I think we'll see how the day goes after our visitors arrive by tender." Grace's mom looked at her watch. "They should be arriving in thirty minutes or so."

"Gabrielle?" Adrian said to get her attention, "Do you know anything about those volcano-looking things?"

"Sure." She walked away from the bar and stood next to Adrian and pointed to the larger one, "That one is cleverly named *Gros Piton* and measures almost eight hundred meters above sea level. The smaller one is *Petit Piton* and measures almost seven-hundred and fifty meters."

"Are they active?" His dad asked with interest. "They look sealed at the top."

"I believe we are looking at the neck of the volcano," she replied, "This morning before breakfast, I read that they are both plugs in the volcano and may be the proverbial cork in the bottle, holding in gasses."

"So, they could explode at any minute?" Grace asked.

"I have no idea," Gabrielle replied with honesty. Then looked at Adrian with a straight face, "I don't know many things that can hold gas in forever. Do you?"

He gave an obligatory laugh then ducked his head, feeling his cheeks grow warm. *OMG, she must have heard me fart in the TV room the other day. I didn't think anyone was around! Oh, this is cringe worthy...*

"I've had my fill of volcanoes for this year," his mom announced, "I don't think I need to hike or explore either of those." Turning to her husband, she asked, "Do you, dear?"

"Oh, I might want to do the big one, which I read was much easier than the shorter one." He paused with his espresso cup inches from his mouth, "I read the views are spectacular."

"That's what drones are for!" Grace injected with an air of

authority, "I don't need to climb any mountain ever again. Just send the drone up! And we couldn't use the drone on our hike the other day because the clouds obscured just about everything. What's the point?"

"The three E's: Exercise, exploration and experience." Her dad dabbed his lips and stood up. "I'll meet everyone back here when the captain's guests arrive. I've got a call I need to make."

"Grace," her mother began as she pushed her chair back, "Want to borrow that nail polish color you asked me for earlier? Now's a good time."

"Sure."

Jane entered the deck and began cleaning up the dishes while Adrian picked at his second croissant. *I wonder who is coming aboard?* Downing the last of his latte, he stood up to leave the table and wandered over to the edge of the pool to look out.

"Can I speak with you for a moment, Adrian?" Chef Zak approached Adrian and signaled that they would walk to the stern for privacy.

"Sure, what's up?" He followed Zak down the steps to the deck close to the water.

"I wanted to talk with you about interrupting me and my staff in the galley when we are under pressure to get meals on the table for both your family and the crew. I screwed up my sauce yesterday and nearly had to start over." While he was talking he was scanning Adrian's response to his words. Adrian went stock-still and his eyes locked on Chef's eyes. "So, to prevent galley errors, I am asking you to text me when you want to ask me something or hang out so I can choose the best time to talk with you. Normally, passengers are not allowed into the galley except by invitation. I've been allowing you to come in and be at home in the galley to learn and bake, but your visits are increasing to the point of distraction. We need to find a better way to time our communications. Are we good?"

"Sure, Chef, I'll text you," Adrian replied in a calm, emotionless voice. "Sorry about that. It was never my intention to distract you."

Zak clapped him on the back like an uncle. "I know. I think you're full of energy, ideas and proactive in making them come to life, but unlike yourself and your sister, we adults are all working twelve to fourteen hours a day to run this yacht and it is mind-altering to have one's focus and concentration broken."

Adrian was frozen to the spot. His gut felt like he was punched. He couldn't speak, but he knew he had to. "OK, I get it."

"Great," said Zak as he leapt up the steps, leaving Adrian behind to stare after him. "I'll see you around. I've gotta get an early luncheon prepared for the captain's guests." And with that he was gone.

Adrian turned slowly to look off the stern deck to the far shore. He didn't want to be seen right now. He wanted to disappear. He felt like diving in and swimming far away and never coming back.

He leaned back against the pool wall and closed his eyes. *Why do I feel like I've done something wrong and lost the respect of a friend? Ugh. I hate this feeling! I hate it!* He slid down to sit on the stern teak floor with the transom wall behind him. Heat rose up to his face and he felt embarrassment flood his cheeks. *Did Pete think the same thing?* He put his face in his hands. *Oh, shoot, did Jimmy act weird with me yesterday because I talk to him too much? I wonder if the crew are complaining to the captain and mom and dad. Ugh.*

I bet they all think I am always interrupting them. His heart sank. It was like he was back home or at school and his teacher reprimanded him for constantly blurting out the answers without raising his hand or busting out with stuff when she was trying to teach class.

I just want to disappear until they all forget I ever existed.

He wasn't sure how long he had stayed on the stern deck, but suddenly the sound of a dog barking and the quiet approach of a motorboat getting closer to the stern registered in his brain. He looked up and saw Raffa and Brian bringing the yacht's tender starboard side to the stern swim platform. He leapt to his feet and forgot his triggered state to position himself to receive the bow line from Raffa.

Sitting in the stern were a white-haired man and woman who were about his grandparents' age or older. *These are the captain's guests.* A flash of white on the floor of the powerboat caught his eye and he saw the woman bend down towards the dog he heard barking a minute ago.

"Pronto?" Raffa asked. Adrian took his eyes off the couple and nodded to the deck hand. Raffa threw the line to Adrian and Brian killed the engine. Adrian pulled the boat in gently. Raffa leapt off the starboard side and took the stern line with him. Together they secured the powerboat.

"Hey, Adrian," Brian called out in a friendly tone, "Come over here so you can meet Henry and Maggie Wright."

"Hallo, Adrian, lovely to meet you." Henry said in a soft English accent. "I've heard very nice things about you from our friend the Captain."

"Hello, nice to meet you, too." Adrian shook Henry's hand and liked him immediately. He turned to shake hands with Maggie but got distracted by the Jack Russel Terrier on a leash that she held firmly. The dog started barking at Adrian and fidgeting impatiently. Ferocious barking continued while everyone laughed and told the dog reassuring words. Maggie's laugh had a musical sound that Adrian perked up at.

Henry shared, "This is our latest dog rescue. Meet Dog."

"Oh!" Adrian gasped with joy and knelt to introduce himself to the dog by putting out his hand, which the dog smelled instantly. The dog barked more, this time like he was telling Adrian a story of having traveled across the sea.

"Nice to meet you, Dog." He looked up and shared genuinely, "And you, too, Maggie. Sorry I forgot my manners, but I didn't expect to see my favorite animal today." He turned to stroke the dog's back and coo over him. "Hello, boy. Are you a good boy? Ah, good boy." Dog barked back and continued to move with unusual energy.

The dog was wagging his tail and licking Adrian's hands. He was sniffing his feet and tasting his skin. "Oh, my gosh! He likes you!" Maggie exclaimed. When the dog tried to jump up on Adrian, who was squatting down and nearly knocked him off balance, she sternly said, "Down dog, down."

Dog wasn't having any of it. Raffa and Brian laughed as Adrian lay on his back and allowed the dog to come over for a little play.

"Oh, my." Henry laughed. "You really do love dogs, don't you?"

"I so want a dog," Adrian confessed. "But my mom won't let me have one."

Brian suggested they migrate up to the next level and he announced through his walkie-talkie that the guests were on board and began moving up to the main deck.

"May I?" Adrian asked for the leash by putting out his hand in Maggie's direction.

"Oh, gosh, yes, of course, love. Here." She unwound the red leather strap off her delicate wrist and handed it to Adrian, who took command of his new best friend and led him up the flight of steps.

"Um, not to be rude or anything," Adrian began with some hesitancy to Henry and Maggie, "but why is his name Dog? I think it is a terrible name for him."

"Well, he's a rescue dog of sorts and we've only just got him. And we just haven't found a name for him yet." Henry explained with frank honesty. "Sometimes you just need to experience a dog before you name it, you know?"

"Yes, I get it." Adrian looked at the dog and wondered what his name would be. "Maybe I can help with that. If something comes to mind, I'll let you know."

"That would be awfully kind of you, dear." Maggie extended with a smile. She turned to her husband, "I see Gunnar! Come on!" She grabbed Henry's hand and they strode over to meet the captain. She opened her arms wide and embraced him with all her heart. He bent and kissed her suntanned cheek that was all smiles. Henry and the captain warmly embraced in a hug, too. *Wow, these are good friends of the captain.*

Adrian hung back to give them space. He wasn't so sure he wanted to talk with the captain just yet. He wasn't sure if the captain was happy with him or not. *Why am I in such self-doubt? Ugh. I just hate to think the captain isn't happy with me right now. And now I'm back to being afraid that I'm in the wrong.*

To take his mind off his conflict, he walked the dog over to the closest chaise lounge and sat on the edge to play with the dog, who leaped up onto the cushioned chair to be with Adrian. He whispered to the dog, "I know I shouldn't let you be up here on the furniture with me, but right now, I am so happy you are here!" Dog licked Adrian's face and he laughed, "Do you smell my breakfast? Do you like chocolate croissants? Even if you do, you aren't getting any because chocolate is very bad for dogs. You know that right? Yeah, you do, because you are a smart dog.

I can tell."

The dog was wagging his tail and super excited. He barked a few times and Adrian stroked his back to calm him down. "Now, now, it's all good." Right away he noticed that the dog's hair was getting everywhere. It was shedding white hair on his clothes, the pillows, the deck and was even stuck to his hands. "Oh, boy. My mom is not going to like this hair everywhere, dog. She likes dogs, but she doesn't like dogs, if you know what I mean." Dog just barked.

"Wow, Adrian, is this Maggie and Henry's dog?" Grace asked as she put out her hand to greet their furry passenger. "He's very energetic, isn't he? And he's shedding like crazy! Mom's not going to like this."

Adrian laughed, "I just told that to the dog! Maybe it would be best if we keep him right here, so we don't track hair everywhere."

"Do you think he needs water or a snack?" Grace asked. "I can get a bowl from behind the bar."

"I think we should ask Maggie first." Adrian said with caution, "We don't have a place for him to use the bathroom. In fact, I don't know what the plan is with this little guy, since he doesn't have a place to relieve himself." The dog was furiously licking Adrian's ear and wagging its tail at rapid speeds. Adrian leaned away and wiped his ear.

"I think he likes you," Grace stated. "But you always did have a way with dogs. Wait here and I'll go ask Maggie what the plan is for him." He followed her with his eyes to watch the interaction she would have with Maggie and the others. He didn't feel like going near them just yet. His parents had joined the captain and several officers and were chatting amicably with the Wrights. Both stewardesses were setting the table for coffee and assorted breakfast pastries and coffee cake nearby. A minute later, Grace and Maggie were walking towards him talking and gesticulating like old friends.

Dog barked at Maggie and took a step back.

'What have we here?" Maggie asked Dog, bending down to pat his back. Dog kept barking and wagging his tail. She turned to Adrian, "I think he is trying to say something. I wonder what it could be?"

"I agree. He is trying to talk," Adrian shared. "I wish I could take him ashore and go for a run or something. Maybe he wants to go home? Or use the bathroom?"

"He took care of his business before coming aboard," Maggie chuckled, "I promised the captain I would do that."

At that moment, his mom showed up and invited everyone to partake in coffee at the table. Adrian hung back and stalled for as long as he could while a group formed around the table. He kept his barking friend on the leash and talked to him in soothing tones. Jane approached him and said, "Hey, Mate, I'll watch this little cutie, so you can join the party. Alright?"

With great reluctance, Adrian handed her the leash. "I'll be back soon, Dog." He bent down to soothe the terrier and whispered, "I'll try and find you a treat, OK? You be a good boy!" Dog licked his ear in response. Adrian laughed and stood up. "Thanks, Jane. I hope to be right back!"

"Aw, no worries, mate. I've got the little love. He's in good hands. Right?" She knelt to offer her hand for Dog to sniff. He looked up and kept barking. He strained to follow Adrian, who looked back and saw Dog trying to get to him. *Well, that's nice to see. At least someone wants me around here.*

His mom raised her arm to signal he should sit next to her, where she saved him a seat. Grace and Maggie were deep in conversation, as were Henry and his dad. Mom and the captain were smiling.

"Like him, do you?" the captain asked.

"Yeah, I do," Adrian said wistfully while placing his napkin on his lap in preparation for a midmorning snack with their guests. "I've always wanted a dog."

His mom laughed and patted his knee, "I know. I know. I'm the one keeping you from having your dream come true."

"You can say that again," Adrian invited moodily. He folded his hands in his lap and looked across the table to his dad and Henry. They appeared to be talking about university experiences. Turning to the captain, he asked, "How long are we staying here in St. Lucia?"

The captain exchanged a glance with his mom and Adrian turned to look at her. He had an odd sensation growing in the pit of his stomach. "What?" he demanded. "What's going on?"

The captain laughed, "You are very perceptive, Adrian! I'll let your mom tell you."

His mom gently took his hand and shared, "Your dad and I and the captain would like to ask you if you would like to spend a week or so ashore with Henry and Maggie...and Dog. It would be..."

Adrian cut her off, "Yes. When can we leave? I'm ready. Just tell me when." He pushed his chair back from the table and pretended to stand up, "I'll pack now. I'm serious. Let's do this!"

While the captain, his dad and Henry were smiling, his mom was seriously taken aback. "Why, Adrian! If I didn't know better I'd say you were anxious to get away from the boat. Is that true?" Her deep concern was written all over her face as she twisted sideways in her chair to talk with him.

Exasperated, Adrian looked up at the ceiling and took a deep breath, "Look, Mom, no offense, but I wouldn't mind getting away for a while and hanging out with a dog...who won't judge me and just have some fun. That's all I'm saying." He closed his eyes for two long seconds and when he opened them he saw all the men looking at him with interest. "A change of pace, you know...?"

"Yes!" Captain Gunnar declared with enthusiasm as he leaned forward to clap Adrian on the shoulder in a friendly manner. Looking back and forth between his mom and dad, he shared, "A change of pace would be marvelous for Adrian! And Henry and Maggie are the perfect hosts for him. He will have a wonderful room in a lighthouse he can share with Dog, learn to row a boat, train Dog –because he needs it! He'll probably meet some local kids his age and explore the island on his own." He turned to look at Adrian, "How does that sound to you, Adrian?"

While Adrian was figuring out his response, Henry quietly shared, "Oh, and Adrian, you will love our place. And I can teach you a thing or two about rowing." He smiled and the sea breeze ruffled his white hair, making him look somewhat angelic. "I do know a thing or two about rowing, don't I, Gunnar?"

"You sure do," he laughed, "Henry taught me how to row. You'll never hear him blowing his own horn but he's a champion rower. Now he builds the best row boats ever." The captain's enthusiasm for Henry was powerful, "Adrian, you should see his woodworking shop! It's amazing."

"Oh, yes," Henry waggled his index finger up in the air before he pointed it at the captain, "That reminds me...I am just about finished with the Whitehall two-seater rowboat, but it needs a name. Perhaps you might have some ideas, Adrian, for this new boat of mine? What do you think? Would you like to come ashore and spend some time with us?"

With gratitude for the mental and emotional rescue and description of what he might experience, he grinned and said in a winsome tone, "Sounds like paradise! When can we leave?"

Chapter 5
Jaxon

Wright's Lighthouse
St. Lucia, British Commonwealth
West Indies, Caribbean Sea

Adrian wasn't sure what he was expecting as he arrived at the Wright's property, but the guesthouse shaped like a lighthouse looked intriguing. The lighthouse part of the building was easily thirty feet tall and capped with red roofing material that matched the roof of the garage, which was a long, wide rectangular shape. Painted white, with varnished wood window trim and doors, it appeared like a tall salt shaker atop a box.

Following Henry's instructions, Adrian dropped his gear bag full of clothes and his backpack on the concrete path outside the side door that led to the guest quarters over the garage, and returned to the front of the building. Looking up, he noticed the top of the lighthouse was all windows. *I wonder if I can get up there to look out...*

With a grand gesture, Henry pulled open two large carriage doors and the early afternoon light poured in to reveal a complex but organized shop surrounding a long wooden rowboat. The rowboat appeared to be finished. It had two seats for rowers, was balanced on wooden sawhorses, and secured to the ceiling with pulleys and ropes on a track system that was tied into the bow and stern metal plates.

Every square inch of space from the ceiling to the walls and floor was used to store wood planks, tools, buckets, cleaners, rags, paints, and varnish. Nautical flags hung from the rafters, adding a touch of color and festivity to the space. Adrian rushed in toward the rowboat and ran his hand along the top rail. "Wow! You built this, Henry?"

Henry nodded and watched Adrian take in his accomplishment, which was close to being completed and ready to launch. Dog ran circles around the rowboat and barked at Adrian constantly. It was difficult to talk with the dog trying to talk, too. Henry snapped his leash back on, walked the dog outside and tied him to a tree branch. Dog did not look very happy and started pawing at the ground as Henry reentered the workshop.

With a sweep of his hand, Henry indicated that Adrian should explore the workshop, "There's nothing in here that can break. Feel free to touch anything you like." He walked over to a wall where tools were hanging from pegs and wooden blocks. He took down an old-fashioned hand cranked drill and passed it to Adrian. "Do you know what this is?"

"Uh, no sir." Adrian admitted with a shrug as he pointed the tip towards the ceiling and turned the crank on the round gear painted red. "My dad doesn't use tools, so I never grew up around them."

Henry grinned. "I'll bet you his tools are his mind, a computer, phone, and a car. Could that be true?"

"Nailed it! Don't forget the espresso machine!" Adrian nodded with a smirk. "But to my dad's credit, I have seen him use a power screwdriver to hang a picture on the wall for my mom. And you know what?" He paused to tilt his head and look up at Henry with a smile that showed his amusement, "He looked kind of pleased with himself when he was done."

"I know what you mean," Henry shared with a smile. "Every time I use the right tool, the job gets done with tremendous ease, and I find myself smiling on the inside." He paused and took in the wall of tools. Adrian's eyes followed his gaze and he saw neat rows of tools from floor to ceiling. The only things he recognized were hand saws and hammers. Henry turned to face him, "How would you like to learn about some of these tools and use them this week?"

"I, uh..., I could do that." Adrian felt hesitant because of his recent chat with Chef, which, upon recalling the bad feelings from earlier, instantly killed his excitement at the offer before him and brought up his anxiety. *Dang. I hate this feeling.*

"Marvelous! I like your spirit, Adrian." Henry enthused and Adrian stood up a bit straighter and took a steadying breath. "So, that eggbeater looking tool you are spinning around in your hand is what your grandfather would have used to hang a picture on the wall. That belonged to my father. It's here today because my dad and I took good care of these tools. That means we cleaned them of sawdust, inspected and oiled the wood or the metal pieces before putting them away, if they needed it. What you take care of takes care of you. Remember that."

Adrian was trying to open the chuck at the drill bit end. "This is where the drill bit goes, right? Does it also have a screwdriver bit?"

Henry chuckled, "No, but that would have been something back in the day. There was a tool my father once had called a compound screwdriver that had a built-in compression system. You hit the top of it with a hammer and the force drove the screw or bolt head down deep into what you were working on." He extended his hand out to take back the manual drill, which he replaced on the wall of tools.

"What are all these wood and metal box things in every size?" Adrian picked up a narrow box-shaped tool with a wooden knob on the top at one end. He turned it over and saw the opening at the bottom. "Whoa. Is that a blade or something?"

"As a matter of fact, it is." Henry's long white finger covered in freckles touched the box, "This here is a called a planer. You run it over a stretch of wood, and it peels layers of wood off a plank, based on the height of the opening." Adrian nodded and placed it back on the shelf. "And these?"

"Those are steel chisels." Henry paused and looked up as if considering something. "I think I'm almost ready to inscribe a name on this rowboat and I will use these chisels to remove some of the wood on the stern, so I can inlay gold leaf on wet size. We can do that together."

"You use real gold leaf on a boat?" His eyes widened at that thought. "Isn't that a bit much? I mean, what do I know? It just seems like gold leaf is for picture frames or something..."

"It's called gilding and it has been used for hundreds of years on boats. The gold lasts for twenty to thirty years if it gets a clear coat of varnish on it."

"So, it's not delicate?" he asked while rubbing a finger on the smooth varnished rail.

"Oh, no, it's soft and it will scratch, so it is an area of the boat that we need to treat very carefully." Henry amended, reaching up to take down a packet of four-inch square papery gold leafing separated by parchment paper of the same size, "Since it will be inlaid and won't be floating on the surface of the wood, it may last a wee bit longer, lad."

"That's a gold leaf?" He reached for it and Henry pulled it back quickly, making Adrian cringe with embarrassment, as if he had done something wrong. "Oh. Sorry."

"Oh, it's okay, and I didn't mean to startle you. I didn't want you to touch the sheets which are so fragile your breath can tear them."

"My breath can tear it? No way!" Adrian exclaimed with disbelief. "You're joking."

"OK, perhaps I exaggerated a bit there," Henry chuckled, "but it is so darned sensitive, if you look at it with your eyes crossed it seems to put a dent in it."

Adrian gave a slight chuckle. "Gotcha. I'll let you touch it."

"Come along, now. Let's get you settled in upstairs and see what Maggie has planned." Henry suggested. "Shall I show you upstairs?" His eyes were back to twinkling, and Adrian wondered what he was about to see next.

"Sure! Let's go!"

Henry opened the mahogany ship's door with brass hardware and an eight-inch diameter porthole. It had a very nautical look to it. Inside the door was a flight of stairs. Everywhere he looked was varnished mahogany like an old sailing ship. Brass hurricane wall sconces lined the stairwell and Adrian visualized them flaming like torches in the night. Halfway up the stairs, he looked out the window on his left and saw palm trees and a small peek of the sea. *The view at the top must be amazing!*

On the landing, Adrian's mouth fell open as he gazed upon his new living quarters. "Oh. My. Gosh. This..." He was at a loss for words as he took in all the details. "This is amazing! You built this?!"

Henry was grinning from ear-to-ear, and he rocked back on his heels and nodded his head. "It took me three years, and I had help from Gunnar and many other friends who visited."

"Really? The captain helped build this?" He asked with incredulity in his every word as his bags slid out of his hands to the floor. He slowly reached out to touch the built-in desk with intricate drawers, doors and a roll top. He moved past the built-in sofa to look out the pair of windows that had a view of the garden below and green hills. The walls had a collage of framed family photos. He spotted one that had to be Gunnar as a teen with his arm thrown around a pretty red-headed girl his age. "Who is with Gunnar? Is that a girlfriend?"

"That's Alice, our daughter. They are good friends and the same age." Henry joined him at the wall and touched another frame. "You know Bryce Fraser, right? The IT specialist on your yacht? That's our grandson, Alice's son."

"Oh! Oh, wow, Henry, that's right!" He tapped the photo of Bryce Fraser, and he nodded his recognition of his, "I forgot the captain introduced him to me when I first got onboard as his nephew. He and Pete hang out so much in the engine room in their office, I rarely see him or talk with him."

"Same for us. We said hello on the yacht, but he had no shore leave available to come see us this week. This is me in my college racing days," Henry straightened a long rectangular photo on the wall. It was an old color photo that was faded but captured the entire crew in university uniforms and their rowing shells by the river. He was lean and appeared to have red hair.

"Amazing. You're just a little bit older than me in that photo, Henry." Adrian scanned many of the other photos and then looked straight up at the opening in the ceiling letting in all the light. In the middle of the room was a spiral staircase going aloft to the observation deck he saw from the outside. "May I go up?"

"Yes, yes, of course!" Henry laughed with a congenial wave of his hand, "Go on up!"

With a burst of speed, Adrian leaped to climb the high and narrow wedge-shaped wooden steps with his left hand on the rail and right hand on the central mast that went all the way up to the roof. On the landing, he observed the balusters that formed a perfect circular railing to keep people from falling down the opening of the stairs. All sides of the octagon-shaped building had double-hung windows that were varnished and gleaming in the bright afternoon sunlight.

Henry shouted to Adrian, "Take your time, Adrian. I'm going down to check in with Maggie. Meet me outside when you're ready."

"OK!" he shouted back.

Pressing his nose to the window close to him, he could see he was above the taller palm trees on the Wright's property and the hillside rose behind the building and disappeared down towards the sea. Moving to his right, he could see the red tile rooftops of houses cascading down the hill towards the beach. Hotels and resorts were nestled into the hillsides. Continuing along, he saw the water stretch out for miles. Sailboats, yachts, and fishing boats were at anchor, and he picked up the powerful binoculars hanging from a hook on the wall to get a better view. Now he could read the names on the boats in the harbor but didn't recognize any of the big yachts. *I wonder what they're doing aboard the Arabella right now. Grace would love this place!*

He glanced down and looked at the roof of the garage and the expanse of lawn and driveways leading off the land. Walking to the next pair of windows, he peered over and saw Maggie exiting the house and calling to Dog. *Oh, that is such a terrible name. What is your name Dog? What would you like to be called?* He rested his elbows on the windowsill and his chin on his hands and followed the dog with his eyes. *What does one call a Jack Russell Terrier? Jack? JR? JT? Russ, Russell? No. Too formal for this guy. Rusty? No. Wrong color. He's just so playful...* Adrian watched Dog race around the yard and then try to jump up on Maggie, who commanded him down. When he obeyed, she rewarded him with a treat.

He opened the window and yelled, "Hi, Maggie! Hi, Henry! Hi, Jackson!" He waved his arm like crazy to get their attention. "I'm over here!" Three pairs of eyes looked up at him. Maggie returned his wave. Dog barked.

"How do you like your new home for the week?" she hollered up to him with a knowing smile.

"I love it!" he shouted to them. "It's the most amazing thing I've ever stayed in."

"Adrian, come on down," Henry instructed him, "And you might want to bring a hat. You're going rowing today."

"Cool!" he responded with enthusiasm. "I'll be right down." He turned to race down the stairs but heard Henry call out to him. Turning back to the open window, he stuck his head out once more.

"Yes, Henry?"

"Close the window before you come down. You don't want mosquitos eating you in your sleep."

"Oh, sorry. Good idea!" Adrian moved to lower the window and turn the clasp to lock it. He felt a bit irritated at himself that he didn't think of closing the window. With a tiny wave to the couple watching him, he dashed down the stairs and met them outside.

"So! Jackson, is it?" Maggie greeted him with a lift of her eyebrow. "Is that what we are naming him?"

Adrian paused and knelt to stroke the hair on the dog's back. "I dunno. It just kinda came out of my mouth." Turning to look the dog in the eyes, he spoke with the dog. "What do you think? Is your name Jackson? Maybe Jackson with an X in it? Huh, Jaxon? What do you think? Do you like being called Jaxon with an X?" Jaxon's ears perked up and he started turning circles and barking. He leapt up into the air and began licking Adrian's ear. "I would say, Eeew, Jaxon, but since it's you, and I think you like your new name, I'll let you lick my ear." He giggled as Jaxon's tongue tickled his ear and feeling a little silly, he finally told Jaxon to stop.

"Well, I think we have a name for this dog, Maggie," Henry began. "What do you think?"

"I believe we do!" Maggie laughed and handed Adrian a small plastic snack bag with dog treats and the leash so he could snap it into Jaxon's red collar. "Here, you're going to need this. When you give him a command, reward him with a treat. At first, give him a treat every time he obeys you, then make the size of the treat a tiny bit smaller and smaller. If you can, alternate praise with treats. The goal is to stop using food as soon as possible. Got it?"

"Got it!" Adrian smiled and stood up, tucking the treats in his pant's pocket. "Where to, Henry?"

"The harbor!" Henry announced with a smile, "But first we have to collect our gear." Turning to Maggie, "Oh, by the way darling, we won't be home in time for tea, but we should be back by dinner time. Is that alright with you?"

"Of course, my love, that's fine." She leaned in and kissed

Henry's cheek. "Run along and have fun. I don't think Jaxon is obedient enough to go for a row, so I'll keep him here."

Walking into his workshop, Henry paused to consider his needs and took a moment to smooth his trim white beard with his right hand. "Let's see...let's see. We'll need some oars." He walked over to a far corner and reached for a pair of matching oars out of many stacked along the wall and walked back to Adrian. "Hold these, please." Silently, Adrian took the oars and watched Henry. *I'm not going to distract him. I'm going to let him focus on finding what he needs.* He lifted an oar and felt the weight of it. He swiveled it in his hand to look at all sides of the blade.

"Um, Henry?" he asked with some hesitancy. "May I ask a question?"

"Yes, Adrian! Of course!" Henry looked over at him with some surprise. He saw uncertainty and a hint of wounding on his young friend's face. Smiling with invitation and enthusiasm, he said, "Fire away, young man! There's nothing I like better than questions."

With visible relief, Adrian let his breath out in a gush. "I, uh, I was wondering...how did you know to pick these out of the stack? You have a rather large collection of oars over there!"

Nodding, Henry walked to the first pair of oarlocks on the rowboat between them and let his right-hand rest on the portside oarlock while he pointed with his left to the starboard one. "You are going to need oars that fit between these two oarlocks. We actually say rowlocks in competitive rowing because the oarlock has a small gate across the top that keeps the oar in place."

"Wait a second," Adrian stopped him, "Go back. How do you spell, what did you say...rawlicks?"

Henry laughed. "R-o-l-l-o-c-k-s is the old word. We Brits pronounce it the old way, which was probably the way some sailors with heavy accents said it back in the late eighteenth century." He adopted a more serious tone when he began to share history. "Many of our English words came from Old German and Dutch words. It can be spelled r-o-w-l-o-c-k, which is more modern, but even so, it is pronounced with the old spelling. Now where were we?" He removed his boating hat and ran a hand through his white hair and fanned himself.

"The distance between the two rollocks?" He liked how that rolled off his tongue. "You were teaching me about how to pick the right oars for the boat."

"Oh, yes, yes." He put his cap back on and pointed out the distance. "Measure the distance between the port and starboard oar sockets in the gunwale. We call this the "span" between the oarlocks. Now, there is a rather famous formula for this, and many people use it to this day. It's called the Shaw and Tenney Oar Length Formula.

"You divide the span by two, and then add two to this number. The result is called the 'inboard loom length' of the oar. Then you multiply the loom length by twenty-five, and then divide that number by seven. The result is the proper oar length in inches. Round up or down to the closest six-inch increment." Henry looked at Adrian whose eyes had glazed over. "Did I lose you?"

"Kinda," he answered honestly. "What's a loom? Because I know we are not weaving fabric here!"

"No, we are not!" Henry chuckled. "The loom on an oar is the part that rests on the oarlock. That's the fulcrum point. Do you know what a fulcrum is?"

"The balance point?" he guessed.

"How about the pivoting point, since the oar is resting on the gunnel edge like a lever?" Henry offered with no trace of *make wrong* in his voice. "And by the way, while we're going over the boat and oar parts, the post on the oarlock that goes into the gunwale is called a tholepin."

"Let me make sure I've got this. The rail is the gunnel and the space between rollocks from rail to rail is the span?" He got a nod. "The part of the oar on the inside is called the loom." He paused and touched the inboard end of the oar, "Is the handle part called the handle on an oar?"

"Aye," Henry smiled, "And the part in the water is called the blade. Or spoon, depending on the type of oar. These ones are blades."

"Makes sense." Adrian nodded, then asked, "What's this leather around the loom? To keep the rollock from chafing the wood?"

"Yes. That is called the collar and the raised piece is called the button. The button helps keep the oar in the rollock." Henry indicated to Adrian to pass him one of the oars which he placed in the rowboat. He angled the oar with care, so it didn't touch the wall and workshop supplies. "Now, if you were to place the other oar into the gunnel, which you can't because we don't have enough space in my workshop, you would find that these handles have a slight overlap."

"Then how do you row? Wouldn't you keep hitting your

hands?" Adrian was confused. "Shouldn't there be a gap?"

"In rowing, there is an ideal ratio-to-row for almost all boats. The leverage ratio is seven to eighteen. If you take the length of this oar and divide it into twenty-five sections, seven of those sections would be inboard and eighteen of those sections would be outboard. What would those fractions be for inboard and outboard?"

"Seven-twentyfifths inboard and eighteen-twentfifths outboard of the rollocks."

"Correct," Henry affirmed, "If you have sized your oars correctly, your hands will be one to three inches apart as you pull towards your stomach muscles."

"What if you get the ratio wrong? And where did the twenty-five parts of the oar come from?"

"First, some oar math magic."

Adrian laughed, "That sounds like *more mathematics*. Same thing, I suppose."

Smiling, Henry agreed. "The total length of the oar equals one-seventh of the oar's inboard length times twenty-five.

"And to answer your ratio question, your oars will pop out of your rollocks if they are too short."

"And what about too long?" He couldn't help but ask with a hint of a smile. "Any advantage?"

"Interestingly, some rowers like to have oars that are about six inches longer for an overlapping grip." Henry said and demonstrated with his hands pantomiming the action, "on the return, when you are feathering your oar, most will place their left handle over the right one and adjust on the sweep through the water."

"This is getting a bit complicated for me, Henry. I think I need to draw this out on paper."

"I think you need to get out on the water and pull the oars and forget about the math."

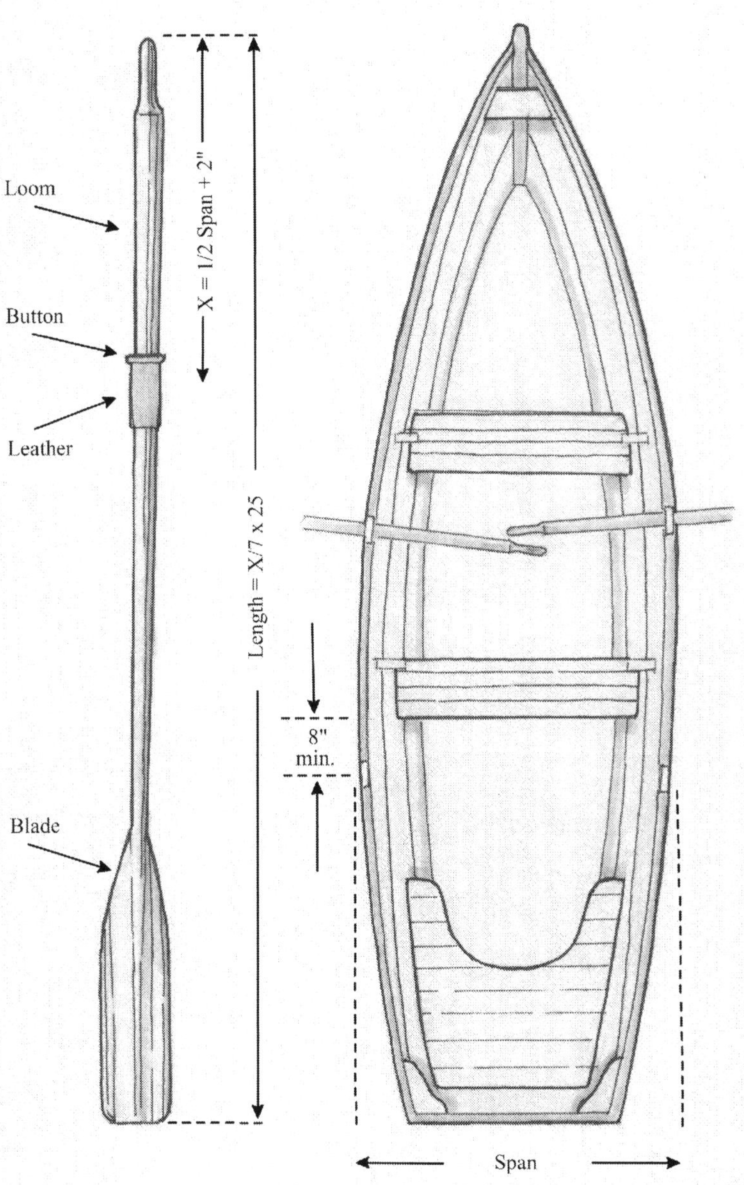
Loom
Button
Leather
Blade
X = 1/2 Span + 2"
Length = X/7 x 25
8"
min.
Span

"Good idea! Let's go." Adrian enthused, lifting the oar out of the oarlock and turned to carry both outside into the bright sun.

Yacht Harbor
Marigot Bay
St. Lucia, Caribbean Sea

Henry drove down to the harbor and spoke to the harbormaster on duty and left word of their plans to row northwards along the island. He explained to Adrian, as they walked over to the far end of the yacht club parking lot where he kept his rowboat, that it was a wise practice to share with someone on land who was going out in the boat and for how long.

Adrian's phone vibrated in his pocket. Pulling it out, he quickly read a text from his mom.

Mom: Hi Adrian, how are you sweetie? Everything going well?

Adrian: Really cool place, Mom! You'd all love it!!! Henry's taking me rowing now.

Mom: Did you let go of your conflict?

Adrian: Um, no. Didn't want to focus on it.

Mom: Did you stuff it down?

Adrian: Duh! Of course, I did. What did you expect?!!!!!!!!!!!!!!!!

Mom: Want help?

Adrian: Maybe later. Gotta go!

He turned off his phone. Then, thinking twice about it, he turned it back on and asked Henry to take a selfie with him to share with his mom. They posed with the backdrop of the yachts at the dock and Adrian sent it off to his mom, then shut down his phone. He knew he was conflict-avoiding his feelings with the chef and possibly all the crew and stuffing his feelings, which his mom would never let him get away with at home. *Sorry, Mom, I know you don't like it, but this week I'm on vacation from my family and the crew. Dealing with these stupid hurt feelings is the last thing I want to do. It can wait.*

They approached a long white fiberglass rowboat covered in a blue canvas cover, resting on a portable aluminum frame dolly. He invited Adrian to help him fold the warm canvas into thirds so he could make a neat bundle, then he set it in the bow of the boat. They placed the oars inside the boat, with a pair on each side, and water bottles. They both snapped on a personal floatation device worn as a belt around their waist. Henry lifted the rubber-covered handle and invited Adrian to take the other side and together they began rolling the boat to a sandy beach where he backed it stern first into the water until it floated free of the dolly. Adrian held the bow steady while Henry walked the dolly over to a palm tree and secured it with a bike lock.

"Go ahead, Adrian, and float her out a bit and spin her around." Henry called from the shade of the palm tree. "I'll be right there."

The glare off the water was strong. He was happy with his ball cap, which provided some shade for his eyes.

"OK! How about I sit in the bow, and you sit in the stern? This way I can match my oars to yours while you're learning." Henry moved deeper into the water as the boat rocked in the gentle surf, hitting the shore. "Alright, go ahead and climb into the middle and keep your weight low in the boat." Henry invited as he held the edge. "And maybe reach across to hold the opposite side as you bring your other leg in."

Adrian gingerly leaned across the long wiggling boat and placed his left foot in the middle and felt the boat go down a bit deeper into the water as the stern keel touched bottom. "Are we aground? Do we need to move out to deeper water?"

"No, don't worry." Henry laughed, "When I put my weight in the bow, it will pop up and balance itself." He waited and watched Adrian settle himself on the bench seat. "Now, place an oar in one of the rowlocks and drag the loom into the boat. Then do the next one."

After placing the oars in place, he held the handles and looked down the length of both oars. He spun one of the oars to make the blade vertical and held them out. "Like this?"

"That looks about right." Henry agreed. "Now, can you place the blade tips into the water to hold the boat steady while I climb in?"

After a bit of rocking and rolling in the water, Henry was lifting his oars off the deck and placing them into the remaining two tholepin holes in the gunwale. "OK, Adrian. Here's how this is going to work..." He took a long smooth pull on the oars to move them away from the shallow waters of the beach.

"Tuck your feet under the wooden brace, then lean forward just enough so that your handles are forward and somewhat level with the gunnel. Then you will gently pull back towards your belly button and lean back slightly. You want to use your back more than your arms. On the return, you want to dip the handles a little bit and move them forward."

Following Henry's instructions, Adrian pulled and leaned back, and both oars popped up out of the water spraying water up into the air as he nearly fell backwards. If it weren't for the foot bracing on the floor of the boat he would have fallen into Henry's lap. "Whoa!" he called out and rushed to sit up. As he did so, his left oar popped out of the rowlock and his right one splashed water.

He heard Henry chuckle, then felt a kind pat on his right shoulder. "It's all good, lad. I can tell you have a lot of power in your stroke!"

Adrian rushed to get his balance back, and his left oar back in the rowlock. He leaned forward and looked left and right to make sure his blades were vertical and ready to pull the boat forward. He took a breath and leaned back. One hand pulled faster than the other, creating a drastic spin of the boat, and he quickly tried to pull the other but angled the oar too deep. "Arrr!" He ground out in frustration. "Clearly, I'm not getting it. What am I doing wrong, Henry?" He dropped his head and awaited more instructions.

In a low, soothing voice, Henry made a suggestion, "OK, how 'bout I pull for a few strokes, and you listen and observe the blades above and below the water." It was more of a statement than a question. Adrian gave a curt nod of his head and looked straight out over the stern to see how far they had come since leaving shore. Three boat lengths. Not far at all. He scanned the beach and saw some boys and girls watching him. One boy in a neon blue and white sports top gave a laugh and it floated across the water to his embarrassed ears. *They better not be laughing at me.*

The steady rhythmic pulling of oars through the water brought him back into reality and the beach moved farther and farther away. Very carefully, he turned while keeping his balance in the center of the boat and looked over his shoulder to see where they were headed. *Out to sea?!*

"How about you put your thumbs on the rounded end of the handle, get the palms of your hands around the handles so they don't slip around, and pull nice and easy on the oars." Henry's voice was calm and his instructions clear. Adrian felt the smooth wood of the handle under the fleshy part of his knuckles and tightened his grip. He lowered his oar blades just enough to put them in the water and gave a slight pull. The boat moved forward slowly. *I feel it moving! I feel the boat move forward! I did it!* He positioned his blades behind him again and lowered them into the water and pulled in unison. *I did it again! I'm doing it! Finally!* He allowed himself a small smile of personal satisfaction and did it again, this time for a much longer pull on the oars.

"You got it! You're doing it!" Henry sounded rather excited this time. "Now try this: when you bring your blades across the water to prepare for another stroke, see if you can roll your wrists forward just a little bit to feather the blades so they don't scuff the water."

"Like this?" He demonstrated with his next stroke.

"Just...like...that!" Henry's voice continued to be low, gentle, and encouraging. "You've got it! Keep your pace, I'm going to join your rhythm without breaking your concentration." Henry gave a gentle and quick row to get his oars out of the way. "Easy now. You're doing great. Feel the oars as an extension of your body."

He let Adrian pull a few more times and as they came closer to the entrance of the harbor, then he guided the boat closer to the north shore to stay out of the lanes of boat traffic. "Keep rowing, you're doing great." In sync, they pulled for a hundred yards then began to travel north along the coastline of the island. "How are you feeling? Let me know if you need a break."

"I'm great! I can't believe I finally got it." Adrian's excitement filled his voice. The rowboat went up a swell and he felt the boat lift and slide down the backside as their oars swept across the water. "Where are we headed?"

"Oh, I thought we could wander up the coast a bit. Do a little sightseeing." He laughed. Adrian knew what he meant. There was nothing to see, per se, as it was all vertical cliffs and trees down to the water, and small ledges of sand met by the sea.

"It's very beautiful. And really green!" Adrian banged his oars on Henry's as he took his eyes off the centerline of the boat. "Oh, my gosh, I'm so sorry."

"No worries, lad." Henry chuckled. "I've clacked oars with many guys until we got in sync. How are your hands? Tender? I don't want you to get blisters."

"Umm," He took a quick glance at his left hand. They were a hot pink color. "I think I'm OK." He checked his right hand. "Yeah, I'm fine. They do feel hot."

"What have you noticed about rowing so far?" Henry asked. "It can be anything at all...a feeling, a thought..."

Adrian rested on his oars and let Henry continue pulling. Water dripped off the blades while he contemplated the question. He tuned into the experience and considered everything so far. "Well, I like the feeling of human power cutting into the water to move the boat. I'll admit, I was overthinking it in the beginning. And I think, maybe, there is an art to rowing, but I am not there yet."

"It's an art but it's also a lot of things. It's exercise, meditative, collaborative, competitive with self and others, it's poetry in motion..." He paused. "One cannot control the water. One participates with the water. Remember that."

"You sound like the captain," Adrian said with a hint of a smile, to which Henry laughed.

"Who do you think raised him? Maybe the apple didn't fall far from the tree."

"What about you, Henry? What do you like about rowing?" Henry stopped rowing and Adrian took it as an invitation to resume rowing, which he did. His hands felt some real heat in the skin, but he tuned it out.

"It has a meditative and relaxing quality once you get into a steady rhythm." Then he laughed, "Well, let's be clear, once you are out here with no one around, does it become relaxing. Rowing in a busy harbor requires paying attention to everyone's movements."

"How long have you been rowing?

"Oh, it must be around fifty-five years now," he mused. "I've been living by the sea forever and a day. I think I learned how to row when I was eight years old."

"Must be nice," Adrian agreed. "I can't believe I didn't want to come on this family expedition, but it's turned out OK."

"A year, or more, at sea is what young men your age did for thousands of years." He glided back into sync with Adrian as they pulled together near the cliff walls. "Every young man your age knew their basic seamanship and it was an acceptable form of school. The type of school you and your sister attend has only been around over a hundred years."

"You're joking."

"No. I'm not joking." Henry replied with all seriousness. "Remember, back in the day, fathers, if they weren't in a white-collar job like a banker or accountant, they were farmers, or ranchers...or they were operating a shop. The others were in shipping, also known as commerce. Many were fishermen -even whalers. Fathers and sons went to sea so the teenagers could learn the family business and take over some day or provide for their family."

"Oh, yeah, well...that makes sense," Adrian conceded. "So, they didn't learn math or science, language or literature?"

"Oh, no, they did," Henry returned, "Sometimes they took books with them, sometimes they learned while on shore. You needed to know math if you were going to sell fish, negotiate transportation of kegs of liquids, bales of cotton, wool, or other agricultural products. And remember, gold and silver coins were the money of the day."

"If I got transported through a time machine to those years, I would be completely lost," Adrian declared with a self-deprecating laugh. "I wouldn't know the first thing to do to survive."

"Come now, don't be so hard on yourself," Henry chided gently, "You know quite a bit! And think of it this way, too: if a boy your age from a few hundred years back was teleported into your world, he might feel quite lost with our technology."

"Huh." Adrian gave that some consideration. "Yeah, I guess he wouldn't know about cell phones, email, video games, computers, or even credit cards. This world might be harder to come into."

"It might."

"Gosh, he might not even know what electricity is!" His voice reflected the shock he perceived they would experience.

"And you might not know how to trade with indigenous people, start a campfire, tan hides or convert seal or whale blubber into lamp oil."

"How far back are we talking?" Adrian asked over his shoulder.

Henry laughed. "There are young people today who can do all those things. They are just more hidden from your view."

"No," Adrian argued with a hint of laughter, "I don't believe you!"

"I'm quite serious. There are young people who live in the Arctic regions and their tribal elders keep traditions alive. And over in the far reaches of the Norwegian sea, the people of the Faroe and Shetland Islands, even Iceland and Greenland in the North Atlantic sea, many know the process of rendering blubber into oil for lamps."

"Do you know how?"

"For what it's worth, I wouldn't make lamp oil if you paid me." Henry was grinning and Adrian could hear it in his voice.

"Why not?" he asked with curiosity.

"I'm not sure I would be able to handle the smell of a dead whale." Adrian could hear in Henry's voice that he was serious.

"That bad, huh?"

"Well, I've read numerous stories about how bad whales smell after they've died, as they lie rotting on a beach. They often explode from the buildup of gases in their belly. It's quite dangerous, actually."

"I'm pretty sure they get the blubber out before the whale rots, Henry. It can't smell that bad if it is fresh. Fresh seafood doesn't smell bad at all."

"I'm not sticking around to find out." Henry stated with firmness. "I can think of better things to do than render blubber for soaps and oil lamps."

"Yeah, that wouldn't be my thing either," he confessed with total honesty, "I can think of a million other things I would want to do first."

"Me, too." Henry agreed. "We've been out for about thirty minutes. We ought to turn back. We'll be heading into a light headwind. It was flowing to the west when we started, but now it has changed direction. Let's stay along the cliff wall to see if that helps. Hold your oars astern, please, as I turn the boat."

Henry pushed his left oar and pulled with his right. The rowboat spun in a circle with diametrically opposed efforts. "There now! Continue rowing, Adrian, we ought to be home in no time."

They pulled together and Adrian felt the pull on his stomach muscles, thighs, back and arms. He was getting tired, but he loved how he felt rowing. His hands were starting to sting where he held the oar handles. He didn't want to glance at his hands while he was doing so well, and yet he sensed he might be getting a blister or two.

"Henry?" he began. "How do you know about exploding whales, and why are they dangerous?"

A deep chuckle came from behind him. "Well, my brother had somewhat of a wake-up call in his younger days when his beach patrol unit was called to pull a dead whale off a beach in England. Let's just say that it didn't go so well, and the guts of the whale shot across the beach and covered bystanders who were over two-hundred and forty meters away."

"No way!" He said with excitement, "That's incredible! What caused it to explode?"

"Rapid decomposition, from what my brother had to say." Henry began, "When a whale dies, it begins to decompose, and the stomach contents putrefy, which creates gases. Want to guess which ones?"

"Methane?"

"That's one." Henry agreed. "What else? Here's a clue...it smells bad like rotten eggs."

"Oh! No way!" Adrian threw his head back and chortled. As he sobered, he gave it some thought. "How about hydrogen sulfide? That's pretty stinky."

"Yep!" Henry confirmed, "Good guess. What else?"

"I have no idea. Tell me," Adrian invited.

"Ammonia," Henry shared. "The whale's body inflates like a balloon, and all that gas is just trapped in all those layers of skin and fat with nowhere to escape."

"Then...Boom!" Adrian finished his sentence with a loud booming sound. "I'd like to see that. And definitely from a safe distance, up wind." Then added with great haste, "But not at the expense of a whale. That wouldn't be cool."

"No, thank you, I don't need to see it. My brother said he had to throw out his clothing and the beach smelled for weeks after that."

"Eww."

"Yeah."

They rowed in silence until they came into the entrance of Marigot Bay and Henry encouraged Adrian to take his oars out of the rowlocks and slip them along the deck. He suggested that he jump out of the boat carefully and pull it ashore the last couple of meters. Henry caught Adrian looking at his palms and asked him, "How're your hands?"

"Uhh," Adrian uttered, as he put them in the cool saltwater, "They'll be fine."

Henry stepped out of the rowboat and put out his hand for Adrian to put his hand in his for inspection. The skin on the fleshy pads below each finger was whitish and forming a raised spot, but not too bad. "OK, you'll be fine, but you may need gloves if we go out tomorrow. I've got some back home you can use. You're one step closer to blisters, and we don't want that to happen."

"I'll be fine," Adrian insisted, "Let's get the dolly and load her up."

Back in the parking lot, Henry wheeled the rowboat over to a freshwater hose and allowed Adrian to spray down the outside walls of the boat and the oars. Henry used a damp rag to wipe out the salt water on the inside. They sprayed their feet to remove the sand and together put the boat cover back on. Returning the personal floatation device belts and oars to the car, they chugged water in silence. "Ahhhh." Henry sighed with pleasure. "That hit the spot! Shall we go home now?" To which Adrian nodded. He felt the good kind of tired...the kind of tired from using every muscle in his body, fall-into-bed-without-a-shower tired.

After chaining the boat and dolly to a post, they let the harbormaster know that they had returned without incident. They drove back to the lighthouse in a comfortable silence, as the sun set over the sea and cast an orange glow on everything.

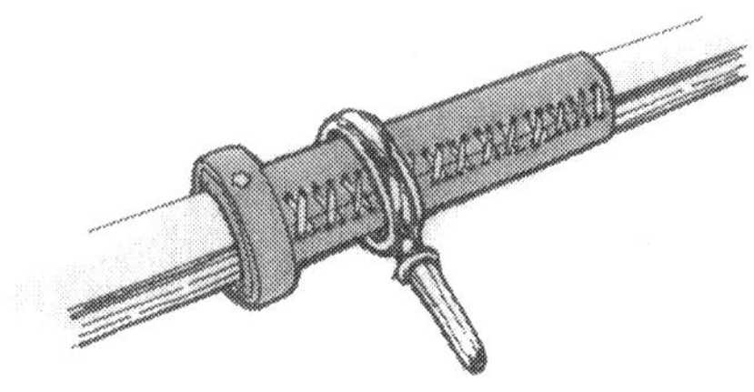

After a cool shower and change of clothes, Adrian walked over to the main house. Maggie was peeling potatoes at the kitchen sink and gasped with shock when she saw Adrian. It startled him and he went into fear of make wrong, as his mom liked to say. "What? What's wrong?!"

"Adrian, go change, now. You can't have camouflage clothing on the island. It's against the law here in St. Lucia and if you get caught you get a serious fine." Maggie spoke quickly. "It's only for law enforcement and the military." Pausing, she asked, "Do you think you will need more clothes?"

Adrian looked down at his cargo shorts covered in navy blue and gray camouflage print with multiple pockets and zippers. "Are you serious?" He wanted to laugh. He'd never heard such rules for citizens.

"Yes, please change."

"OK, wilco." And he turned and left for the lighthouse. On the way, he turned his cellphone back on. His mom had written.

> **Mom:** OK, I emailed you how to clear "make wrong", which is what I think you went into. Great pic of you and Henry! Say hello for us. XOX
>
> **Adrian:** TY! I need it. Now Maggie's upset bc I wore cargo pants w/camo print. Camo's illegal on St.L. Can you believe it? LOL TTYL

He reentered the kitchen less than ten minutes later and asked Maggie if he could help. She handed him a large salad bowl to place on the table and a pepper grinder with a rueful smile. "Thanks for changing, love. Forgive me, but I'm still a rule follower, Adrian. It's a hard one to break. I guess I fear the punishment model your mom speaks about?"

"Oh, yeah! I know all about it." He smiled back at her as he took the bowl and grinder into his hands. He paused, then confided, "Punishment is part of my anxiety. I hate being judged for doing something wrong because of whatever punishment might happen to me...the punishment, even if it's just someone's criticism of me, like a teacher's or my classmates laughing at me, leaves me feeling horrible. My mom calls it triggered 'cause I get so upset. And you know, Maggie?" He looked at her in earnest, "Every student knows that their school's punishment model means getting kicked off a team, put in detention, expelled or being grounded by their parents. My folks don't believe in grounding me, thankfully, but when they express being disappointed in me for not getting it right, well...it doesn't feel good in my body."

Maggie nodded and let him continue talking. "You know, she

texted me today to tell me that she wrote out a clearing process for me to follow to self-heal my conflict with some of the crew. If you want a copy, I'll forward it to you if you think it helps. You basically acknowledge the conflict, let go of all judgments, forgive stuff, notice you're free of it and energetically share with others that they can be free of the conflict, too."

"I'd love that. And maybe we will find out that you can teach an old dog new tricks." She laughed and placed on the table a platter with roasted vegetables and a serving spoon. Adrian placed his items on the table, too. "I'll get the last platter. Can you call Henry in from the front yard? He's talking with the neighbor boys and has Jaxon."

"Sure!" Adrian spun on his heel and headed towards their home's main entrance and walked outside. At the end of the drive, Jaxon was barking at two boys and Adrian squinted hard as he spotted a familiar neon blue and white sports shirt. *I know that guy from the beach.* "Hey."

The boys grinned broadly. Blue shirt spoke first, "Heyyyy. We know you. You da one out wid Mister Henry today." He put knuckles out for Adrian to fist bump, which he did with a cautious smile.

"Yeah, I saw you on the beach and heard you laughing."

"Oh, dat must a been Jazzy making me laugh. Dat girl is so darn funny." He passed a hand over his mouth to keep from showing his full grin.

The other boy, who appeared to be younger, spoke up, "I'm David. He's Jayden. Do you play football?"

"Not really. I play soccer."

"Mon, dat's the same thing." David shared. "We have a casual game tomorrow afternoon if you want to join in."

"I don't have cleats or anything..." Adrian shared with great hesitancy.

"Come on, mon, we don't wear no cleats here. We play in the sand." Jayden was smiling and shaking his head in disbelief.

"Oh." Adrian suddenly grinned. "OK. I'll play. Where and what time?"

"After school, Roseau Beach." David nodded with acceptance of the plan. "Henry, you can bring him?"

"I'll have him there." Henry committed with a small salute to the younger boy. "And I'll bring Jaxon."

Jaxon yelped at the sound of his name. Reaching into his pocket, he pulled out the treat bag. "Jaxon! Quiet." Jaxon talked even more. He held up the treat above his nose. "Jaxon! Quiet." He finally got a clue and watched Adrian's hand holding the treat with sudden interest. "Sit." Jaxon barked. "Quiet." Jaxon's tail wagged like crazy. All eyes were on Jaxon and Adrian. After three seconds, Adrian gave him the treat. "Good boy! Good job! Good being quiet."

"Henry! Adrian! Dinner's on the table!" Maggie waved to them with a touch of impatience in her voice and returned inside.

"Coming!" Adrian shouted back. He put out his hand to touch his knuckles with the boys, who then bent down and gave Jaxon plenty of pats and praise. "See you tomorrow. And thanks."

"Have a nice evening, lads," Henry said as he waved goodbye.

"See ya, Mister Henry."

"Ya, bye," said David.

Jaxon barked the entire walk back to the house. Henry and Adrian looked at each other and shrugged. "I rather think he wants his dinner, Adrian. Wouldn't you say so?"

"I think so, Mister Henry!" and they both laughed.

At the table, Adrian took a long sip of sparkling water flavored with chunks of juicy mango. "Excuse me, Maggie?" When she made eye contact he asked, "Is there anything else forbidden on the island?"

"Actually, there is. You are not allowed to insult anyone or use bad language." She was matter of fact about it.

"Really!" He leaned forward in his chair with a half-smile on his face. "What happens if you do?"

"Honestly, I don't know." Maggie laughed, "I'm not one to talk like a sailor. Henry? Do you know?"

Henry put his fork down and looked up to his left and thought about it. "I believe it is one-thousand dollars to get out of jail for the use of profanity. Do you like to swear, Adrian?"

The question took him off-guard for a second. "Who doesn't?"

Maggie looked at Adrian for a long second. "A better question might be: do you use bad words to hurt people?"

"I try not to," he said, a bit uncomfortable with the Wrights both looking at him. His right leg started jiggling under the table and he didn't like this conversation very much. "Are you worried I might say something while I'm on the island?"

"Oh, dear me, no!" Maggie laughed. "If you are playing soccer, as you call it, tomorrow with our neighbors, is there a chance that you could lose your cool and say something unpleasant to another player?"

"No. No, I don't talk bad with other players," he declared a tiny bit defensively, "Although, I know some who do, and none of my friends or I like it. It's bad sportsmanship."

"Maggie, I don't think we need to worry about this." Henry leaned back in his chair and winked at Adrian. "He's got the low down on the rules. He's a smart lad and I trust him. St. Lucia'll not get a dime of his money!"

Adrian grinned. "Correct!"

"Just remember the old adage, 'When in Rome, do as the Romans do!'" Henry said with a smile as he picked up his fork to resume eating.

"Anything else I need to know about this island?" He held his breath, hoping it wasn't going to be bad news. *Why do I always assume the worst? I'd like to let that go!* He watched Maggie gather her thoughts.

"Well," Maggie began, "We like to believe she's the only country in the world named after a woman, even though I believe Ireland is, too. And she used to be called The Helen of the West Indies because she changed hands between the French and the British fourteen times in the seventeenth and eighteenth centuries."

"Sorry, I don't get it. What's the Helen bit about?"

"It's a reference to Helen of Troy. She was considered the most beautiful woman in Greece and the cause of the Trojan War." Maggie raised her eyebrows and looked at Adrian from underneath them and added rather seriously, "In mythology, she was also the daughter of the God Zeus."

Henry interjected, "But the main reason is that she assisted both sides of the war. It's the back-and-forth part that history is referring to when they call our island The Helen of the West Indies."

"Oh. Gotcha." He nodded his head in understanding. "That's quite a title, and a story. So, this island has been under British and French control? Did I get that right?"

"Yes. The local Carib Indians, the Arawaks, allegedly were here first, then came the French in the mid-seventeenth century. Then, as the British always seemed to be at war with the French, it was constantly changing."

"Who was Saint Lucia then?" Adrian asked. "How did her name get used to name this place?"

Maggie leaned towards him and shared, "Rumor has it that some French sailors were shipwrecked on the feast of St. Lucy of

Syracuse, and they named the island in her honor."

"And Christopher Columbus?" Adrian asked with a titch of suspicion. *Somehow, he always has something to do with these islands.*

"Not a clue." Maggie shook her head and looked with interest at Henry, who shook his head no. "Really, darling? You've got nothing?" She giggled, stood up, and picking up her dinner plate to move it to the sink declaring, "Really, that's a first!"

Tired from a long day, Adrian climbed the lighthouse and sat down on the edge of his bed. Jaxon had come with him, and he leaped up on the bed. "Oh, that's a bad habit, my boy, but I am not going to say no to you!" Jaxon barked in return. "Quiet."

Jaxon stood defiantly on the bed and wagged his tail. He seemed to be sniffing the air. He took a step forward and nudged Adrian's pant pocket.

"Oh, you are a smart one. Good boy. Good boy, Jaxon. I've got a treat for you." He pulled out the bag and pinched off a tiny bit of treat. The dog appeared to have some training. He placed the bag on the upper bunk where Jaxon couldn't get to it. Then he emptied his pockets onto the bedside table. He turned on his phone and found his mom's email waiting but didn't open it. He brushed his teeth, turned off the light and fell asleep within seconds with Jaxon on his feet.

Chapter 6
Soccer

Adrian awoke to Jaxon barking and nudging his chin. Jaxon leapt up onto his bunk that was built into the wall and varnished to a high gloss. Drawers with brass finger pulls were embedded in the base of his bed and above him was another guest bunk bed held up by a pair of chains and bolted to the wall. The guest's bed was actually a full-size bed and the upper bunk a single. He wished one of his friends was here to enjoy it with him. *Maybe Grace would like to visit at the end of the week. She'd like this a lot.*

"OK, Jaxon, I'll take you for a walk so you can do your business, but first I have to do mine." Within minutes, he grabbed his shorts from the night before and quickly pulled them on, tucking the plastic treat bag into it. Pulling a t-shirt over his head, he slipped into some slip-on skateboarding shoes and headed down the staircase with a very excited Jaxon clicking his nails on the varnished wood steps.

He snapped on the leash before exiting and Jaxon nearly pulled him forward in his haste to relieve himself. "Whoa, boy! Easy there. Come. Let's go over by the bushes." Jaxon followed him to an area that was not a part of the formal gardens and he took care of his business. Adrian praised him and gave him a treat. "Good job! Good boy! You're so good, you waited. I'm so proud of you." He gave him a pat on the back and Jaxon barked a few times.

"Morning, boys!" Maggie waved from over by her rose garden. "I've got breakfast waiting in the dining room. You can leave Jaxon with me. I've got his food and water on the patio."

"Thank you, Maggie." Adrian rejoined and passed her the leash. "He relieved himself away from the garden and I gave him both praise and a treat for going where I picked."

"Very good!" Maggie bent down and stroked Jaxon's back. "Are you a good boy?" Jaxon started barking nonstop and they laughed at his desire to have a conversation with Maggie.

"I'll be quick, Jaxon. I'm going to eat my breakfast." Adrian gave him a little wave and walked off. He spotted Henry behind the sliding glass doors of the dining room, as he slipped off his shoes and entered.

"Morning, Henry! How are you?"

"Fair to middlin'." He picked up his teacup and smiled over to his guest. "Have a seat."

"Um, what is fair to middlin'? I've never heard that before. Is that an English term?" He pulled out his seat and sat down to a bowl of fresh tropical fruit, a cup of yogurt and granola that Maggie had placed for him.

"Oh, that is just an antiquated figurative term that means slightly above average. I picked it up from a dear old friend who was a produce shipper in the States. He used it to not only describe the quality of goods he exported, but also how he felt in his body." Henry chuckled, "You would have liked my friend Jack. He was quite a character."

"I bet! So...the expression is American?"

"I believe so. It was part of a spectrum of words used to describe the quality of farm produce. At least that is what Jack told me. He said there was fine quality, good, fair, middling and poor-quality farm produce."

"Fine must have been the best of the best?" He munched the coconut and almond granola as he reflected on the words. "So, are you not doing well today if you are middlin'? I'm a bit confused. I thought you implied fair means slightly above average."

Henry laughed, "Well, Adrian, words change meaning over the years based on who is using them." He lifted the lid off a china teapot, smiled and asked, "Would you care for some very fair English Breakfast tea? I just made a fresh pot."

"I'd love some!" Adrian passed his china mug over to Henry who poured out the steaming golden brown liquid. He spooned sugar and added cream. "What's the plan for today?"

"How would you like to pick another name?" he asked with a coy smile. "A four or five letter name."

"Jaxon's five letters. Do you and Maggie not like it?" Adrian was full of concern in mere seconds.

Henry let out a bark of laughter. "Oh, dear me, no!" He spread his hands on the table and leaned in. "We love Jaxon's name. It's for the new rowboat!"

"Ohhh! I get it!" Adrian felt sheepish for assuming it was a problem with the terrier's name. "Whew. I thought...never mind. What are you thinking would be a good name?" *Ugh. I better clear make wrong programming in my thinking. I keep assuming people are telling me I'm doing it wrong... Note to self: read mom's email tonight.*

"Well, I try not to be attached to my projects. Perhaps that is because I don't think it is a good idea to name your non-human babies." He leaned back and studied the young teenager before him. "What do you think?"

"Oh, gosh. Uh...well, let me see." He looked up to his right to access his creative mind. He and his friend Brody were always good at brainstorming for creative projects. "How about...Star? Brave? Fast? Rad? Zeus? Helen?"

"Wow, you are quick. Let me get paper and pen." Henry pushed his chair back and walked to a sideboard where he grabbed a notebook and pen. As Adrian recited the names he already listed, Henry wrote them down. "Anything else?"

He rode backwards on the two back legs of the chair and Henry was quick to correct him, "Adrian, all chair legs on the floor, please."

"Oh, sorry." Adrian leaned forward to lower his forward chair legs to the floor. Ignoring the feeling of make wrong in the etiquette department, he suppressed the anxiety that he was rude for rocking back on the chair legs. "How about Bolt?"

"That has potential. What's similar to bolt?" His pen poised over the notepad, he looked up at the ceiling. "Run? Race? Sprint? No, that quite won't do, will it?"

"Dash?" he asked with a slight smile and a twinkle in his eye. "I kind of like that one. As in, I'm gonna dash across the harbor."

Henry rolled the word around in his mouth. He murmured it, with several nods of his head while sketching the name in a Times Roman style font. "Like this?" He turned the pad around for Adrian to see.

"Yes! That's it!" Adrian, who had practically leaped forward over the white tablecloth to see it up close, sat back in his chair. "Do you like it Henry?"

"I rather like it, I do." Henry leaned back from the drawing and smiled. Looking across at Adrian he shared, "We have a name, we have a boat and today we are going to carve the name and paint it with gold leaf, if we have the time. What do you say?"

"I'll let you do the gold leaf." He smiled at the white-haired man across the table and stood up. Leaning across it, he put out his hand. Henry stood up and took it. Shaking it, Adrian said, "Henry, you got a deal. Let's do it!"

After clearing the table and placing dishes in the dishwasher, Henry and Adrian went over to the wood-working shop. Henry got some painter's tape, a white grease pencil, a small table to hold tools, a low stool on wheels, a couple chisels and a small wooden mallet.

"Now then! How wide do you think we ought to space the letters across the stern?" Henry stood with his arms crossed and his left forefinger on his lips.

Adrian squatted before the rowboat and held his hands equal distance from the edges of the stern. "I think you need a good margin and to center it in the middle. Is that pencil what I think it is?" He reached for it and felt the tip. It was waxy and somewhat soft. "Do you have a measuring tape to find the middle?" Henry's forefinger left his lips and shot up into the air, "Coming right up!"

Together they found the middle from left to right and from top to bottom. A small plus sign marked the center of the wineglass shaped stern. "How tall should the letters be, Henry? Maybe five inches?"

Henry opened the tape measure and held it against the stern. He extended it to six inches and then five and a half. They both took in the height and hemmed and hawed. "Let me see five and a half again?" Henry opened the tape another half inch. "Yeah, I think that's the right height."

"Five and a half it is!" He turned to Adrian and asked, "Do we print letters and trace them or freehand?"

"Oh, I think we ought to print them, so they are uniform in size and scale."

Henry nodded at the suggestion. "OK, back to the house. Let's print, cut, tape and get busy." They started walking back to the house and he asked, "You know how to work a computer, right?"

"Oh, yeah!!" Adrian had a super confident tone to his voice that was borderline braggadocious. "I know them inside and out. I've even built them from scratch with my dad."

"Maggie's more techie than me." He gave a little laugh. "I'm a bit of a Luddite. I knew you'd know." He slid the sliding door open and let Adrian go first. He closed the door behind him and guided Adrian to the office where Maggie had her computer and printer setup on a small desk.

Adrian sat down, fired the computer up, and quickly scanned the list of programs choosing a common graphics program to open. He created a new document and began making five and a half inch tall boxes and added a capital letter D to the first box, sized it up and bolded it. Turning to Henry he asked, "What do you think?"

"Print it!" He gave a confident thumbs up sign in front of the monitor.

"Well, hang on, Henry, I've got to make three more!" He laughed and worked some digital magic. Soon Henry had four papers in his hand, and he signaled to Adrian to shut down the computer.

Back in the shop, Henry handed Adrian a pair of scissors and had him cut out the letters. They started in the middle of the stern and using a bit of tape rolled back on itself, stuck the letter A and S in the middle. Next they added the D before the A and the H after the S. They stood back to look at their handiwork. Henry turned and walked to a wall and lifted off a level from some pegs. "Let me just check this to make sure it's straight." He put the level on the top of the stern gunnel, and it was level to the floor. He checked the floor and Adrian agreed it was level. Then he checked the letters by holding it under the row of letters and aligned it with the lower serifs on the letters.

"I think it looks good. What do you think?"

"They are optically spaced, and I believe they look good. I say we begin to trace the letters." Henry declared stepping forward to pick up the grease pencil to hand it to Adrian. "The honor is all yours."

Taking the pencil into his hand, he gave Henry a suspicious look. "Are you sure about that? I've never done this before."

"I handed you a grease pencil, not a permanent marker," he said with a smile and trusting tone, as he picked up a rag off a shelf. "If it gives you any comfort, here is a rag that you can wipe it off."

"Huh." Adrian sat on the stool and began to trace the letters with care. When he was done, he peeled off the letters and saw the faint outline of the name DASH on the shiny varnished wood. "Wow, that is cool. I like it, Henry."

"Indeed. Now, I want you to draw a centerline in the middle of each part of the letter. That's where the trenches will be, and that line will be our stop cut." He watched his young apprentice carefully draw more white lines. "You can add some 45-degree lines in the right-angle corners, like the legs of the H and A, the beginning and end of the D and S." He drew the first one for Adrian to understand and let him complete the task. "OK, now I'm going to cut into the wood with this small V-chisel and if we do things well, we can go to the next step tomorrow, which is to do the gold leaf."

They traded places and Adrian grabbed a wooden crate to sit on while Henry placed a small wooden mallet and an assortment of chisels between them and started in the middle of the letter D and made a vein in the wood as a guide for the rest of the carving. When he got to the letter H he passed the narrow v-chisel to Adrian. "Think you can do it? Just keep the angle the same as I showed you."

"We'll find out." He took a steadying breath and positioned the v-chisel at the top of the H and pushed it into the wood with just his hand strength. "Whoa, I didn't expect it to cut in so easily. It's very sharp."

Henry picked up a wide double beveled chisel and gently hammered it into the centerline of the D. He continued to work his way around each letter until he got to the H. He passed the tools to Adrian whose eyes were gleaming with anticipation. He tapped the chisel into both legs of the H and looked at Henry. "All good?"

He leaned in and inspected the centerlines. He pointed out the top of the left leg of the H. "I think you can go closer to the beginning of the serif. Serifs are those lines that make the letters fancy. You can always put a slight breakout at the end of the centerline, so you don't cut into the 45-degree angle part. I like to use a small fishtail chisel for those, or a knife, but a knife can bend and wander if you aren't careful. Try nudging that a little deeper and higher up the leg."

Concentrating on his task, he applied just the right amount of pressure. The wood gave way and the desired depth and length of cut met with Henry's approval. "OK, what's next?"

"Well, now we use a broad chisel with a bevel on the back. That allows us to carve at a 60-degree angle. We are going to start in the center and work on the A, then the S, which is more difficult. That way, our letters get better with time. Everyone looks at the first letters and if they are not well made, the rest of the name doesn't look so well made. Woodcarvers start in the middle and alternate their way to the outside." Henry gave a soft chuckle, then added, "I quite suppose that it is more interesting for the woodcarver to do this."

"Don't wait for me, Henry, lead the way!"

Maggie and Jaxon came out to the shop to find them hard at work on the letter D. Jaxon barked and barked. Adrian quickly reached into his pocket and took out his small treat bag. "Come here boy." And he nearly pulled Maggie off her feet in a rush to get to Adrian. "You're so good. Good boy." Jaxon barked and barked. Adrian quickly said, "Quiet." And when Jaxon did not comply, he used a sterner voice and said, "Jaxon! Quiet!" Jaxon stood still wagging his tail. Adrian counted the seconds, then said, "Talk!" And Jaxon started barking. He gave Jaxon a small treat for that.

"Wow, Adrian, when did all this training take place?" Maggie was pleasantly surprised at how much training Adrian was actually giving the dog. "You've only been here two days!"

"Well, every chance I get, I teach him talk and quiet. He loves to talk." And he burst out laughing. "I don't think I've ever met a dog like this. He's unbelievable."

"Yes, Jack Russel Terriers are quite the talkers," Maggie agreed. "Teaching the command to be quiet was a great idea. While you've been working on that, I've been working on sit. Try him."

"Jaxon! Sit!" Jaxon sat on command. "Wow! Good boy! Give me five!" Adrian held out his hand for him to place his little paw on it, which he did. "Oh, my gosh, you're such a smart boy. Do you want a treat? Talk!" Jaxon barked and Adrian treated him.

"You're quite something. You've a gift for training dogs." Maggie shared.

"Maggie's not one to compliment lightly, Master Adrian. Her family has been raising and training dogs for generations." Henry had spun on his stool to take in the activity. "He's listening to you. You must have reached him on some level."

"Well, maybe it's just my love for dogs, you know? I just feel what they are feeling and try to treat them the best I can." He shrugged his shoulders and bent down to pat Jaxon's back and scratch his ears a little bit. "I always ask myself, What would the dog like? Sometimes I can just tell."

Maggie exclaimed with delight, "Oh! You're an animal whisperer! I love it!"

"A what?" Adrian was confused.

"An animal whisperer is someone who is empathic with the animal and can feel, hear or perceive what the animal wants or needs." She explained, then asked, "Do you think that could describe you?"

"Yeah, I think so."

"Well then, that is one of your gifts! Dogs are a passion of yours, right?" Maggie asked with all sincerity. "You know...the reason why connecting with dogs is so easy for you?"

"Um, I guess because I feel an affinity or something with them." Adrian wanted some clarity, "Why do you call it a gift?"

"Because you are endowed with a gift of being an animal empath, especially in the area of dogs. Not everyone has this gift. You can talk to dogs, teach them, comfort them, and maybe even heal them." She paused, "You basically shared with us when we met you that you love dogs. Why is that?"

"Loving dogs comes easy to me." He shrugged again, "I just do. I always have."

"Right! Our gifts are easy to notice when it comes with ease and flow or love. It doesn't mean that you don't have challenges with your gift, because it can be a very sad time when an animal you love passes away. I know that on such a deep level."

"I know. Don't laugh, but I was sad for weeks when my first fish died." Adrian smiled back at the memory of when he was six years old. "I didn't know that the warm weather in Los Angeles would heat up my room and cause the bacteria in the water to grow so fast, and my fish just couldn't take the heat or the dirty water. I felt so guilty for letting him die. I almost couldn't forgive myself."

"Adrian," Maggie said with a big smile, "I love you already!"

Adrian felt his eyes get a bit watery just knowing that she understood him and his love for dogs. He felt quite touched. His mom and dad certainly didn't want pets because they loved to travel. He just wanted to stay home and have a dog or two. He petted Jaxon while Maggie told them she had made sandwiches and lemonade and left them in the fridge for when they were ready to take a break. She was going to go shopping and leave the dog with them if that was ok.

"Of course, Maggie," Adrian rushed to say, "I've got him. We're not going anywhere until about 2:30PM, right Henry?"

"Oh! Yes, yes, of course, I didn't forget," Henry rushed to say as he put two and two together. "I think I can knock out this last letter and call it a day soon. What says you, Adrian? Shall we finish this first?"

"Absolutely!"

Maggie left and Henry continued working on the D cutting the serifs in neatly. He asked Adrian if he was ready to give it a try on the H. "I suppose so." He tied Jaxon to the leg of a workbench and sat down. He placed the flat chisel at the top of the H on the inside of the left leg, took a deep breath and hit the hammer lightly on the top of the chisel.

"Very good. Not too much pressure. Keep that 60-degree angle. You're doing great." Adrian lowered the chisel and tapped another section out. "Excellent. Now start at the end and work back up towards the middle." Adrian put the point of his chisel where he wanted it to stop and tapped it in. "Well done!"

He straightened up with pride and smiled. "I did it! Can I do the other leg the same, then move to carving the reverse side?"

"That will work, too. Go ahead."

Adrian did a lot of work on the legs of the H and, with guidance from Henry, made the necessary cuts to the cross bar and serifs. Henry took over for the nitty-gritty parts that required expert control, which Adrian was OK with, as he was pleased with his first wood carving efforts. "We did it! The D-A-S-H looks great!"

"I'll let you clean up the tools with your rag and place them on the table there. There's a small dust broom and pan. You can collect all the shavings from the floor and place them in that bucket over there. Then I suggest we eat lunch!"

"Roger that. Wilco!"

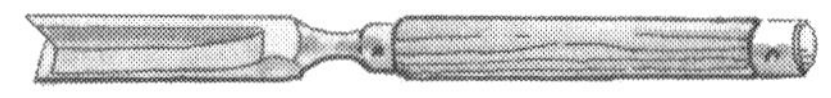

At a quarter past two, Henry, Adrian and Jaxon piled into the SUV and took off for the beach in Rosseau. They arrived just before 3PM and parked off the road. "I would imagine that we go down that path to the left and see where they are. We're a little bit early, but we can have a look-see around the place."

After a while, they heard voices, and several youngsters were standing under a tree that provided shade from the hot Caribbean sun. "Hallo, Adreee-ann" he heard Jayden call out to him and saw the familiar neon blue sports shirt. Adrian walked over to the shade and said, "Hi guys." Dark-skinned knuckles came out from all directions to greet him, and he met them all.

David spoke up, "This is just a friendly game of pick up. Others may join us. We'll see. We can't exactly play on the resort or hotel beaches and people leave us alone here. Here we can kick up as much sand as we like. Right guys?"

"Yeah, mon!"

"OK, Adrian, you play with Jayden and David." A tall youth suggested, "Me...I'm Noah by the way; me, Eugene, and Charles can play together." They grabbed their shoes and flip flops and marked boundaries and goals. "OK, let's go." He dropped the ball in the middle of the playing field, and everyone rushed it.

Not sure where to turn, Adrian kept his eyes on the ball and stayed with Eugene, as suggested by Jayden. He was used to play-ing middle and knew his way with a full team.

Two more teens showed up. Francois and the other was a girl by the name of Dizzie. Adrian's team got Dizzie. She was fast as lightning! The game picked up speed and dynamics as they all sorted out each other's playing abilities and style. Adrian got the ball and passed to David, who scored. They played offense better than defense and the other team scored on them. When they called it quits, Adrian was soaking wet with sweat and bent over trying to breathe. Playing in the tropics was hard work. He felt a hand on his back and stood up straight. It was Dizzie. "Hey, you play well."

"Thanks, Dizzie. So do you. You're very fast out there!" His admiration shone through his words.

"How do you think I got the nickname Dizzie?" She laughed out loud, and he grinned back at her.

"I gotcha."

"Come on, guys...now the best part! Run!" David yelled as he headed for the surf line. All the teens rushed into the sea and splashed away at each other. "It don't get no better than dis!"

"No, it doesn't." Adrian agreed. "Hey, do you and your brother need a ride home?"

"That would be nice. We usually take de bus or hitch a ride. Somebody usually knows us."

"I forget that on an island, everyone pretty much knows everyone."

Henry left the shade of a palm tree and brought Jaxon close to the water. He was unleashed, barking and dancing with excitement at the waves coming on shore. All the teens came in closer to say hello to Jaxon. David knelt in the water's edge, reached out to pat his back and said, "Hey, lil buddy. How are you, my friend? Remember me? I'm your neighbor." Jaxon jumped up on his wet shorts and licked the salt water off his face. Then he moved to lick his ear. "Hahaha, hahaha" David laughed at the sensation. "Why you do dat, my friend? Dat's crazy!" He smiled at Jaxon. "But I still like you a whole ton!"

Adrian and Henry smiled at each other. Jaxon's secret way of saying he liked someone was to lick their ear. Next thing they knew, a large swell crashed ashore, knocking David forward on Jaxon, who yelped and jumped away and was still overwhelmed by the waves. "Oh, no. Lil man, it's okay. No worry, my friend." David was up and calming the frightened dog. "Come. It's not so bad." Jaxon shook his hair dry and barked a long soulful story about what just happened. David lay back on the sand and laughed until his sides hurt. "What?! You think Mister Sea did all dat to you? What about me? Do you hear me complaining? No, sir! I'm laughing!"

Jaxon stopped barking and cocked his head to consider David. He took a tentative step towards him. Water was lapping his feet and legs where he lay, but his upper body and head were out of the surf. "It's okay, Jaxon." Jaxon sniffed him and licked his ear, which set David rolling over and laughing. Jaxon barked and started wagging his tail. "OK, Jaxon, I am going in to clear all dis sand off of me body. You wait here." Jaxon barked and kept wagging his tail. He jumped up on his hind legs and dog-paddled in the shallow water. He walked tentatively after David and Henry let him explore the water some more. While Jaxon quickly figured out how to swim in the waves with the boys surrounding him, he yapped and barked with glee.

Adrian ran over to the bushes and poked around looking for a good stick to throw for Jaxon to retrieve. He found a well-worn piece of driftwood under some bushes and ran back, calling to Jaxon. Wading into the very shallow water, he let Jaxon see the stick. He dog-paddled over to Adrian and sprang off his hind legs to grab the stick. "Good boy!" Adrian praised him and patted his back. Jaxon swam over to David with the stick in his mouth. He dropped it in the water where it floated seconds before David grabbed it and threw it a short distance away. Jaxon turned on a dime and swam to it and moments later he was back to David with the stick.

Laughing out loud, Adrian said, "Well, David, it looks like you are going to get a different kind of workout today!"

"Yes," he agreed, "Dis here is a real fun dog!"

Henry suggested they get out and start drying off before they got in the car. The boys wrung out their shirts and the sun and sea breeze helped with the rest. He tossed them some towels he kept in the back of the car and instructed them to line the car seats before sitting down. They waved goodbye to their friends and headed back up towards Marigot Bay before the sun started to go down.

Chapter 7
Secrets

Back in the lighthouse, he pulled his laptop out of his backpack. He hadn't turned it on in days. He plugged his charger in and fired it up while sitting at the built-in captain's desk. His hair was damp from the rain shower he took after returning to Henry and Maggie's home. He had two hours before dinner, so he let his hosts know that he was going to shower and check emails.

The desk had a roll top cover, which he had raised and placed his computer on the dark green leather desktop. The desk was full of mystery. He pushed his laptop to one side, and tentatively pulled out drawers and opened the multiple cabinet doors. There were pigeonholes everywhere and pull-out trays on shelves made of wood. He pulled one out all the way and looked in the vacant space. It was deep and dark, and on inspiration, he used his cell phone flashlight to look in. With a short intake of breath from his surprise, he saw a bunch of papers at the back. *There is no way my hand is going to fit in there.*

He pulled out all the trays and considered his options. *What the heck? How do I get to those?* He opened all the doors, drawers and looked for access. He tried to lift off the top of the desk, but it didn't budge. The floor was littered with trays full of pens and other stationery supplies. *I've tried the front and the top.* Excitedly, he snapped his fingers. *The sides!!*

Running his hand along the sides of the desk, he pressed and prodded every corner and edge, and nothing moved. *How the heck did those papers get in there? The bottom? No. The back? No, it's built into the wall.* Just in case he missed something, he felt along the back edge and then returned to run his hands inside the different sections looking for anything that might suggest a release mechanism.

How would Henry solve this puzzle? A sudden inspiration had him considering the tic-tac-toe grid of shelving that held the trays. Bracing his hands on both sides of the grid, he pulled gently towards himself with equal pressure on all sides. It slid forward. His heart leaped with excitement. The whole thing came out and he carefully set it on the floor. Opening his flashlight again, he looked in and pulled out the stash of papers, which he set down on the desktop.

A big envelope with an adoption agency name in England was printed in fading ink on the corner and addressed to Henry and Margaret Wright. He carefully slid the papers out of their protective sleeve and scanned the first page.

Dear Mr. and Mrs. Wright,

Enclosed please find a replacement Certificate of Adoption in the case of Gunnar Erik Johnson, born December 24th, 1982, in Stockholm, Sweden...

"Whoa!" Adrian let out a low whistle and stopped reading. He shuffled the paper and looked at the next paper, which was the actual certificate.

This is to certify that Gunnar Erik Johnson has been formally adopted into the Henry and Margaret Wright family. Witnessed by Mary Jane Smith. On this 14ᵗʰ Day of February 1996. Signed, Henry R. Wright and Margaret E. Wright.

The next page was a letter from a Brighton foster program in England, dated 23 December 1995.

Dear Mr. and Mrs. Wright,

We have found and positively identified the young boy that you have been searching for. He was in our system but is now currently detained in a juvenile offending system in Worthing. He is in good health, but without parents or guardians in foster care.

Our records show that Master Johnson's mother, Anna Mossberg, is recorded as deceased on 4 April 1995, from injuries due to a car accident. The father is listed as Thor Sixten Johnson, but we have been unable to locate him at this writing. Both names appear to be of Swedish origin, and Master Johnson received his citizenship in 1995 under his mother's name. His father does not appear in the United Kingdom records of birth, marriage, divorce, or death.

Furthermore, our records show that Master Johnson was picked up by the constabulary for petty theft and given a warning. He was hauled before the courts after being picked up again for breaking and entering a vacant building. He was homeless, penniless, and truant from his school when he was arrested.

Please contact us at your earliest convenience.

Respectfully,

KW

Mrs. Katherine Wainswright
Office of Records
Brighton, England

Adrian stopped reading and put the papers back in the envelope and put it back in the back of the desk's interior. He opened the last envelope, which had a Dartmouth post office stamp of 2000. He opened the folded paper covered in small tight letters in blue ink and read the letter to Henry and Maggie.

Dear Henry and Maggie,

Well, here I am! I made it to Naval College, if you can call it that. It has an amazing history, but I guess you knew that.

Are you sure I'm in the right place? Everyone is so formal! I know I passed all the academic, medical, physical, and mental aptitude tests, but honestly, the formality is totally ridiculous. Do I really have to go through this? Can't I just get on a boat and work?

The food is so-so. The beds are hard. It's freezing in the dormitories. Are they testing our fortitude? I'm seriously thinking many will fail because they are softies. Ha! None of these blokes have lived on the street like I have. My silver lining...?!!

Anyway...just letting you know I made it and check-in was easy. I made two new friends. A guy named Adrian Thompson who is from the Bahamas and Ben Martin from Wales. Both are my age, and we room together.

I'll write again soon. Fingers crossed I can make it through this 30-week program. I'd sure love to have you here at my graduation.

Love,
Gunnar

Adrian put the letter back in its envelope and tucked into the desk with the other one. In the last envelope he opened, it held a formal engraved invitation to attend Gunnar's naval college graduation. A small piece of ruled notepaper tucked in with it read,

> Hi H&M, I did it! And I have a job at sea if I want it, on a cargo ship running the North Sea between Sweden and England! Being bilingual has its advantages. Hooray!!!! Now I can start getting my sea time in. Excitedly yours, Gunnar

Adrian stuffed the final envelope into the desk and began replacing the wooden trays. Once reassembled, he sat down with his mind spinning and his heart racing. *What secrets have I stumbled upon? Shoot! This is bad. Arrrgh! Why did I have to stick my nose where it doesn't belong? I didn't even stop to think if it was wrong...*

He sat down at the desk and stared at his laptop. *Mom's email.* He opened his account and read the letter.

Hi Adrian,

I suspect what you have been going through the last few times you've been corrected by someone, or someone suggested you were wrong to, for example, distract someone or interrupt them is because you haven't cleared Make Wrong Consciousness from your mental operating system. It's a software bug, if you'd like to hear this in your lingo.

Remember I said to you that there are five basic perspectives of relating? And this is how we all source fear when relating? Well, here they are as a reminder:

1.   Me to Myself
2.   Me to You
3.   You to Me
4.   Me to a Group (2 or more people)
5.   The Group to Me

It helps to know who is sourcing the fear and what the fear is called. I believe you are suffering from the one I call Make Wrong.

You see, if you beat yourself up for doing something wrong, or don't get something right, you are talking to yourself, which is perspective number one.

In number two, you source the fear that someone did it wrong and judge them for their thoughts, emotions, actions, or behaviors. Especially their lack of integrity and point your judgment in their direction. Remember how you hated me telling you that your homework was messy? That was me sourcing perfectionism fears and directing them at you. Now you know how the recipient feels.

Reverse number two and you have number three: Someone is telling you that you have done something wrong. Remember how you would tell me to stop telling you to wear a jacket when it was cold outside? That was my fear that cold weather created colds in children without jackets and I directed it at you.

In number four, you are telling others they were wrong. Do you remember being in first grade and how you would tell Grace and her friends they were wrong for leaving you out of the hide-and-seek game when you couldn't play with them?

And in number five, you are the receiver of a group telling you, you are doing it wrong.

Remember all of these judgments destroy relationships. It creates bad feelings everywhere.

So here is how you clear it:

First, imagine the person is before you. Now share with them from your heart and mind, "I acknowledge I have a conflict with Make Wrong Consciousness and all the ways that you have told me that I did it wrong, can't get it right, didn't give you what you wanted, wasn't good enough in my effort, didn't follow the rule and maybe kept the conflict stuck. I now choose to let all that go from my awareness."

By the way, Adrian, I encourage you to release all your self-judgments first, so you have clarity about the conflict. If you recall, these types of statements start with "I can't believe I felt powerless in the moment and couldn't speak to share my perspective" (I know you so well, that you often freeze up and with this one cleared, the rest will flow.) Self-judgments start with:

I can't believe I...
I wish I had (not)...
I could have...
I would have if...
I should have...

Then go to your inner guidance. For example, "I wish I had checked in with my inner guidance to know if it was a good time to talk with Chef and I release that from my conscious awareness." (Was there anyone else you barged in on or distracted? Just add it to the clearing.) Be sure to say the healing words, "I release all my self-judgments from my conscious awareness."

Honey, can you try and find the words for why you think the conflict happened? It might sound like, "People should be clearer about what their expectations are of people, so they can't be made wrong when they do something the other person doesn't like."

After you've identified all the judgments and let them go, a simple forgiveness statement clears the remaining energetic rubble from feelings and emotions. "I forgive all judgments from all angles, levels physical, emotional, mental and spiritual, all dimensions of awareness, and from all perspectives of relating." You will probably feel more peace by the time you get to this third step!

Now you get to energetically share with the person, "I declare myself free of this conflict and commit to clearing any judgments that come up in the future around make wrong."

Step five is remembering your true nature of love and shining the light of truth to the other party that you have cleared your judgments. But the most important thing in this step is that you energetically share with them that they can be free, too, because that is what love does. Love sees the highest potential in someone and focuses on their true potential, not their lack of integrity or bad side.

You can ring me by phone if you need more help.

Love,
Mom XOX

PS: Identify emotions by name and breathe them out as you go!

Adrian didn't even try to clear the Make Wrong Consciousness that his mom had pointed out. He forwarded a copy to Maggie, who had given him her email earlier, and closed his laptop. He put the dog treats on the top ledge where his furry friend couldn't get them and climbed onto the bed which he had loosely made up in the morning. Jaxon was snoring at the foot of the bed, taking a nap. He and Henry had given him a freshwater hose-down and quick towel-dry before he went upstairs.

What are my self-judgments? He stared up at the ceiling with the center staircase opening. *I hate that I freeze up when people tell me I'm wrong.* He rolled off the bed and walked back to the laptop and opened it. *What do I do with that self-judgment again...?*

"I release from my conscious awareness that I hate when I freeze up when people tell me I am wrong." He took a deep breath and ended up yawning. "I let that go. Boy, do I ever let that go!" He yawned again. *Heh heh heh...that feels better.*

"I release from my conscious awareness that I can't believe I didn't check in with my inner guidance if I should have been interrupting Pete, the captain, Chef, Mom, Dad, Grace, Jimmy... Jimmy." He stopped and felt the feelings of his relationship with

Jimmy come right to the surface.

Sitting in the burgundy leather desk chair, he rested his head on the top of the swivel chair and looked up at the ceiling. *I feel confused.* He breathed out confusion. *I feel sad, disappointed, and separate from someone I believe is my friend.* He breathed out those feelings. *I feel like he hasn't been my friend. What is that emotion even called?* He sat and thought about it. *Betrayed? No. I'm being denied something...like friendship? Yeah, that's closer. He went into competition with me, lied about his skill level and then gloated when he won. I guess...I guess I feel hurt.* He breathed out all the hurt from that incident and felt a small shift from the event. Now all the hurt from the strained reactions of Pete, Jimmy and Chef Zak came into his awareness to be dealt with. *I thought they didn't really like me anymore.* He sat there searching for the truth.

"I release my self-judgment that I can't believe I thought they didn't like me anymore, that I was a bad person for interrupting them, did something wrong to tick them off, and wasn't very likable. I let that go." As soon as he said the words, he yawned so hard his jaw cracked and he smiled to himself. His mom always said yawning during a clearing process was a good sign.

"I let go of my self-judgment that I believe certain people on the boat don't like me. And that I am annoying when I distract or interrupt them." Something was shifting inside him, and he felt lighter.

"I let go my...what is it?" He used his right index finger to scroll up on the laptop keypad to the part of the email where his mom talked about letting go of the judgment of the conflict. "I release my judgment of the conflict that people who act like my friend shouldn't be mean to me." *Why did I believe that? Because I believe if you are a true friend, you always treat your friends nicely. Oh, wait. So, when someone I think is my friend isn't being nice, I believe they're being mean and not my friend? Well, duh...no wonder I thought I lost friends this week!* He started laughing. Jaxon barked and jumped down from the bunk and leaped up to rest his paws on Adrian's leg. "Hang on, Jaxon. I'm almost done. I think I am figuring out something important out here."

He scratched behind the dog's ears while he reread his mom's email. He found the part about saying forgiveness and it felt so easy to read after he let go of the judgments he had held inside himself. He made a commitment to recognize when he felt make wrong or saw it in others, so he wouldn't judge it and if he did, he would let go of the judgments he made about it. *I'm going to have to be careful how I talk to people, so I don't make them wrong when I see something I don't like. Sheesh. That could be hard.* A little voice inside his heart shared, *not really when you can come from love and not perfectionism.* And he nodded his head. *Yep.*

He closed the laptop and Jaxon stopped his investigation of the bathroom to fly out the door and bark. "Want to go for a walk? I think we have some time." Jaxon ran for the stairs and his nails made the loudest noise ever on the way down. Adrian burst out laughing, "Jaxon, I think you are waaaay too active for Henry and Maggie."

He found Henry and Maggie sitting with a glass of white wine on the patio and let them know he was going for a walk before dinner. He had on running shoes. He wanted to see what Jaxon's interests were in the outdoors.

On the hill, Jaxon was very interested in running, not walking. Laughing, Adrian allowed him to run and pull him up the hill on the leash. *Who is running who here?*

He turned the corner near David and Jayden's home and saw them shooting basketballs into a hoop. They stopped playing, put the ball on the concrete and went towards him. Jaxon galloped across the road to say hello.

"He practically dragged me up here to you." Adrian shared with a big smile. "I think he likes you guys."

"Yeah, we like Jaxon." David replied and bent down to receive an ear lick from his new buddy. "I love this dog."

"Me, too."

Jayden looked at Adrian, who was looking at David, and asked him, "You keepin' this dog?"

"Oh, no!" he said with some surprise that he was even asked the question, "He's Maggie and Henry's dog. I'm just the lucky guest who gets to play with him for a week."

"Yeah, but Miss Maggie says she no want no hyperactive dog." David supplied. "I don't think she can run him every day. Dis dog needs to run....run sideways and all ways." They laughed at the visual.

"What do you think is going to happen to him?" Adrian was curious and just had to ask. "Are they going to give him away?"

"We don't know." Jayden replied, then touched his shoe gently on his brother's foot where he was bent down playing with Jaxon. "Come on, bro, don' get too attached. Dat always happens to you." Turning back to Adrian he asked, "You takin' him for a run? Wan' company?"

"Yeah!" he replied with genuine enthusiasm, "Let's go!"

The boys guided Jaxon up a steep hill and as the light faded, they turned around and jogged down the hill back home. A bat flew low across the road and Jaxon put a burst of speed on and zipped left to go after it. "Whoa! No!" Adrian shouted with dismay as Jaxon took off down the street a bit faster than he would have liked. The leash was fully taut between Adrian and Jaxon and the tension around the dog's neck was extreme. *Holy smokes, this dog is a tiny racehorse!*

"Jaxon, stop!" David shouted, and miraculously, Jaxon yelped and stood still. The dog trembled from excitement and faced the shrubs and trees where he wanted to chase the bat that was now long gone. His barking was non-stop. "Quiet. Jaxon, quiet!" Jaxon stopped barking but stayed tense and ignored the boys.

"Good boy, Jaxon. Good boy for staying quiet." Adrian was at the ready with a treat and Jaxon turned around to receive it. "Good listening to David. Yes, you did good." Adrian and David smiled with their eyes and shook their heads over the back of the terrier as if to say, "I can't believe this dog!"

"Here." David extended his hand for the leash. "Let me take him down the hill."

Adrian, a bit uncertain about the transfer of power, extended the leash over to David. "You sure?"

"Yeah, mon. Give it here." David took it while Jaxon was calm. "Now we walk down. The light is almost gone, too."

Looking around, Adrian noticed it was very dark. He didn't have his watch on, so he pulled out his phone and looked at the time. "Oh, no, we gotta get back. It's dinner time."

They marched down the hill at a good pace and when the boys got to their house, David handed the leash back to Adrian and said, "Hey, we'll see you tomorrow."

"Yeah, sounds good." He took the leash, said goodnight, and headed down the hill.

Back at the house, he walked around to the back patio and tied the leash to the patio roof post near Jaxon's water and food bowl. Then he slipped off his shoes and entered the sliding doors where he found Henry and Maggie seated at the dinner table starting to eat.

"I'm so sorry I'm late," he began, "Jaxon took off after a bat and David and I nearly lost control of him." He took in the faces that paused eating to take in his explanation and seeing no stress on their faces, he rushed to say, "I'll wash up and be with you in a minute." He ran into the kitchen and washed his hands and using the paper towel he used to dry his hands, wiped his face of sweat. He placed it in the wastebasket and entered the dining room quietly, taking a seat.

"Maggie," he started in with caution, "May I ask what your plans for Jaxon are?"

"Well, to be honest, I'm not sure. I rescued him and thought I would train him, but beyond that..." she gave a slight shrug and took a sip of water. "I don't know. I know we can't keep him. He's too much for me and Henry."

Henry swallowed and took a sip from his wine glass and then rested his wrists on either side of his plate. "Do you have some thoughts about it?"

With some hesitancy, Adrian put some thoughts together for their consideration. "Well, um, you know how good David is with dogs? I mean like me, you know? He has a passion for taking care of them, and he wants the best for them. I, uh...I was kinda thinkin' that maybe he could take care of Jaxon if his parents and well, uh, you two were okay with Jaxon going to their home. It's just an idea. I don't know if you like it or have considered them, but I would put Jaxon in their care. I trust them." Adrian reached for his water glass and took a long sip, then put it down.

While Adrian reached for the bowl of mashed potatoes followed by the gravy boat, Henry and Maggie exchanged a smile. Maggie passed him the plate of roasted chicken and handed him the serving fork. "Why, Adrian, that is a marvelous idea and I love it!"

He perked up at Maggie's praise, "You do?"

"Of course, we do, don't we love?" She turned to Henry and placed her right hand on Henry's.

"Yes, yes, of course! Splendid!" Henry beamed at his wife. "Problem solved." Turning back to Adrian, he asked, "We ought to talk to their parents first and make sure they are okay with a young terrier entering their lives."

"Oh, man, Jayden and David are going to be so excited!" Adrian's eyes gleamed with happiness at how happy his new friends would be. "I can't wait to tell them! David's going to be so, so...overjoyed."

"I know that young man loves Jaxon." Henry smiled over at Adrian. "He's very good with him, like you are. I'm glad you found a solution for us. He's an excellent choice for this dog."

After dinner, Adrian went and sat on the patio with Maggie and Henry and Jaxon sat on his lap. The sky was clear, and a multitude of stars shone down from the dark blue tropical sky. He sighed as he listened to the tree frogs, insects and the breathing of the dog. "I love this. This is sweet."

"I agree, dear." Maggie reached out and patted Adrian's arm. "We're so happy to have you here with us this week."

"Do other people stay with you?"

"Well, yes, they do, but it is always during Christmas and

summer holidays. Not everyone can take time off when they'd like," Maggie replied.

"Um, I have a random question," Adrian started and looked them both in the eye. They turned to look at their young friend with open, receptive faces. "How do you know the captain?" Then he held his breath waiting for the story to come forward with the explanation he was hoping to get.

Maggie gave a soft laugh and then got a bit serious. "When I was a young girl, my parents sent me off to a boarding school in Switzerland and I met his mother, Anna. We hit it off like wildfire. After graduation, I went back to England, and she went home to Sweden.

"She met a young handsome sailor who was a couple of years older than her, who was about to graduate from the Royal Swedish Naval Academy. They fell in love, got married and had Gunnar.

"Unfortunately, Gunnar's father was ambitious and pigheaded; he wanted what he wanted and there was no middle ground." Her voice had turned cold and flat. Warmhearted Maggie was gone, and she continued the story in a voice devoid of emotion. "At twenty-two years of age, Thor took off as a commissioned sailor with the Swedish Navy and left Anna with a newborn."

Henry placed a hand on her arm and gave it a squeeze as he continued the story, "Adrian, Thor was very determined to become a licensed captain and get his own ship. He was the kind of guy that put conditions on his life and figured everything would work out in the end."

"What do you mean by conditions?" Adrian asked with genuine curiosity.

Henry stroked his beard for a moment and then asked him, "Do you ever say to yourself, 'When this is behind me, I'll be happy?' and you live through something painful without being happy, waiting for the day that it is all over?" Adrian nodded yes, and Henry continued, "Well, Thor was always saying, 'if I can just get a thousand hours of sea time logged, then I can cut back and spend more time at home.' Or 'When I can make enough money, then I can take time off.' Well, his conditions were met all the time, but instead of coming home, or taking a break, he had replaced the old conditions with new ones. He never made it home."

"Wait a second." Adrian knit his eyebrows together in consternation, "Are you saying that Gunnar never knew his father?"

"Something like that."

Maggie's face was stone cold. Her lips were pursed, and she looked pained. "One day, Anna asked if she could bring Gunnar to stay with us in Brighton for the summer and I said yes. Henry and I were married about the same time as her and Thor, and our daughter Alice was about the same age as Gunnar. They came over and stayed. My parents had their own business and they helped her by offering her work and getting her a visa. She lived in my old bedroom and had the love and support of my family."

"But what about Anna's family? Who sent her to boarding school?" Adrian asked.

"Her grandmother," Maggie shared, then shook her head. "Her parents died in a freak boating accident when she was young. Her maternal gran took her in and raised her. She didn't have siblings and there were no other relatives. So, when her gran died, she was without support in raising her son, who was almost twelve at the time."

"We were thrilled to have Gunnar and Anna in our lives." Henry added. "He was always a good kid. And smart. You want to talk smart? That young man had quite the head on his shoulders! I always knew he would land on his feet."

"What happened?" Adrian was glad it was dark, and they

couldn't read his facial expressions.

Maggie looked at Henry and held his hand for support. She bent her head and took a deep breath, then raised it. Turning to Adrian, she said, "We left for America where Henry got work as a university rowing coach. We spent our holidays here in St. Lucia every year between semesters. One day we got a call from my parents that Anna had been killed in a car accident."

"Maggie's parents were much older, and her mother wasn't well," Henry said. "Her father wasn't in a position to support Gunnar and things fell apart."

"I went home to Anna's funeral and Gunnar would barely speak to me, much less look me in the eyes." She shook her head at the memory as if it haunted her. "He ran off after his mother was laid to rest and, for a long time, we didn't hear from him."

"Months later Maggie's mother passed, and we went back to England for the funeral and learned that he had come back to the house long enough to pack a bag and run away. Maggie's father hadn't reported anything due to his burden as a caregiver and running the family business. It's a long story and we need not go into it, but you get the idea. Gunnar sort of fell between the cracks. And no one seemed to know where he ran off to."

A heavy silence fell between the three and Adrian didn't know if he should speak or not. Finally, Maggie spoke, "We called the department of children's services and asked if they had heard of his whereabouts. He had been found and placed in a foster home, but apparently it was a challenging situation, and he ran away again."

Now Henry's lips were pursed, and he was nodding his head in the darkness. The wall sconce shone a soft golden light onto his white hair. Adrian could see the tension on his face.

Maggie sat up and declared in a bright voice, "The good news is that we found him after much effort and we brought him to St.

Lucia, which we had decided to call home. We became his stewards after that and resourced and cared for him as best we could."

"We sure did!" Henry smiled, "He was not unlike you, Adrian. He was always smart, capable of so many things, and had all the signs of leadership. He loved sports and was quite an athlete but didn't want to compete. And he loved the water!"

"I love the water, too." Adrian shared with enthusiasm. He was glad the tone of the conversation had turned around and become light again. The captain's story was stressful to hear. "I don't always care for competition, I just like people I play with to have fun. We don't need winners and losers."

"Oh, I agree with you on that!" Maggie smiled.

"So, everything worked out with the captain, huh?" Adrian asked, hoping for a bit more of the story.

"You could say that," Henry said. "We raised him until he went off to Dartmouth, the British Royal Naval College, and we almost never saw him again."

"Why is that?"

"He loves being at sea. He has salt water in his veins. He went from one ship to another gathering experience on all kinds of vessels until he could go take his hundred-ton license to be a yacht captain. I think he unconsciously followed in his father's footsteps."

"Oh." Adrian weighed his options. *Do I ask more about Gunnar or go down the path of the father?* "What happened to his father, do you know?"

"No," Maggie said, shaking her head. "He was never located, although we tried for one year. We even hired detectives in several countries and got nowhere. We gave him up for lost. After that, we stopped looking for him."

"Did Gunnar ever look for him?"

"I don't know, to be honest." Henry said, "That's a good

question. He was so angry after losing his great grandmother, leaving his homeland, never seeing his father and then his mother dying...that he wrote everyone off and was a troubled boy for quite a while. Anyone would be."

"But the captain is so...normal and nice." Adrian declared with a touch of defensiveness for the leader of *M/Y Arabella*. "Everyone loves him, and he is so respected by the entire crew and my family."

"Oh, yes," Maggie agreed, "He's a good man with a kind heart and clear head. He's so much like his mother, which is a good thing!"

"People say I am, too," Adrian confessed. "Like my mom, I mean."

"I can see that," Maggie nodded, "You are sensitive and intelligent. It's a good combination if you ask me. Just don't get stuck in your head and forget your heart."

"Thanks for telling me about the backstory of the captain," Adrian said, then with a light tone asked, "Anything else I should know?"

Henry waved his hand to dismiss the question. "Ah, you're good. You got the highlights." He stood up and stretched. Jaxon lifted his head at the movement. "I'm going to bed. Maggie, are you ready to turn in?" He extended his hand to his wife and helped her up. "Good night, young man. We'll meet here for breakfast and then get that gold leafing done. What do you say?"

"I'm in!" He stood up and gave hugs to Maggie and Henry and said good night. He took Jaxon for a quick walk and then went inside the lighthouse for the night.

Upstairs, he threw on a pair of shorts that he liked to sleep in and padded across the wooden floor to the kitchenette. Opening the under-the-counter refrigerator, he opened the door and found bottles of mineral water inside and chose a lime-flavored one that was fizzy. The night was warm, and he was feeling restless.

Opening his laptop, he replied to his mother.

Dear Mom,

Thanks for the email. It was really, REALLY helpful. I feel much better having let go of my self-judgments. I think now I could even face the guys onboard again without feeling weird...so that's good!

Hey, what do you do if you know a secret...and it's about someone you know, and they don't know that you know and let's just say I found out something that I probably wasn't supposed to know about and now I know more than I need to...arrrrrrgh! I just wish I didn't know what I know!!!!!!!!!!! Can you help me? It's eating me up.

Say hi to Dad and Grace.

Love you,

Adrian

He lay down on his bunk, tossed and turned for a minute or two before he punched his pillow in exasperation that his brain wouldn't shut off. He stared across the room to the window where a small sliver of moonlight was coming through the white curtains. *I don't have a clue what to do with this secret about the captain. He never introduced Henry and Maggie as his adopted parents, just "my good friends"...how can I act normal knowing what I know? And arrested? Troubled boy? It just doesn't seem like the captain.* He continued to stare at the window, listening to the distant sound of tree frogs, until his eyes closed on their own.

Chapter 8
Gilt

The next morning, Jaxon was barking and jumping on Adrian's back. He licked his ear until he promised to get up. "OK, OK, I'm getting up!" Adrian felt a bit moody and tired from stuffing his emotions the previous night. He took care of his needs first, then went downstairs and stuffed his feet into his shoes. Adrian held the leash with a firm hand. "Wait. Good boy!"

Opening the lighthouse door, Jaxon sped outside, pulling Adrian behind him. He got to his favorite area and sniffed the bushes and trees a bit, then relieved himself. Adrian rewarded him with more praise and a few pats on the back. Jaxon kept trying to nose his pocket and Adrian told him, "I'm sorry buddy, I forgot them upstairs. Come on, let's go find Henry and Maggie!"

He tied the leash to the post in the patio near the dog bowls and watched Jaxon begin to eat and drink. Next, he slipped off his shoes and entered the house. "Morning, Maggie, how are you?"

"I'm wonderful, Adrian. How are you?" She passed him a platter of roasted breakfast potatoes with rosemary, ham and bacon, and several hard-boiled eggs. "It's hot on the bottom, be careful. There's a trivet in the middle of the table. You can put it on the trivet."

"Where's Henry?"

"Oh, he's out in the shed, I believe. He may have the door shut, but he can hear you if you call him from the door."

Adrian stuck his head out the sliding glass door and called to

Henry in a loud voice. "Breakfast!" A carriage door opened, and he emerged, brushing his shirt and shorts of dust. As he got to the house he shared with Adrian, "I'm almost done carving out the serifs in the name and sanding it. It looks really good, if I may say so myself."

"Cool! I can't wait to see it!" He moved away from the door and took a seat at the table. Maggie was already seated and spooning food on everyone's plate.

"Oh, hello, love, that looks rather wonderful." Henry placed a kiss on the top of her head and continued to his seat. "Adrian, I've been meaning to ask you how your hands are today?"

He held his hands up, revealing tiny pink circles under each finger on the palm of his hand. "No blisters, no peeling."

"Oh, that's marvelous." Henry nodded and seemed pleased. "We'll go rowing later, I think."

After breakfast, Henry and Adrian worked on the rowboat by taking ultra-fine sandpaper and cleaning the inside of the carved letters as best they could. Henry took an air compressor and blew the stern clean and made sure there were no particles in the letters. Then he prepared some size, which was an interesting mixture of rabbit skin glue gelatin crystals and very hot water. He stirred it in a small tin can that he recycled. Adrian was fascinated with the size as it dissolved and became a clear beige liquid.

At the stern of the boat, Henry had the table cleared of tools except for a small box with the gold leaf, and what looked like his mom's makeup brush for her cheeks, a small detail paintbrush, clean towels and a polished stone-tipped tool on a wooden handle.

Sitting on the crate, Adrian waited. Henry handed him the paintbrush and size. "Here you go. You may do the honors and paint a thin layer of size into the letter A, and while you do that I'll create some static electricity with this sable brush to lift up the gold leaf sheet and then touch it to the glue. Ready?"

"Ready as I'll ever be." Adrian dipped his brush into the warm size and wiped off the excess on the edge of the tin. He'd painted model airplanes before and knew what a thin coat of paint meant. He carefully started at the top of the A and made sure that the serifs had every nook and cranny filled with size. "Am I doing this okay?"

"You sure are," Henry stated. "You have model building experience?" It was more a statement than a question.

"Yes, sir." Adrian was glad his dad and he had done a few fun projects together. "It was an F-16 Blue Angel. Turned out pretty good, I'd say. And in cub scouts, of course, my first project was the Derby race car. My dad did most of the work to shape it, but I painted it."

"I can see you know what you are doing."

"Thanks, Henry." Adrian said, "You sure are easy to work with. I mean that."

"Well, that is kind of you to say. Thank you."

They worked in silence and as soon as the size was completely in the grooves of the A, Henry ever so gently lifted a single sheet of gold leaf and let it float onto the wet glue. The wet size grabbed the fragile gold metallic paper and using the sable brush very carefully, Henry touched it in such a way that the gold adhered and lay flat in the grooves carved in the wood.

"Wow. I see what you mean by fragile." His voice held his awe at the material being held by static electricity to a crafting brush. "What about the excess that is covering the A? Don't you want to take it off?"

"We'll let it dry a bit, then brush it off. Be careful with the S. It's easy to go beyond the lines on curves."

"OK, thanks for the warning."

In no time they were complete, and Henry carefully went in and rubbed the gold with the polished stone on the end of a wooden handle. Adrian watched in fascination as he pressed and burnished the gold into the glue without tearing it. Little by little, the unused portion of the gold fell into the little box that Henry held below the letters. The name looked so good, Adrian was whipping out his camera to take a picture of Henry dusting off the H.

Standing up to review their work, Henry put an arm around Adrian's shoulder and said, "Well, now, that is a proper job!" Adrian put a hand on Henry's other shoulder, and he bobbed his head in excitement.

"Oh, man, Henry, this looks dynamite!" He chortled with glee and then knelt on one knee to take a photo of the stern. He turned and gave Henry a high five. Henry was looking mighty pleased with himself.

"Young man, I cannot wait to get this boat on the water." He bent to pick up his tools and set everything on a side work bench. "Wash the paintbrush in the palm of your hand with soap and warm water until the size is gone. Tap the water out gently, then reshape the tip. You can clamp it upside down over there on the tool wall to dry with those other brushes."

While Adrian washed the brush, Henry put things away and gave the floor a little touch up. He put the compressor hose back on the wall and moved the canister under the bench. "I love the name, Adrian. Inspired! We chose well, I believe."

"Yeah, I love it." He was smiling with pride. "I hope I get to go out in it before I leave. What else do we need to do with it?"

"After the size dries, we can give a coat of varnish to it. Then after that dries, we can hoist her up, remove the chocks she's resting on and run a trailer under her to pull her out of the shop."

"Oh. That's great." He looked it over and walked around it, he touched the bow. "Handling lines?"

"I made two. They're somewhere in here. I'll find them and you can clip them on."

"The big question of the hour is, shall we go for a row or a hike?" Henry asked.

"Row."

"Good. Let's have a quick bite and then go." Henry stopped in his tracks. "Do you think Jaxon is ready to go on the boat? Maggie left for several appointments in the city. Shall we give him a try?"

Adrian bit his lower lip and thought about it. Last night's episode of his being out of control was a consideration, and it did make him hesitate for a moment. *Maybe being in a boat was not going to be a problem.* "Let's take him. I'll be sure to have some rewards for good behavior."

"I think he'll be fine. He did rather well on the motorboat when we went to your yacht."

After eating sandwiches, Adrian grabbed the four oars and brought them out to the SUV while Henry brought the two clip-on personal floatation devices, bottled water, and a small plastic bowl for Jaxon to drink water. Adrian made sure to refill his plastic bag with treats. They both grabbed hats and applied sunscreen in the shade of the patio, then headed to the harbor munching crisp green apples along the way.

Jaxon barked at the harbormaster, who laughed and added a note to his book that they were going out. At the water's edge, Jaxon pranced and jumped through the water that broke on shore with such joy. Henry shrugged and ordered Jaxon to get in the boat. The terrier barked and barked. Adrian went to the other side of the boat and held up a snack. The terrier paddled over to Henry, who lifted him up and let him leap inside, tracking water everywhere. "Where do we want him to sit?"

Henry pointed to the bow, and Adrian held a treat near the inner triangle without giving it up. "Sit." Jaxon barked. "Quiet." Jaxon stopped and looked expectant. "Sit." He didn't budge, and he didn't bark either. "Sit, Jaxon." Jaxon put his rear end on the forward triangle that was a seat for a small person. "Good boy! Good boy!" Adrian gave him a tiny piece of a treat and moved the boat out a bit further. "Want to get in first, Henry? I'll hold the boat."

"Sure." He stepped across the starboard stern quarter and stepped over the bench seat Adrian sat on the last time and sat down. Adrian moved the boat out another few feet and climbed in himself. He drew his oars out and inserted the tholepin into the rail. He positioned himself for success and swiveled his oars until the blades were vertical and ready to dig into the water. "Ready?"

"Go for it!"

Adrian leaned forward and let his blade get as far back as possible before he allowed them to cut down into the water and he pulled with a sense of familiarity. His oars gushed out to the stern, and he sprayed water. He laughed and shared, "I guess I'm just too excited and trying to go nowhere fast!"

"It's OK. You're warming up." Henry gave a nice slow and steady stroke to move the boat in the direction of the harbor opening. The tholepins made creaking noises and the steady sound of the oars moving in the rowlocks was rhythmic and pleasant to hear. They got in sync quickly and at the entrance Henry turned the boat due south. "I figured we might try and enter the river down here. If the water level is high enough, we can get through. Or we can float the boat over the couple of inches of water at the mouth of the estuary. It's a nice place to row. You'll see."

They left Marigot Bay and rowed south towards Roseau River. The water was glossy, a sublime color of pale blue green and super clear to the bottom. Adrian could see schools of fish under the water and witnessed fish jumping out of the water several times. While they were halfway to their destination, Henry pointed out a couple of dolphins having a lazy swim towards Marigot. Adrian rowed and focused on their location as he took it all into his awareness. Jaxon barked when a flying fish leapt out of the water nearby.

"OK, we're almost there. This sand bar moves with storms and river runoff. Let's see if the water depth is going to hold as we go across the sand bar." Henry announced. Together they brought the boat around and headed into a small opening in the sandbar. "If we get stuck, we just get out and float the boat into deeper water."

"Roger that." Adrian looked at the water and noticed the differences in the color. The river was bringing silt and golden-green colored water into the aqua blue sea.

"That's the river meeting the incoming tide and creating turbulence. There's not much room here because of this narrow bend in the river. I'll row and bring us up the river a bit. It opens up rather quickly. Most of the time you have to walk your kayak or boat across the sand."

The boat went aground without warning. Jaxon barked to alert the crew. Henry and Adrian laughed and stood up and told Jaxon to stay put. They sloshed through the very shallow water and moved the boat into deeper water. Henry got in first, and Adrian pushed the boat out to deeper water before climbing in.

In a few strokes they were in the middle of the river. It was wide, hot and serene, with the northern hillsides covered in low tropical foliage right down to the water. Grasses grew in the shallow water that was brownish green. A red pickup truck drove down the road on the starboard side of the boat and Henry asked Adrian if he recognized the location. "No, not really."

"You were here yesterday afternoon playing soccer on the beach. This is the river alongside the road we drove down and parked on to the side."

"Oh, wow, I follow."

They rowed deeper up the river and the mangrove trees appeared, the water turned brown like black tea, and a dense canopy of leaves covered their heads, providing some much-needed shade.

"It's really hot out here." Adrian complained. "This shade feels good." He twisted to get a glimpse of Jaxon and saw he was curled up on the bow with his jaw resting on the gunnel panting to stay cool. He was sniffing the humid air and he was alert.

"Yes," Henry replied, "This type of activity can create a nasty sunburn. The water reflects the rays of the sun and intensifies the ultraviolet light we are getting right now. How's our friend in the bow?"

"He's good. He looks hot." Adrian said in a quiet low voice, "Henry, look at that blue-gray bird on the rock by the shore." He pointed out what appeared to be a rather large Great Blue Heron on his left while balancing his oar across his lap. The back of the bird's head had a long feather that hung in the heavy air. Neither one of them spoke or rowed as they watched the bird watching them.

They continued rowing and entered an area of water flooded with sunlight and littered with millions of leaves and flowers that looked like gold flecks on the water. Twisting his head around, Adrian looked over the starboard side and up the river to see the source of such magic. "Wow, it looks like confetti on the water."

Minutes later, the river narrowed and became a quiet, dark channel that was peaceful yet buzzing with insect and bird activity. "Adrian, on your left. Shoulder level." Henry's voice was soft so as not to spook the wildlife he spied.

A Little Egret stood on a dense grouping of gnarled brown

roots of a mangrove tree a few feet above the water. It was snow-white and stock-still watching the water below. The compressed s-curve of its neck produced a hunched predator appearance centered on long black legs. He unzipped his pants pocket and took out the waterproof bag he kept his phone in. With deep care, he turned it on out of sight, added zoom and raised it with no sudden movements and took a picture. "Wow, it's beautiful," he whispered. "Good find, Henry."

Henry took a slow pull on his oars to keep moving the boat along. Adrian didn't bother to row while he was mesmerized by the egret and the tranquility of this part of the river. After a while, he picked up his oar handles and matched Henry's blade stroke for stroke.

Guiding the boat down a tributary, they made their way down a section lined with coconut, banana, and breadfruit trees. A large cloud crossed overhead, making the estuary channel darker than normal. Birds called to each other throughout the treetops. "The weather's changing. Ready to turn it around?" Henry asked while he rested on his oars and consulted the sky. They were floating in a quiet spot that was wide enough to spin the boat around with ease. "How about you have a go at it?"

Dipping his right oar down, he pulled on his left, and the boat began to turn nicely. Feeling confident, he moved the right oar into place and pushed against it while pulling the left oar. He repositioned the boat so they could exit the upper section of the river and head to sea.

Both pairs of oars pulled at a comfortable pace with Henry watching over his shoulder for where they needed to go with one eye on the sky. Parrots cawed overhead and made a racket that ignited Jaxon to bark. His bark was loud and caused a multitude of birds to leave the trees in a rush. "Quiet, Jaxon." Adrian ordered, without looking back. He let Jaxon settle himself down again and then gave him praise. There wasn't another whimper from him until they got to the beach, and they let him out to run around and relieve himself. He barked incessantly when Adrian ordered him back into the boat.

"I believe our little friend believes it is his turn now." Henry surmised with a patient chuckle. "Go find a stick to throw; and maybe let him cool off in the water."

They made sure the boat was beached properly and looked for driftwood suitable for throwing. For ten minutes, Jaxon ran after a stick and splashed in the water. He loved prancing in the incoming waves. "We ought to get going. The sea is getting a bit choppy." Henry looked out to sea and turned his gaze south and north, focusing on a bank of clouds that wasn't there earlier. "Let's get a move on. Jaxon! Get in the boat."

Jaxon shook himself free of water and sand and stood there barking. Henry dragged the boat with Adrian to the seashore. "Now!" He pointed the bow to the dog. There was a sternness in his voice Adrian had never heard before. Jaxon obeyed by leaping up and scrambling into the bow. *Oh, he's good with dogs.*

Henry got in and held the boat steady with his oars while Adrian both shoved off the sand and climbed in. He had barely sat down and was reaching for his oars and Henry was already pulling at full strength against the incoming tide. They rode up and down over the swells, which were coming into shore in faster sets. Adrian got his oars in and began to pull. Up and down, pulling against wind and tide. Adrian broke a sweat after ten minutes. "Wow, Henry, it wasn't this hard coming here."

"We rowed with the wind and tide." He answered, "It's changed. We need to row hard and fast. Rain is coming. I'll pace with you. Do your best."

Salt spray doused the bow and flew over Henry's head and hit Adrian in the back of the head. He smiled. *This is exciting!* Jaxon barked and climbed down onto the floor of the bow where he was safer. He continued to look out over the gunnel standing on his hind legs. He barked each time a wave came across the bow and hit him.

Sometimes Adrian's oars never got into the water as they couldn't catch atop a swell. The entire time, they never saw another boat. Clouds were crossing the sky and they moved under shadows and light as they stayed far away from the cliffs covered in cactus getting sprayed by waves whipped up by the approaching storm. The first heavy drop of rain hit the back of Adrian's neck as they turned the corner of Marigot Bay. Soon they were rowing with the incoming swells, and it took no time to cross the bay, now the color of lead.

Soaked to the skin in the warm tropical rain, Adrian felt the bow of the boat go aground on the beach and he popped out his oars and stored them inboard. There was a couple inches of rainwater in the bottom of the boat. He slogged through the swells on the beach and pulled the boat up higher after Henry got out. He returned with the boat dolly and together they hauled the boat onto the trailer with the wire cable winch. Jaxon stayed in the bow watching the activity. Walking the boat around to the boatyard parking space, they hosed it down and Henry produced a bailing scoop and towels from the SUV. Adrian climbed in and scooped fast, dumping water over the side. "Stop, Adrian. We've got more rain coming. Look." He pointed out an opaque gray wall of water that moved from the bay entrance towards them.

"Oh, yeah. Forget it." He jumped out. "Just cover it and come back later?"

"I'm afraid so." They covered the boat with the blue canvas cover and returned the hose to the wall after giving Jaxon a quick wash. Thunder and lightning cracked in the bay, and they were all startled at the sight and sound. Jaxon yelped and tried to climb up into Adrian's arms. Picking up the wet dog, he comforted him with calm, soothing words. He was about twelve or thirteen pounds dry, but now he was a wriggling wet mess of dog hair that was trying to climb up onto Adrian's shoulders in fear. Henry locked the cable and ran to the SUV and opened the doors. Adrian put Jaxon down on the pavement so he could climb in. He shook himself then leaped up. "Good boy!" Then he hopped into the front seat next to Henry. He wasn't used to being on the left side of the car next to the driver, or the "wrong side of the road." Today he didn't notice. "Wow! We got in just in time. That was fun, Henry."

"That could have been dangerous." His voice was low and full of concern. "I checked the weather last night. The chance of rain was only twenty percent. I didn't check this morning before going out."

"Nothing happened. We got a little wet..." he wanted to assure his new friend that there was no make wrong.

"Rowboats can turn into bathtubs in these storms. I forgot to bring the bailer or a portable pump. And you never want to be out with lightning, if you are the only object it can connect to."

"That makes sense." He faced forward and watched the road through busy windshield wipers. He heard thunder nearby and Jaxon barked. No one said quiet. He just kept barking.

"Henry, I had an amazing time. Even with the rain." Adrian looked at his hands. With some excitement, he held out his palm in Henry's direction, "I even have my first blister!"

A small smile crept up the left side of Henry's face and he took his eyes off the road to take a quick peek at the blister, then at the bright eyes of the boy next to him. He made a fist and put it out for Adrian to do knuckles with him. Returning his attention to the road, he navigated into his driveway. "It was a beautiful excursion. I'm glad we did it. And you did fantastic rowing back to port. Quite good, actually."

Earlier in the day, while racing back to port, Adrian sensed he had done a good job rowing for his second time out on the sea. He took Henry's praise into his heart and felt an inner glow of happiness. He flashed Henry a smile of gratitude and put his hand on the door handle, "Ready to make a mad dash to the door?"

"Absolutely!"

"Three, two, one...go!" He wrenched the door open and grabbed the handle behind his door for Jaxon to jump down and slamming the doors shut, they ran across the driveway. Under the eaves, Henry looked at them and said, "We had best go around the back to the patio. We can't go in like this." Racing around the wing of the house, they rushed to the patio. Maggie slid open the door and gasped when she saw three bedraggled boaters.

"Oh, my. Look at each of you." She covered her mouth and started to giggle. Henry and Adrian looked at each other and the dog. Their clothing was drenched and t-shirts transparent. Nothing was dry anywhere. Jaxon looked woebegone. He barked and shook himself. Everyone jumped back with a laugh. Three humans said in unison, "Jaxon!!" And he barked back at them.

"OK, wait here. I'll get towels." She turned, "And I'll put the kettle on!"

"Now that's a British person for you," Henry smiled with deep affection, "If you are cold and wet or warm and wet it doesn't matter; you're getting a cup of tea."

They shared a chuckle and sat down on a bench and Adrian pulled out his baggie of crushed dog treats. Jaxon quickly came to attention in front of the baggie and barked. "Quiet!" He stopped barking and wagged his tail. "Talk!" He barked. "Ah, you are a good boy!" He gave him a treat. "Shake!" He put out his right hand and Jaxon placed his paw in it. "Dang, you are smart. You learned that quickly." He gave him a small nibble. "Sit." He sat and got a treat. "Beg." Jaxon looked confused. Adrian put both hands in front of him and barked. Jaxon sat back and raised his front paws and barked. "Quiet." He got praise for holding the pose. "Niiiice." Adrian gave a tiny bite to reward the new trick.

"Very intelligent, isn't he? He learned that quickly." Henry observed. "It's almost like someone had worked with him before."

"I think so, too." Adrian scratched the back of Jaxon's neck and patted him. "I'm going to see what else he knows." He commanded the dog to come by slapping a wet short pant leg. Jaxon looked up at his human.

"Jaxon! Come!" Adrian patted his leg and Jaxon jumped to attention before him. He gave him a treat. "Sit." He sat. "Oh, joy, you are a good boy!" Adrian gave him a pat on the back. "Shake," and put out his hand. They shook, "Nice to meet you, Jaxon!" Jaxon barked. "Quiet." He stopped trying to talk back. "Talk." Jaxon resumed barking and continued to sit. "Good sitting, good talking!" He noticed Jaxon eyeing the treat bag. "OK, I'll give you a treat. Stand up!" Jaxon lifted his front paws. "No, that's beg. Stand up!" Adrian raised the treat over the dog's head, and he leapt up high and took it out of Adrian's fingers. "Wow! You are an amazing animal!"

"We need to talk to David and Jayden's parents and learn if they would be willing to take Jaxon before you leave." Maggie opened the door and came out bearing towels. The guys toweled their hair and faces. They stepped out of their water sandals and dropped their hats and wet t-shirts on a bench. Wrapped in towels, they sat down on the chairs.

"Tea?" Maggie asked.

"Oh, yes, please!" Henry looked over at Adrian and raised an eyebrow.

He gave a dramatic and regal nod of his head and said in his best British accent imitation, "Why, yes, Maggie, that would be quite perfect."

She got a wink from Henry and returned with a tray of mugs full of steaming black tea, with cream and sugar and a few plain biscuits.

"I'm thinking showers, and then we meet back at the shop. What do you say, Adrian?" Henry dunked his tea biscuit a second too long and it broke off. Straightening up, he looked deep into his cup and said, "Oh, dear. It appears that I've lost my biscuit." Maggie passed him a spoon and soon he was fishing it out from the bottom of his mug.

"Sounds good to me. The rain has stopped. Do you think we need to give you-know-who a bath?"

Maggie looked at the dog resting at Adrian's feet. "Let's wait. I suspect he'll be digging in the garden mud in a moment. That's the one thing I struggle with when it comes to terriers. They love to dig."

"Yeah, a dog like this wouldn't like living aboard a boat. There's nowhere for them to dig." He looked at this young digger and smiled, "I'll bet David and Jayden know plenty of places he can dig!"

"Maggie, I was thinking we could take our little fur baby here and Adrian for a hike tomorrow. What do you think?"

"I love it. We can do some birding, what do you think?" She turned to her young guest, "Have you been bird watching before?"

"Well, today, we saw several incredible shore birds. Is there more to it?" he asked.

"Oh, my, yes! It's a very competitive sport," she exclaimed with excitement. "People race all over the world, counting all the different birds they see in one year."

"My lovely Maggie loves birding," Henry shared with a broad smile. "We've traveled far and wide in search of rare and common birds."

"Really!?" *Chasing birds is a thing?*

"Oh, it's like a treasure hunt and very challenging." Maggie shared with pleasure. "Haven't you ever gone looking for something specific and found it? There is a certain thrill involved."

"Maggie is quite the bird detective!" Henry added, "She can listen to the birds and know who's who in the zoo, see a bright spot of color in the trees, a flash of wings in the grass...she's got the instinct. One year she spotted nearly six-hundred different types of birds."

"Wow, that's cool." Adrian said, still not convinced that he would find this hobby engaging. "I wouldn't know where to look, although today the birds were just so obvious, it would have been hard not to notice them.

"I did get a cool shot of one of them. Here, let me show you," he fished his phone out of his back pocket and flicked it on and pulled up the Little Egret. Passing the phone to Maggie, he shared, "He was an easy subject because he didn't move, and the contrast is extreme."

"Adrian, this is quite a beautiful shot! Well, done young man. You've got the eye." Maggie passed his phone back and he breathed in the praise.

He laughed, "Thanks. I hardly use my camera for anything anymore. I'm too busy participating and focusing that I forget to take a few pictures."

"That is wonderful." Henry nodded and was listening deeply. "It sounds like you become very present with yourself and others -or your activity- which is a gift you give yourself. Did you know that?"

"No," he replied, and then gave a short laugh, "You sound like my mom, now. Or the captain. Is this my fate? To one day sound like all the adults in my life to the teenagers in my life when I'm older?"

Maggie and Henry roared laughing at his question and Maggie wrapped her arms around him in a very endearing sideways hug. "Adrian, you make me smile. You can sound any way you want to sound. Deliver your wisdom with your voice."

"I plan to!" he shared with a smile. "Hey, Henry, are we going to finish the boat today?"

"Yes, and we need to return to the harbor and clean out the rowboat, which won't take but an hour or less." Henry stood up, "Let's get a move on. Only so much daylight left. Best to use it."

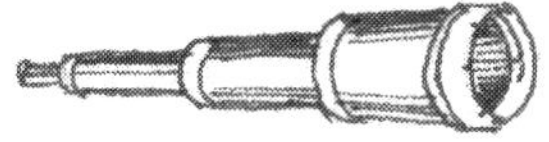

Chapter 9
The Big Hike

Quilesse Forest Reserve

Anse La Raye

St. Lucia

Adrian woke up to his alarm and a dark room. Jaxon barked at the unfamiliar sound. "Quiet, Jaxon" he ordered in a soft voice. Surprisingly, the dog obeyed. "Good boy!" He reached for the treat bag and gave him a tiny piece. "I don't think you really need these anymore, do you boy? Huh?" Jaxon headed down the stairs, but Adrian hung back to gather a few items and shove them into a backpack. Jaxon began barking to get Adrian down the stairs faster.

"Stop being so demanding, Jaxon. No one likes it!" he yelled down to the dog. The dog was incessant and so was Adrian. "Quiet!" He yelled from the bathroom, "No one likes demanding energy, Jaxon. If you keep that up you'll never have friends, and no one will like you!" Then he started laughing. "Oh, my gosh, I sound just like my mom... this is terrible!" Chuckling, he threw his ball cap on, slung his backpack over his shoulder, grabbed his multisport water sandals to put on downstairs, and hustled down. "I swear, Jaxon, if my mom was here she'd tell you that you need to let go of your fear that you won't get your needs met and then the need to be demanding goes away."

Slipping on his shoes while sitting on the bottom step, Jaxon tried biting his Velcro strapped rubber hiking sandals and Adrian swatted him out of the way. "Hey! That's not a chew toy!" *I wonder if he has a chew toy...I need to ask Maggie.*

Snapping his leash on, he exited the building and Jaxon raced over to his favorite spot in the untamed tropical foliage. The sun was starting to crack over the horizon and a beam light across the sky. Adrian pulled out his phone to check messages while his friend did his duty. His friends were all too busy to write. *Unless you're on a server or playing a video game, you're out of touch. Is this what it has come to? We're not friends if we're not playing video games?*

Jaxon pulled him towards the house, and they entered the patio area together. He tied him to the post and took his food and water bowl into the kitchen where he cleaned them and filled them. The hungry dog set about wolfing down his breakfast.

Maggie was the first out and she immediately thanked Adrian for taking care of the dog bowls. "No problem," he replied, "What else can I do?"

Handing him a padded cooler bag, she suggested he fill it with snacks for the car. Apples, grapes, cheese, protein bars, granola if he wanted some, and suggested he fill four travel bottles with water. She moved through the kitchen making breakfast while he took care of the hiker's needs. Setting everything by the door, he wandered back to the dining room table and put out mugs for tea, flatware, and napkins.

The smell of breakfast wafted through the house and Henry emerged at last with slightly damp hair, dressed for the trail in cargo pants and a long sleeve travel shirt with epaulets on the shoulders. "Good morning, Adrian. How are you this fine morning? Sleep well?"

"Yes, Henry. Thank you."

"Very well. I will be interested to see how we do birding today." He placed his own backpack by the door with a first aid kit. "Darling, do you have your illustrated bird book of St. Lucian birds for Adrian to use today?"

"I do!" she responded, "It's in my bag."

"Marvelous." Henry sat down and poured tea. "Where we are going today is a veritable bird heaven for bird watchers. It's really the heart of the island, a thousand feet above sea level, and there are over thirty birds that can be seen there."

"Five of them," he continued, "are endemic species, meaning they are only found on this island, which makes them truly unique."

"Their names all begin with St. Lucia. There's a St. Lucia-Parrot, Oriole, Pewee, Wren, and a Warbler. Our parrot was brought back from extinction in the 1980s. We're lucky to still have it. There's a good chance that we'll see three or four of these endemic species today. The wren you'll have to look for in dry scrubby areas. But it is important to go early in the morning, which is why we are up before the sun."

"How long will the hike be?" Adrian asked.

"Oh, maybe two hours. It's only 2.8km, which is less than two miles," Henry supplied. "I'm afraid we have to leave our dear friend, Mr. Jaxon, here because he will make birding impossible." As if on cue, he barked, and they shared a knowing glance.

They ate quickly and loaded up the car. Maggie made sure Jaxon was comfortable, then ran around closing windows and doors before slipping inside the front seat next to Henry. "OK! Let's go!"

The forest reserve was lush on all levels. All shades of green, yellow, and brown collided with each other and grew towards the blue sky that was speckled with broken clouds. The air was buzzing and humming with insects, lizards, birds and more. The walking trail was a simple dirt trail wandering over roots, rocks and not unlike his recent volcano hike. The canopy of leaves overhead was full of squawks, trills, and chirps. Adrian didn't know where to begin. "Do we just start walking or...?" He let his question hang in the air as Henry fished a pair of small binoculars out of his bag and passed them to Adrian.

"First, take a look around and observe the tropical forest. Watch for a flash of wings, a movement of something." Henry leaned over his shoulder and pointed to a tree dead ahead of him, "Right there. What do you see?"

Squinting into the binoculars, he shared, "A gray bird?"

"Wait for him to turn," Henry said with patience in his voice. "Wait for it."

"Oh! Wow! He has bright yellow feathers on his chest!" Adrian exclaimed with surprise. "What is it?"

"St. Lucian Warbler. Your third bird, I believe." Henry smiled at the excitement he heard in Adrian's voice. "Would you like to write it down?"

"Yeah, I guess so." He pulled out his phone and opened a note taking tool and wrote in SL Warbler.

"Add the date, time and location," Henry suggested. "On birding blogs, forums, and websites, if you see something rare, you want to share the location so others can come look at it, too. It's possible the nest is nearby. Birders are quite a generous bunch and share their discoveries."

"Roger that. Wilco."

"Look, Adrian!" she excitedly whispered. "Eleven o'clock, black as night, on a giant tree fern..." Her voice was soft, and she had her binoculars trained on a small bird.

"I see it. What is it?" He opened his phone to enter the next name.

"Black Finch. Endemic."

"Got it. Thanks." He slipped his phone into his back pocket and began walking with his eyes scanning the trees.

Towering dark green philodendrons had wild orchids in white and lavender pink growing off the trunks and greenish-pink and red-toned anthuriums grew in the humid air on the forest floor. Stepping over a trickle of water that ran across the red dirt trail and down the steep hillside, Adrian paused and looked across the gap in the trees to the steep mountains across the valley. "Henry? Do all birds have a nest?"

"Well, that is an interesting question. Let me ask the expert. Maggie!"

Stopping on the trail, she turned to see what they wanted. "Do all birds have a nest?"

"No, not at all. Some birds don't have a clue, like some humans. It's amazing they survive at all." She laughed. "Let me give you some examples. Common murres lay their eggs on flat surfaces and huddle together. Father penguins hold the egg on their feet for months until it hatches. And some birds use other bird's nests rather than build their own."

She shivered, "And then there is one I still can't believe...super parasitic."

"Like what?" Adrian encouraged her to tell him.

"The Common Cuckoos will lay eggs in a variety of nests, but especially the Reed Warbler's nest."

"What's so horrible about that?" he asked, wondering why she had experienced a horrified shiver from calling up info about the cuckoo bird.

"These newborn cuckcoos that don't even have feathers and are blind, instinctively know to eject the Reed Warbler's eggs out of the nest, killing their young. And then the baby cuckoos demand to be fed." She shook her head to clear the story from her thoughts. "Imagine the one who kills your young baby, demanding you feed them. Impossible!"

Henry laughed and put an arm around his wife's shoulders. "Now, love, let's focus on the lovely specimens on the trail before us and put your least favorite bird out of your mind, who is simply living by instinct not conscious choice."

She hitched her backpack tighter to her body and raised her chin. "Something must be wrong with those birds. It's not normal and it is tolerated by other birds. If the Wrens just refuse those cuckoo eggs, the population would just die off."

"So, are you suggesting that the Reed Warbler's should kick out the egg of the Common Cuckcoo? Like 'enough is enough,' we're not taking your bad behavior anymore?" Adrian asked to gain clarity with a hint of humor.

"Something like that." She turned and continued up the trail. Adrian shrugged and Henry winked to say that everything was fine.

"Henry, how does a baby bird, absent of its own biological parents, know how to kick out the other bird's egg? That's just incredible. Could it be genetic memory? What causes this to even happen?"

"Adrian, if I knew I would tell you," Henry began earnestly, "And I would help my lovely wife get to peace on these types of conundrums on the trail of life. The truth is, I just don't know."

"I forgot to ask...where do parrots nest?" He looked sorry for bringing it up and made a cringey smile at Henry.

"Hollows of trees. They like holes in trees and will stay there year after year." He looked around for a tree but didn't find what he was searching for. "Chestnuts and gum trees usually have holes. And you can hear the screeching. They make a fierce noise. I'm not too fond of the sound, if you know what I mean."

"Los Angeles has lots of parrots and they remind me of green fighter jets when they glide through the sky. They're pretty cool. Not quite flying in formation, but close."

They continued their walk and at times the path was steep, wet, muddy, or arduous. They stopped at a railing that kept the hikers inside the trail and away from the precarious edge of the hillside. The view was developing below and across the valley, as the sunlight burst through clouds and mist. Birds flew from treetop to treetop and it was electric to hear so many bird sounds from the valley floor.

"The noise is incredible! I love it!" Adrian excitedly took out his camera phone to record the sound and make a panoramic video. "Hey, what's that? It's gold-toned on the breast and sort of brown-gray on the back."

"That would be the Pewee!" Henry said with some excitement, "Good eyes, Adrian. That's three natives you've spotted. Look for that blue head and medium green body...that would be the parrot colors you are looking for. His local name is Jacquot!"

"Jacquot?" he asked without looking up from his phone, where he entered notes on the last bird. A movement on the tree near him caught his eye and he moved closer to search for the source. "Henry! Look! Check out this lizard! It's huge! And it's blue and green. Holy smokes, this thing is huge!" He took a few photos of it and entered it into his digital diary.

"That is a Caribbean Lizard that you find in the Antilles. They're fairly common." Henry rushed to turn Adrian around and pointed out a large bird of prey crossing the canopy away from them. "I think that might be a sea eagle or an osprey. Hard to see from here." He held his binoculars to his eyes and tried to find the bird, but it was difficult. "Drat."

Maggie came back towards them on the trail with a big smile on her face, "Did you see the osprey?"

"Yes!" Henry and Adrian said in unison.

Together all three stood in silence and looked out across the top of the rainforest to Mt. Gimi, the highest peak on the island. Maggie's right hand reached out to grip Adrian's arm, and she whispered, "Don't move. Look out about twenty feet and to the right. See that dark yellow sort of olive-brown colored bird on the branch with the moss? That's the Pewee!"

"I just saw that same bird moments ago. Might be the same one."

"Do you have any idea how shy that bird is, and many people come up here hoping to see one and go home without seeing one?" She threw up her hands to the sky and turned to walk on. "Adrian, you are on a roll," she said over her shoulder.

Smiling, he followed her footsteps and after a few steps he

said, "Wait. I hear something." They all stopped dead in their tracks and listened. The wind had picked up and the treetops were creating a swishing sound. They all looked at each other and continued to pause. Adrian looked for the source of the cawing sound he thought he heard. "I dunno. I thought I heard a par..." Just then a green parrot swooped down out of the branches to his left and glided over the trail and down the steep canopy of branches and leaves into the valley. "There!"

"Bravo!"

"We'll make a birder out of you yet, Adrian!" Henry clapped him on the back, and they continued down the trail.

This is amazing. I can't believe this is fun. He smiled at how his whole being was attuned to the rainforest, listening to the sounds, and his eyes watching for the slightest movement. In a clearing they saw both a Green- and Purple- Throated Carib Hummingbird.

A park ranger was putting out coconut halves and several finches were investigating, along with some green butterflies. They all said, "good morning" and kept walking.

Maggie pointed out a few different types of doves. "You know the yellow birds in our garden?" Adrian nodded, "Those are Bananaquits. They love sugar and are found all over the Caribbean."

"Do you have a favorite bird, Maggie?" Adrian asked.

"Oh, that's a tough question." She responded, "I have several favorites depending on the environment. I love hummingbirds, but also birds of prey. All birds are rather interesting, even the parasitic ones."

"Well, that was a great hike. Thank you for taking me. I bet my sister and parents would have loved this hike, too. We do these types of activities as a family." He sounded a bit wistful. He was wondering on the ride up here if his family was having fun without him or missing him.

"Are you ready to go back to the yacht?" Henry asked over his shoulder, as he clicked his seatbelt into place. "You can go back early, if you choose."

"Oh, no, I'm good." He assured them, "I can call them anytime. I'm just enjoying the break. I think they may all be enjoying me being off the boat, too. I seem to get on people's nerves lately." He looked out the window as Henry pulled onto the mountain road and began his descent out of the rainforest.

"Why is that sweetheart?" Maggie asked with kindness. "And please pass me the cooler bag, love. I could use a nibble."

"Well, I have a habit of bursting in on people working and disturbing their concentration. Or something like that." He passed her the bag and then stared at the greenery going by in a blur to his right. His thoughts went to the chef. He felt OK, which surprised him a tiny bit. *And Jimmy? No triggers. And Pete?* A little tiny bit of insecurity rushed back and flooded his awareness, and he felt a pang of something. *Was it because he never said anything, and I just assumed he didn't like my interruptions?* He squirmed a bit in his seat. He always got uncomfortable when he discovered he assumed stuff about people and got called on it. *I guess I have to let go of making assumptions or this will be a lifelong curse.*

He sighed and noticed Henry was asking him a question for a second time. "I'm sorry, Henry, what was that?" He caught Henry's eyes in the rear-view mirror. He saw some concern.

"Do you want to go anywhere or head back to the house?"

"Back to the house is fine. I'm wondering how Jaxon's doing." He moved the focus off himself and onto the dog. "Have you talked to David's parents yet?"

"No, we'll do that tonight." Maggie assured him. "I'll bake cookies and we'll take them over with us."

"Sounds great." He thought his voice sounded a bit flat, even to his own ears.

"I was thinking of having your family spend the evening with us, two days from now. I know your parents are looking to get a move on to the next island. You can go back with them, if you like, or spend one more night with us and then we can bring you to the harbor. It's up to you."

"I really like it here. I like being with you both and Jaxon." He was surprised to hear himself say this to this nice couple that, in all honesty, he barely knew, but really liked a lot. "I'm going to miss the lighthouse. I really love having my own space and a dog." His voice was wistful at the thought of leaving so soon. He let out a big sigh.

"Sweetheart, you are always welcome to come back and stay with us," Maggie shared with so much generosity in her voice. Adrian knew it was a genuine offer.

"Thank you. I might take you up on it if my parents agree." He smiled into the rear-view mirror to Henry. "Maybe you can teach me how to build a boat from scratch, Henry!"

"I'd be delighted to!" He declared, "Speaking of boats, we have a boat to launch!"

"Are we going to take it out today?" Adrian sat forward with deep interest. "Is it ready?"

"Not quite, but early tomorrow morning would be perfect for her maiden voyage."

"Far out! I can't wait!"

Back in the lighthouse, Adrian sat at the captain's desk after lunch and opened his laptop. Jaxon was resting at his feet and being quiet. He found an email from his mom addressing the secret issue.

Dear Adrian,

If you know a secret about someone and they did not share it with you, you need to be direct and have a one-on-one, authentic, and transparent conversation with them about what you know. It is the best approach to your problem. Otherwise, you carry a burden in your heart and mind that will eat away at you and the other party will sense that there is something being withheld inside the space of your relationship. Secret Consciousness is loaded with mistrust and needs to leave this planet. It shuts down the energetics of the relationship.

Also, you need to set the listening for the conversation you are going to have with that person. I recommend you a.) let go of your self-judgments (aka fears) that you can't be heard and may be judged, and b.) judgments you have of the other person that they won't hear you, so your judgments are not in the conversation on an energetic level. Got it?

Call me if you need more help.
XOX

Huh. He leaned back in the office chair and thought about how he would share with the captain how he knew about his past. How about… "Um, Captain, there's something I have to tell you, I know you're adopted." *No, too direct and doesn't sound nice at all. Ugh.* "Hi, Captain, can we talk? There's something I have to tell you."

No, better to give some back story. "Captain, I was looking through the desk in the lighthouse…I accidentally found your adoption papers and thought I had better let you know." *Why does having this conversation sound like I am super nosy and now I have some info on him that I could blackmail him with?* He shuddered. *Why does this sound so painful and hard to do?*

He closed his laptop after he wrote a quick thank you to his mom. Jaxon jumped up on his leg and Adrian ordered him to get down. He did, and was praised.

What does authentic really mean? Hmm. What is transparent? Not hiding anything? He leaned back in the seat and spun around a few times, annoying Jaxon, who yelped and jumped out of the way. *Mom would say, I didn't mean to find them, but I did. And now I feel like I am carrying a personal secret of yours. Is that true? Is your adoption a secret?* He let out an exasperated growl. *Why in the world am I making such a big deal out of this!?!*

"Want to go for a walk, Jaxon?" For a response, Jaxon jumped down the stairs two at a time. Adrian followed and put his shoes on and snapped on the leash. "Let's go, boy!"

He stuck his head in the shop and told Henry he was going for a quick jog. He waved and wished them well. With Jaxon in the lead, they headed up the street and ran through tree-lined streets, past big houses and wound their way around hilltops until the heat and humidity caused Adrian to call a halt. "OK, buddy, we're cooling down now, got it?" Making their way back, he began to feel that gnawing anxiety growing in the pit of his gut. Twenty minutes later, he had the hose out and was spraying Jaxon down to help him cool off. He tied the leash to the post and added water to his dog bowl.

He wandered over to the shop and found Henry sharpening some tools. He had a ceiling fan on, and the back window air conditioner was running. "Is it me, or is it hotter than yesterday?"

"Oh, it feels hotter than yesterday!" Henry didn't look up as he continued to move the edge of a chisel across a whetstone. He was wearing a pair of reading glasses. "Are you ready to get *Dash* on a trailer for tomorrow?"

"Yeah! What can I do to help?"

Wiping off the sharpened tool with a rag, he set the chisel down and turned to face the boat. "Well, now, let's see. I suppose we ought to get the trailer first." He smiled and wagged his head in the direction of the exit for Adrian to follow him.

They walked around to a two-car garage that was closed. Henry opened a pedestrian door off the corner wall, and they entered. Maggie's car was parked inside. The other stall contained all kinds of boat equipment, including a trailer. Henry looked a bit bashful when he turned to Adrian, "My SUV suffers a little bit sitting on the carport when it could be in here, but where else will I put all my boat locker items?"

"Oh, this is perfect!" Adrian assured him, "My garage would be full of toys, too, instead of a car. Trust me on this."

They moved boxes, ice chests and picnic baskets, oars, buckets, coiled lines, anchor chain, a small mushroom anchor for sandy bottoms, and an aluminum mast and boom off the trailer and soon it was available to roll out the door. "Are you going to keep the boat in here, Henry?"

"Boats have a way of finding their own berth. We shall see."

Together they wrangled the trailer around the house and put it in the position of centerline to the two carriage doors. Henry opened one of the big doors and they slipped inside the shop, closing the heavy door behind him. It was ten degrees cooler inside and Adrian pulled his sweaty t-shirt off his chest to release more heat.

"Let's find the bow and stern lines and attach them." He scanned the workbench, the tool wall and looked inside some buckets. "Where, oh, where did I place those lines...?" Adrian decided to stop watching and join the search. He took the opposite wall and scanned the supply of wood, the floor and center of the space. Then he looked at the back wall and met Henry in the middle. "Nothing?"

Adrian scanned everything then looked up and started to laugh. "Um, Henry?" He pointed up to the neatly stacked rows of coiled lines that were over their heads the entire time on a rafter in the ceiling. Laughing, Henry got a step ladder and climbed up to reach the two neatly coiled lines and passed them to Adrian.

"Both the same length?" he asked.

"Yes, either one will work."

Adrian set about clipping the lines, which were conveniently eye-spliced with a carabiner at one end to snap into the D-ring mounts at either end. He stored the remainder of the lines inside the boat. "What's next? Hoist it up?" He'd assessed the situation over the last two days. There was nothing in the boat, it was resting on custom chocks on sawhorses and the boat would need to go up a few inches, to pull those supports out, to slide a trailer in under it.

"Yes, but let's think this through because we will need to store those supports out of the way." He turned to look at the back wall and paused to stroke his beard while he thought about it. "OK. Here's what we are going to do.

"We'll raise it up and tie off the lines from the ceiling block and tackle. Then let's carry those pieces under the boat outside and stack them on the path to the guesthouse door out of the way. OK?"

"Roger that."

"Let's take the bow and hoist it first, remove the chocks and then do the stern."

They lifted the bow about eight inches and slid the supports out and readied the space under the bow. Next, they hoisted the stern and carefully lowered the big chock to the floor and slid it out of the way along the back wall. Next, they carried the saw-horse out and opened the second carriage door so they could roll the trailer under the boat while slipping the boat between two side-mounted stanchions covered in thick insulation that rolled along the post. Henry walked around the boat looking carefully at where the boat would touch the carpeted metal structure. He moved to release the stern and lower it to an inch above the chocks. He moved to lower the bow within an inch, too. Then he laughed and caught Adrian's eye, "I think I am being too careful. Release the stern, Adrian, it looks good."

With the stern lowered, he dropped the bow. "Let's get the straps and tie her down."

"Henry, why do they call a boat a her?"

"Oh, that is a very, very good question. Where do I begin?" He spread his feet shoulder's width apart and put his hands on his hips and looked down at the floor considering his answer. None was forthcoming.

"Seriously, Henry?" He laughed, "I'm not asking how they came up with a calendar or time. Isn't it a simple answer?"

"No. I'm not sure where to begin and what I am about to share may be one version of the truth, but it is related to admiralty law. And it is something very valuable to know." He looked up and began with a slow pace, "A ship is involved in commerce, or trade. The ship, like a good mother, carries goods and people across the sea until they land safely.

"The ship comes in and ties up at the dock where its goods are said to be manifested. What is a manifest? It is a document that represents all the goods in the belly of the ship with detailed descriptions.

"And who is in charge of the ship?" Henry paused to give Adrian a chance to answer.

"The captain."

"What is the captain in charge of?" Henry raised a silvery eyebrow, "Think of the word I'm asking about. It's similar to captain. Cap-"

"Oh. Maybe, capital?" he guessed. "Wait, money!"

"Yes, the captain delivers the proverbial baby with the doctor as she sits in her berth."

"Ohhh, I think I get it," he said with excitement, "So, the ship is a she because it is like a mother delivering the goods in a berth with a doctor who gives her a birth certificate! Am I right?"

"A manifesto, to be more accurate. Every item is worth money so the ship needs a manifesto itemizing every object." Henry's smile revealed his appreciation for the bright young man before him who understood words like the people from his generation. "OK, I'm going to give you some info, you tell me how it got to be in our language today. The Latin word for bank is bench. Who sits on a bench?"

"Um, ball players who aren't getting their time on the court."

"Yes, you're on to something. Courts are definitely a racket!" Henry laughed, "But who presides on a bench?"

"I'm not following you."

"Judges sit on a bench. Now, knowing that, what do judges preside over?" Henry paused and waited for him to figure it out. "Remember, the Latin word means bank."

"Oh. Maybe the judges rule the banks?" Adrian felt like he was guessing.

"Historically, yes. Now, where do you find banks in nature?"

"Well, there are sandbanks, and riverbanks. Is that what you mean?"

"Yes. Riverbanks control or direct the flow of the water or the currency." Henry walked to the wall and pulled off a bunch of wide webbing straps to tie down the boat to the trailer. "What else is called currency?"

"Money."

"Electricity, too, I suppose, or whatever is being used to trade or barter," he added. "Anything that carries anything of value, is carrying something worth money or currency. And on this planet we have the law of the land, which is about the culture of that land, and the law of the water or high seas is maritime or admiralty law. It is the law of money."

"Wait a second, Henry," he interrupted him, "You're saying that if I am in the middle of Arizona, surrounded by dry land, doing a transaction with money, I am under the law of the sea?"

"If you are banking, you are under maritime law. Yes." Henry bent down to place a metal s-hook into a hole in the trailer support frame and carefully tighten the strap. "But it gets better."

"Go on, I'm listening." Adrian reached across the boat and accepted the red strap Henry passed him. Henry walked around to repeat his action with the opposite s-hook.

"Where were you born?"

"At a hospital."

"Was it a birthing hospital where your mother was placed in a delivery room?"

"I have no idea. There was a doctor and a nurse with my mom."

"Did her water break before you were manifested into the world?" Henry raised both eyebrows in his direction as he walked to the stern to tug on the webbing on the port quarter. "Did you get a birth certificate?"

"Whoa. Henry." Adrian placed both hands on the starboard gunnel and leaned across. "You're blowing my mind here. You're saying I'm goods from a mothership? I'm confused."

"No, I'm saying that your body, according to maritime international law, is a maritime admiralty product and is worth money as an admiralty product of your mother, because she delivered you through her birth canal." Henry waited for him to digest this tidbit. "A doctor signed your birth certificate, correct?"

"I'm a product? According to some admiralty lawyer?" Adrian asked, a bit confused. "What does this mean?"

"Once upon a time, we humans were all free beings. The word is sovereign. I suspect those who wanted more control over humans figured out ways to use laws to make even more money. It's a bit esoteric," he paused, "Do you know what esoteric means?"

"Not really," he admitted honestly. Cranking the steel cable winch on the bow to make sure the boat was secure to the forward post and the hull up against the rollers on the post. The boat was not going to move. He locked the winch and, as an extra measure, tied the bow line to the post, putting a round turn on the padeye and two half-hitches. It was good and snug.

"It means it is not likely to be understood by many people. So, only those with a specialized knowledge or interest in an area such as admiralty law will know what's what."

"So...I now have esoteric knowledge of admiralty law?" Henry gave a solemn nod, and Adrian continued. "What do I do with this knowledge?"

Henry laughed, "I've been asking myself that for years!" He walked around the boat and tested the tautness of the straps holding the boat in place. "I suppose the next time someone asks you why a ship is called she, you can explain it to them."

"You know," Adrian began with a glimmer of mischief in his eyes as a grin started to spread across his lips, "The very first day I met our First Officer, Jimmy, he didn't have an answer for me. He said I'd find out soon enough." He chortled, "I'll bet you money that he doesn't know!"

"Not many know this, which is why it is..."

"Esoteric knowledge." Adrian grinned, finishing his sentence for him, "Thanks, Henry! It's a fun bit of trivia. Maybe one day I will find out how to capitalize on myself. Heh, heh, heh. You like that?"

Henry waggled his freckled index finger at Adrian with a smirk, "I like the way you think. Now then, we need to tie the oars to the boat and then we can roll!"

The boat was heavier than the one at the boatyard and while

Henry pulled, Adrian got behind the stern and pushed hard. They rolled it over to the garage where they lined it up with the towing hitch on the SUV. "I need to attach the brake light wires under the rear fender. Grab that set of cables, will you?"

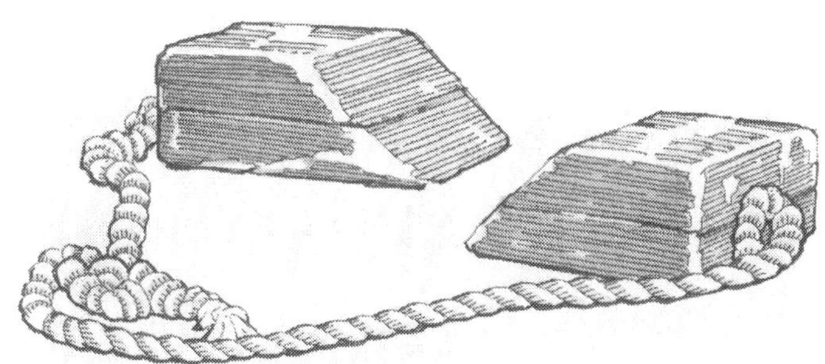

Together they tested the brake lights and made sure the pair of wooden tire chocks, for bracing the trailer wheels from rolling, were inside the boat. Henry had fashioned it himself and drilled a hole through the square part of the block and placed a line inside the hole to make a grab handle. "Let's check to make sure the trailer is level."

Standing some distance away, Henry pointed out the bow and stern needed to be level with both the road and the trailer hitch, or it could cause problems with the load. It looked fine to Henry, so they went back to the shop to clean up. Adrian used the workshop vacuum to clean the floor and Henry brought in the sawhorses and chocks, placing them near the wood supply racks.

"Wow, there is so much room in here." Adrian turned off the noisy shop-vac and stood back to consider the additional space. "What are you planning on building next?"

"That's a very good question, and I have no answer for you, yet. I am giving considerable thought to this dilemma at the moment," he began, "I want to build a small sailing vessel that one can row or sail. And Maggie would like me to make a replica of an antique table -but which project first? We shall see."

Maggie walked into the shop and clapped her hands, "Oh, wonderful! The boat is trailered, and you can make my table now!"

Adrian looked at Henry who smiled and said, "I guess I'll be making that table next."

"I hope you don't mind, Adrian, but I went ahead and made the cookies while you and Henry got the boat prepped. Would you like to go before or after dinner? And by the way," she added, "The parents are home right now, and we have an invite to go up anytime."

"Well, let's go now while there is still light."

"Sounds good to me, let's all freshen up and head out in ten minutes," she suggested. "I'll meet you out front with the cookies."

Fifteen minutes later, they were welcomed into the home of David and Jayden. They walked through the house and onto the back patio. A kidney shaped swimming pool sparkled in the late afternoon sun. "Wow, I didn't know you guys have a pool!"

"Well, you don't ask." Jayden laughed, "When you leavin'? You have time to come swim?"

"Probably not. My family is coming tomorrow. Then I leave the day after that."

"OK, so probably not this trip." David figured, "Next time you visit, you bring your shorts, and we'll have our own Jump Up." Jayden laughed and Adrian was confused. "It's local slang for a happenin' party."

The adults were talking amongst themselves and seemed to be having a good time. Adrian had agreed to keep the dog adoption process a secret until the parents agreed to give Jaxon a home. All four adults walked over to the boys where they were lounging around the pool talking.

The father asked his sons, "So I hear you like their dog Jaxon. Is this true?"

"Dad, I love dat dog. He's the best." David lit up and Jaxon barked. "He's a good dog."

"Jayden, what do you think?" his dad turned to his oldest.

"Ah, Dad, these two don' get no tighter."

"Well, Maggie and Henry have offered to give us Jaxon, and we are okay with that, but you have to take care of him. It's real responsibility. Can you do that?"

David jumped to his feet like a shot of lightning went through him. "Daddy!" He ran and threw his brown arms around his dad's middle and hugged him tight. Turning to bend down to hug Jaxon, he told the dog, "You gunna be part of our family, Jaxon. Did ya hear dat?" Jaxon barked and barked, wagging his tail until Adrian thought it would shake his hindlegs off. Looking up at his dad he shared, "Dad, you can trust me. I'll do everyt'ing for dis dog."

"Jayden? Do you back him up?"

"Sure Dad. Jaxon's cool. I'll help out."

"Is he ever quiet?"

Adrian quickly said, "Jaxon, quiet!" And he stopped barking.

"Good," the boy's dad said in a serious tone. "That's a good dog." He bent down to let the dog sniff his hand. "Welcome to the Joseph family. Your new name is Jaxon Joseph. Now, we have a second JJ in the family." Jaxon barked twice. "Quiet," the dad said in a stern voice. Jaxon went silent. "Excellent! Good dog!"

"Can we take him tonight?" David wanted to know.

"No," his father said. "We must get things squared away here first, get a dog bed, and a few other things. We don't have dog food either."

"Dad, he can sleep with me," David offered.

"No, he needs to learn to sleep in a bed. House rules." His dad turned to Adrian, "I heard you goin' rowing tomorrow in the new boat. That should be a sight on the water."

"I'm excited," Adrian shared back, "I have been learning to row and tomorrow is my last full day here." He turned to David and Jayden, "I guess I can bring Jaxon over here when I leave and say goodbye."

David heard something in Adrian's voice and quickly asked, "You going to be okay with Jaxon comin' here?"

"Of course, it was my idea!" He stated with conviction, "I couldn't think of a better home for Jaxon than with you guys."

"Thanks."

"I'm still going to miss him and think about him, but I'll be alright." *Fingers crossed.*

The Wrights and Adrian made their way down the hill an hour later with Jaxon leading the way. He was racing all over the road. Maggie laughed and commented on what a high-energy dog he is, and Adrian agreed. "He'll do well with David and Jayden, don't you think?"

"Oh, very much so. It was an excellent choice, you know." Maggie added. "We can help them when they travel by dog sitting, and we get to see him every week."

"It really is a happy ending," Henry said with a smile. "I'm just glad it all worked out for everyone's best interest. You got time with a dog which you wanted, we get relieved of having to take care of a dog with more energy than we can manage, yet we can keep in touch with the dog and the Joseph family gets a wonderful dog to love. And let's not forget Jaxon. He gets the best of everyone, so it really was a splendid solution, since no one was left out."

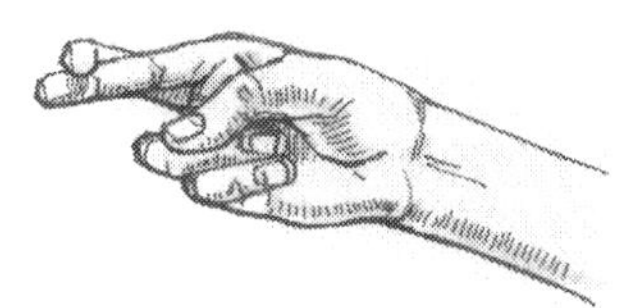

Chapter 10
Sea Trials

Laborie Bay

St. Lucia

Caribbean Sea

Adrian and the Wrights were up early to go rowing. Jaxon was super excited to be going out on the water. "I believe that is a good sign in a dog, don't you, Henry?"

"I would say so. Dogs do love water and have an instinct to swim."

"Adrian, I thought we would do a different adventure today and drive south to Laborie Bay via the east side of the island and make a full day of things, since you are leaving us tomorrow. We can launch *Dash* from the beach next to the pier. It's more than an hour's drive south of here and will give you another perspective on the island. Laborie is a real taste of the Caribbean. We could row west, then north and come back to meet Maggie at the pier for lunch."

Henry double checked the tire pressure on the trailer and the SUV and, satisfied with the rig, he slowly exited their driveway and began the journey across the island. They passed farms as they headed deep into the heart of the island, and the landscape began to change as the elevation increased. Villages were spread further apart and soon they were climbing and winding to the top of ridges and circling the rainforest where the mist had not yet cleared. Henry turned his windshield wipers on so they would clear his view every so often. Tight hairpin turns on steep mountain sides had Adrian twisting in his seat to look back at their trailer to make sure it was handling the roads. So far so good. As they descended altitude, the skies cleared, and they could go through a drier region of the island that was not as lush. Soon, he was getting glimpses of the Atlantic Ocean in the distance and felt excitement growing inside him.

Turning south, they drove with the ocean on their left and went from hillside to hillside all the way down the coast. For a brief while, they drove inland near forest reserves, and he lost sight of the ocean, as the greenery grew thicker. Before long, they were back on the coastal range, passing more cars and seeing the water from a mile away. Henry explained, "The Atlantic is rougher than the Caribbean side. The coast is very rugged in most places. It's not always friendly to swimmers, which is why the west side is favored."

"Just south of the airport is a fort that we don't have time for, but should you ever return to St. Lucia, and we hope you do, we can visit there." Maggie added.

As the houses and businesses got denser, so did the road traffic, and he could tell they were in a city area. They passed signs for the international airport, a university, and a major retailer from the States indicating that this was a highly populated area. He couldn't see any water just buildings and cars.

"We're heading west, aren't we?" Adrian asked from the backseat. "The mountain is on our right, and we went inland, I think."

"Correct," Henry answered, "We've crossed into Laborie and should be coming up on our turn soon. Maggie, darling, keep an eye out for the gas station and Waterfront Road."

He had barely spoken when Maggie said, "Don't miss it, that's it!"

Slowing down, Henry made a tight left turn from the left lane, which Adrian still wasn't used to traveling in. He wasn't sure he would ever get used to it. He kept his speed below ten kilometers per hour as he rattled down the road towards the sea.

"I see water!" Maggie exclaimed. "Do you want to pull into the petrol station and back down to the pier?"

"I think that is a rather good idea," he said as he turned the SUV and trailer around and slowly backed down to the sand. "Maggie and Adrian, why don't you hop out and help guide me?"

A small crowd of locals joined in, and Henry received directions from half a dozen individuals. Laughing, he got out of his vehicle and shook hands with the guys closest to him. "Adrian, you can help with the lock and chain on the trailer hitch. Maggie has Jaxon, so after you and our new friend Eddy here can pull the pin. I'll pull the car forward. Then we'll walk it down to the water."

With many hands helping, the boat was launched. Adrian held the bow line so it wouldn't float off. He did as Henry directed and looked carefully at the boat to make sure there were no leaks. Finding none, he felt reassured that the boatbuilder knew what he was doing.

Maggie allowed Jaxon to leap into the boat and she offered to hold the bow line so he could get life jackets, water, and snacks from Henry. Eddy was helping Henry get the trailer reattached. Adrian walked to the back of the vehicle and took out personal floatation devices better known by its acronym PFDs, a bailing bucket, plastic water bowl for Jaxon and returned to the boat while Henry got permission to park alongside the gas station.

He tucked everything except the belt-style PFDs under the stern bench seat and put the bowl with some water in it for Jaxon behind Henry's seat. He snapped his PFD around his waist, spun it to the back and let his t-shirt fall over it. These were comfortable to wear and out of the way while rowing. Looking out to sea it was calm and glassy. The typical high clouds were piled on the horizon south of the island and a soft shade of cream.

"Maggie, what are you going to do while we're gone?" Adrian asked her with a trace of concern.

"Oh, I'm going to walk the beach for a bit then read a good book over a cup of coffee."

"Glad to hear it." He spotted Henry ambling across the sand. He watched him pass his car keys to his wife and give her a light kiss on the cheek. "Take care of these for me, please. We'll see you later, my darling."

"All aboard!" Adrian called with a smile. "Bye, Maggie! See you later!" He handed Henry his PFD, which he promptly clipped on and moved to his backside.

She waved to them as they pushed off and began rowing. "We'll go parallel to the shore until we get a feel for *Dash*, then we can move out further in the bay."

Dash handled like a dream. Henry was tickled at her balance, speed, and size. "Wood has a different feel to it, Adrian. I can't truly explain it, but it floats differently than fiberglass. It even sounds different."

"I'll take your word for it, Henry. I'm not an expert. One thing I do like is the whole idea that we were first to use it and test it out."

"Take a look and see if there is water coming in anywhere. With all three of us in the boat, we're lower in the water than when you inspected it."

Neither found nor saw anything. "Your oars feel good? I'll stop rowing so I can listen to your tholepins." After half a dozen strokes, he said, "OK, my turn." Adrian turned slightly to look over each shoulder to look at Henry's oars and listen to his set.

"Sounds and looks good to me, don't you think?" He asked Henry.

"I'd have to agree." He began to line up the boat with the end of the pier. "Let's see how well she goes in a straight line. Ready to pull together? ... Pull!"

They rowed across the bay for a dozen strokes before Henry declared *Dash* nice and true. "OK, let's go out to sea a bit and see how she handles the swells."

They rowed well past the point of land and Adrian noticed the sea changing colors. Twisting around, he advised Henry about the reef they were headed for.

"Yep, time to turn and head north." The water had become more of a pale aqua color as they made their way around the first point of land. "How are your hands? Feeling okay?"

"So far so good!" For the next hour, they rowed north past two more points of land when Henry suggested they take a break. "I believe we could just go on forever and row the entire island, but it is good to pace yourself when you are just beginning."

They rested for a while and the boat drifted with the swells and current that ran along the island's western shore. The sun felt hotter, and Adrian felt a trickle of sweat run down his shoulder blades. The sound of a motorboat came into their awareness and Adrian twisted to see where it was coming from. He spotted it in the northwest aiming right for them. "Henry, they're aiming right at us. Should we be worried?" He positioned his oars to ready himself to move quickly if the boat didn't stop.

Henry turned to look and said, "There's plenty of sea room. And I think I hear them slowing down." True enough, the boat slowed down and the tender to the *Arabella* came into sight with none other than the captain in the stern and Jimmy at the helm. Adrian's mouth fell open at the sight. "What the heck?!"

Jimmy throttled back and floated the tender a whole boat length from the rowboat while the captain put fenders over the side. It was a clear indication that they were to tie up together. Adrian hustled to get his oars on board. Henry tucked his oars alongside Adrian's then reached behind him for the bow line to pass to the captain.

"Gunnar! So good to see you, son."

Son? Did I hear that correctly?

"Hi, Captain!" Adrian greeted him with bright energy although he was quite shocked. He toned it down a bit when he addressed the first officer, "Hey, Jimmy, fancy meeting you out here! Hahaha!"

"Hey yourself, how was de row?" Jimmy stood poised at the helm, ready to protect the boats. The captain stood ready to receive the stern line from Adrian. No sooner did he catch it than he was tying it off on a cleat.

"Come on aboard," the captain invited. Henry began to climb out of the rowboat and into the tender. Adrian followed him by climbing into the position that he had just vacated to keep the boat steady. He stood up in the rowboat and held onto the tender's gunwale for balance without leaving the rowboat.

Adrian was the first to speak. "Where did you guys come from? Was this random?"

Henry spoke up and confessed, "Adrian, I'm afraid I am responsible for this unusual meet-up. I thought it would be a nice surprise to bump into them on the water since it has been almost a week. I also wanted to give Gunnar a chance to try out the new rowboat. Try before you buy is only fair."

Adrian turned to the captain and with incredulity in his voice he asked, "You're buying the rowboat?"

The captain smiled, "Let's just say I might be an agent." Changing the subject, he asked, "How have you been, Adrian? We all missed you!"

"Is that really true?" He looked past the captain to Jimmy with a touch of suspicion. "I'm pretty sure everyone needed a break from me."

"Oh, mon, you have no idea how sad we've all been. We almost made the chef walk de plank. He made such a mess of his food this week because he and you got on de outs wid each other. The crew can't take it no more. You have to come back." His white smile stretched across his dark face and Adrian couldn't quite suppress the smile that wanted to break free, so he pinched his lips together as hard as he could, but his eyes gave him away.

"Zak making bad food? I doubt it!" Adrian smiled, "So it's business as usual?"

Gunnar looked at Henry, "How are you Henry? How was your week? Are you ready for a vacation?" He winked at Adrian to imply no offense.

Jimmy passed Henry a cold sparkling water which he took and nodded his thanks. "I had such a marvelous week with young Adrian! In fact, it's one I won't forget for as long as I live."

Adrian was not really surprised to hear this from Henry. He knew he had a great time with Henry and he thought he was great to hang with. He knew that they were compatible together. All along, he felt that Henry had understood him, which was one of the reasons he felt comfortable leaving the yacht and going ashore with the Wrights.

"Thanks, Henry. I agree. One for the record books."

"Indeed! We get along like two peas in a pod." Henry elaborated on how they spent their days while Jimmy and the captain nodded.

"Sounds awesome!" the captain said. "Well, Adrian, how about you sit down, and we take it for a spin? I've been looking forward to this all week!"

"Okay. Where do you want to sit?" Adrian asked the captain.

"Well, I should probably take the stern because I am much heavier than you or Henry. We'll have better displacement."

The captain climbed in and stayed in the center of the boat while Adrian began to position himself to climb into the area just forward of the middle. As he was about to take his seat, the captain took the bench facing the stern. Jimmy and Henry untied and threw the lines back inside the rowboat. Jimmy's barefoot gave them a good push off the tender for good measure. The rowers inserted their tholepins, placed their oars, and began rowing.

They both rowed in silence for a little while. Adrian was not going to be the first to speak.

After they were far enough away from the speed boat, the captain broke into conversation, "I knew you would have a good time with Henry and Maggie."

Adrian still didn't feel like talking. After another few pulls on the oars, the captain complimented him on the boat's name. "Great choice of name, by the way. Henry had asked me for some suggestions, and I gave him a whole page of names in the mail, but clearly nothing landed for him.

"And we all loved the name Jaxon with an x," he added, hoping to warm up Adrian a bit more. Adrian still said nothing, he just pulled on his oars. "Adrian..."

"Excuse me, Captain, but what is the story between you, Henry, and Maggie?" he burst out his question. "He called you *son* when we got on the boat. But he isn't your father, is he?"

"No, he's not my biological father, but he did take me in as a teenager and raised me until I could go off to naval college and to sea." The captain's voice was friendly and open.

"That's it?" he was stuck in the middle of knowing and not knowing.

"What else could there be?" the captain asked, sounding unsure of where the conversation was going.

"When did you first meet? How old were you?"

There was a long pause from the captain. "Where are you going with this, Adrian? I'm confused. Are you fact checking?"

"Uh, never mind." Adrian wished he had never asked.

"No, when you say never mind, that's abandoning ship when you haven't given the ship a chance." The Captain said his words in a neutral voice, then invited, "What would you like to learn about me? Clearly, you learned something, but you want more detail, or you wouldn't have asked. Could that be true?"

"Yes. I just wanted to know your side of the story."

"OK, so I was your age when I met the Wrights in England. My mom worked for Maggie's family farm where they bred and trained dogs. My dad was *persona non grata*, meaning unwelcome by my mom or her grandmother. I only met him a few times, but he lived his life at sea and rarely ever came home. Unfortunately, my mom died in a car accident shortly after we got to England and I..." he paused as he chose his words with care, "I got lost for a while because I believed I lost everything at that point. It wasn't true, but it sure felt like that. So, I believed my feelings were the truth of me, my life and my opportunities. I fell apart and gave up caring because I thought there was no one left to care for me.

"The Wrights never gave up on me, even though I gave up on myself."

"I can see them being that way," Adrian commented thoughtfully.

"Henry was in constant contact with any authority who would listen to him even though he was in America at the time. I lived on the streets, and I turned into a petty thief to get money to buy fish and chips, and I broke into buildings to have a place to sleep when it rained or was cold. I got caught and they put me in a detention center for juvenile delinquents.

"The worst thing in the world, Adrian, is a child believing he is a bad person. Any idea why?"

"I suppose if you think you're bad, you'll go do bad things."

"Right. It's buying into the idea that you are bad, so you set out to prove you are bad and then you get proof that you're bad, but the irony is...you can prove anything to yourself. You could prove you're good." He shook his head and said, "You know, I was acting badly, spoke like a gutter rat, had abandoned my manners–and keep in mind my mother went to a fancy boarding school and taught me how to be with powerful and rich people by the time I was your age–so for me to hit bottom like that? I turned into a real jerk believing I was a victim of life circumstances."

"I can't even imagine not having my mom or dad. That must have been really hard to go through." Adrian offered with compassion, then added, "I'm sorry if I sounded rude when I asked you for your side of the story."

"It's ok. The most important thing to remember when you want to hear someone's side of a story is to let the person know you heard one perspective and you'd like to hear the other person's. Make sense?"

"Yes, thank you." Adrian said. *OK, here goes nothing...* He cringed a little and then said, "I may, uh, I may have discovered a family secret in the lighthouse, and I don't know whether or not I should tell you."

"Really?" the captain asked with some surprise. "You found something I haven't found already?" And he laughed out loud. "What did you find?"

"Some legal documents in envelopes in the desk." He kept his eyes closed when he said it, wishing it would go away and not be the truth. "And a letter you wrote to the Wrights..."

"Really?" the captain sounded uncertain. "What were they? And whereabouts did you find them?"

"Well, let me start at the beginning so you have my side of the story in case this gets me in trouble with anyone." Adrian could swear the captain was shaking with laughter, but he didn't hear a sound. It was hard to tell because he was rowing.

He walked him through how he was attracted to all the pigeon-holes, drawers, and doors and when he slid out the tray and looked in, there they were.

"Ah! Curiosity got the cat!" the captain was laughing.

"And I do this thing, at least when I remember to, when solving problems, where I step into someone else's shoes and ask what they would do?" Then he added, "And I chose Henry and suddenly I knew how to solve the puzzle and out slid the framework, and I was able to access the documents."

"And what were they?" the captain asked with great curiosity.

"Uh, here's where it gets weird," Adrian tried to buy time and he wished his mom were here with him. "I found your adoption certificate and graduation announcement from naval college."

The captain threw his head back and laughed out loud. "Seriously? You found adoption paperwork for me? For real?"

"You're not mad?" he asked, a bit bewildered at the captain's response.

"Oh, Lord, no! That's the funniest thing," he added. "Now, I'm really looking forward to having a conversation with Henry when we get back."

"How so?" He felt nervous energy hit his stomach and worried about the impact this might have on his relationship with Henry, if the captain brought this adoption-reveal to his attention.

"Remember, I was angry at the world, thought the world was against me, I was a bad person, blah blah blah victim talk. Henry said to me one day that he and Maggie would like to adopt me and asked me if that was okay with me.

"Well, I said no. Then proceeded to read him and Maggie the riot act, saying that they would live to regret it. I told them they wouldn't want their good name associated with me in a million years, and if he did adopt me, I would be nothing but trouble and I'd run away to protect them if they didn't want to protect themselves. I warned him not to, and that he didn't have my mother or father's permission to be my legal guardian. I was so full of myself." He chuckled at the memory, "I wizened up and later went back and apologized for all that.

"So, what you're telling me is that they went ahead and legally adopted me anyways and let me think I was in charge of myself, and they still considered me their son? That sounds like something Henry would do!"

"So, you never knew?" Adrian asked, a bit flabbergasted. "That was decades ago. They kept it a secret all these years?"

"Obviously." They continued to row together in a southern direction, parallel to but away from the land. Adrian looked over his shoulder at the tender, which was far away. He knew Jimmy would keep an eye on him and the captain.

"Captain, how did you turn your life around? From what I've seen in my city, most people don't you know."

"Henry had a lot to do with helping me. It's like he did a mind transfer or something." The captain asked him, "You must have experienced it. That's one of the reasons why I wanted you to spend a week here with them. The guy is special. I couldn't have made the leap that I did if he weren't the genius that he is."

"Well, he was a coach, right?" Adrian offered by way of understanding. "He worked with young people and got them in sync on a boat."

"He coached, yes, but did you know he has degrees in history and admiralty law, is an author, boatbuilder extraordinaire and even did some journalism?"

"What? He never mentioned any of those things and aside from the boatbuilding, there's no clues anywhere that he did any of those things." Adrian was in shock. "How," he demanded, "Did he write a book when he can't use a computer?"

"He told you that he can't use a computer?" The captain laughed and shook his head. "Did he use that Luddite label on himself?"

"Yes," he felt like someone had pulled the wool over his eyes but in a good way. "So, he can use a computer?"

"Yes, Bryce and he spent hours on computers together." The captain stopped rowing and drew his oars in and carefully turned to take the stern seat and face Adrian. The boat bobbed up then settled down with the captain's weight in the stern.

"Adrian, look." He held his hands wide as if he were grasping with a concept he wanted to pass onto the young man in front of him. "Henry is super humble, kind, thoughtful, intelligent and takes people's perspectives, which is why people enjoy being with and around him. He's everything I want to be as a leader.

"Before I accepted the contract to work on board the *Arabella*, I had many phone calls with your parents to learn about you and your entire family, your wants, needs, desires and so much more. Your parents wanted to offer you and Grace an opportunity to cultivate your inner leadership. They asked for my help. I was referred to them by a crew agency by what may seem like chance, but there is no such thing when you realize you create every experience in your life. Know what I mean?"

"I'm starting to. For example, I realized that I can choose how I feel and whether or not I want to judge the experience. If I judge it as bad, I create a feeling of bad inside me," he shared. "What

I didn't know until this trip was how to release the bad feeling."

"Exactly," he agreed. "How did you accomplish that on this trip?"

Adrian rested his arms on his oars which he had pulled into the boat up to the collar. "My mom wrote out a process to let go of make wrong. That's what she calls it. I was told by Chef that I did a make wrong, and I didn't know that I went into agreement with him, so I added to it and made myself wrong. I know from past experience that I tend to rush and interrupt or distract people when I get a bright idea and need to get help bringing it to life. I had to let go of my self-judgments, then my blaming, and all kinds of stuff.

"I also remembered to identify my emotions and breathe it all out of my body. That helped me a ton!"

"Excellent. That's energy mastery. I lacked that as a kid. My mom had to work, my dad was missing in action, and I suspect was forbidden from coming around. My great grandmother passed away and we were without support on so many levels. We didn't know how to support ourselves inside," he tapped his forehead, "Or outside," he pointed to Adrian and himself. "I didn't have any knowledge of making relationships work, but Henry did. He didn't teach me, he showed me."

"I know. I've been watching and listening to him with everyone. But..." he paused to gather his thoughts and words, "I can't put my finger on it. It's more than tone of voice or body language. It's like he's speaking inside my head...and my fears melt away, and I get to be me without my anxiety."

"Yes," the captain agreed, "He has a knack of getting people to just be peaceful or happy. He has no judgment on anyone, that I can tell." Adrian bobbed his head in agreement and contemplated the floor space between them.

"Your parents asked me to support your learning at sea, but

especially with being a leader, because they see this in you and your sister. I run a more relaxed ship than most captains and your folks and I decided to be different. For instance, Jimmy would never in a million years be a steward to you because his rank, skills, knowledge, and abilities are to do my job. He already has his captain's license. He could get a job today as a yacht captain. But I talked with him, and he agreed to be part of this unusual arrangement since nothing we are doing is standard to the industry. Not even this conversation!"

Adrian looked up and smiled, "Really? Captains don't go rowing with the owner's son and have man-to-man convo with them?" They both laughed at that. "Seriously, my mom is so unusual, I can't think anything about our family's arrangements are normal or typical. So, um, are you my mentor or something?"

"No, yes, maybe." He gave a half smile, "Please be aware that normal passengers do not have access to the crew spaces except by appointment and with a crewmember present. I and the crew all agreed that you could have full access to all positions onboard to learn from them, if you were able to do so respectfully."

"Ah. And then Chef thought I wasn't being respectful," he filled in. "Did Pete complain, too?"

"Pete? No." The captain looked a bit confused. "Did something happen there, too?"

"No, it was just that I interrupted him the same day as Chef, and...I just assumed he felt the same and maybe said something." He managed to look a bit embarrassed. He needed to let go of making assumptions about people. His mom had been on him for years about this very topic.

"I invited Chef to speak with you privately because his work is affected by interruptions, and not just you. Otherwise, I haven't heard a word from anyone else." The captain looked him in the eye. "Is there anyone you have complaints about? This would be a good time to air them."

"No, not really. I just thought I was getting along really well with everyone and then it felt like Chef was telling me I wasn't playing nice, and Jimmy didn't play nice with the sailboats, and Pete looked a bit exasperated with me...so, yeah, I made up stories in my head about most of it and chose to feel bad."

"Pete's been working on something special for you and Grace. I won't spoil the surprise. And I will say this," the captain made sure Adrian was looking him straight in the eye before he spoke, "My crew and I all respect you. We know you're a good lad and look for ways to give you an opportunity to grow in all the best ways we know how. And we all agree on one thing."

"What's that?" Inside himself, Adrian was feeling emotional at the tangible relief flooding through his body. His throat was tight with emotion, and he blinked his eyes a few times to move out the feeling of wanting to cry from relief of being respected by the crew. *It sounds so silly even to me, but I am so glad to hear everyone's ok with me and I'm not a problem like I thought.*

"Everyone commented on how empty the boat felt this week while you were gone. It just wasn't the same. We all felt it and we're looking forward to having you come home."

Adrian gave a slight smile and hung his head so the captain wouldn't see his emotions. *Home. I just want to go home to the Arabella.* He nodded agreement. Choking out the words, he said, "I'm looking forward to coming home, too." Then he pushed his oars out, signaling that he was done talking. The captain took in his demeanor and repositioned himself with care on the bench and resumed rowing.

"Do we want to row or get a tow? What are your thoughts," the captain asked? "You've already put in about two or three miles today."

"A tow would be nice, but it's not necessary," he said, grateful for the change of subject.

The captain pulled something out of his pocket and said, "Cover your ears." Then he blew a whistle.

"Seriously? You have a whistle in your pocket?" Adrian's voice held disbelief and a touch of humor.

"Well, it occurred to me that it might be a good thing to bring, since I didn't know if you were going to be upset at any point in the conversation and jump overboard and swim to shore hoping to never be seen again."

"What?! I wouldn't do that!" he said with a defensive tone. *How does he know that's my go-to thought?*

"You sure about that?" the captain asked with a hint of laughter in his voice. "I'm pretty sure I saw that in your body language on the CCTV when Chef talked to you on the stern last week. You had me worried for a while."

"You saw me that day?" he asked in disbelief. If it had been anyone other than the captain admitting that he watched the discussion, he would have felt angered. It was a private moment, and he didn't know if he even wanted his mom to know.

"Yes. And I know the feeling well. It's why I left Maggie's family and ran away hoping to never be seen again."

"Yeah, I wanted to dive overboard, and swim ashore and never be seen again." He laughed at himself, "Pretty dramatic, huh?"

"Yeah, you looked pretty sus that day." Adrian gave a friendly punch to the captain's right shoulder and the captain laughed. "Keep it up and I'll go mano y mano with you and you won't like it. You might end up swimming back to shore."

"I hate to admit it, but I believe you!" Adrian felt so restored inside he started rowing back to shore.

"Hey, I thought you wanted a tow?"

"Oh. I guess that's okay, too. Where are they? And where's the *Arabella*?"

The captain squinted in the afternoon sun to see where the tender had gotten to. "Looks like we may need to row ourselves to them or the pier, Adrian. I don't think they can hear us very well. Take your pick."

"Let's row to the pier. And let's row fast, like we're racing," he suggested with enthusiasm.

"You're on!"

They were a hundred yards or so from the west end of the pier when the tender came flying towards them. Jimmy waved and slowed down, the fenders were still over the portside. He took some photos of the captain and Adrian rowing to the beach. He came full circle and tied up next to the pier with Henry's help while Maggie walked down the sand towards them.

Henry lifted Jaxon out of the tender and placed him on the pier, then climbed out. Jaxon ran to the sand and relieved himself, then made a run for Maggie, followed by a romp in the water to get to Adrian. The captain and Adrian were hauling the boat up onto the damp sand so it wouldn't drift off. The stainless-steel keel plate that ran the full length of the boat impressed the captain. He turned to Henry and said, "Nice job on the boat, Henry. Love the keel plate."

"Yes, yes, that was a necessary item to protect the bottom from hitting a rock or coral. And the sand isn't very good for it either, so I was happy when the local milling place was able to fashion it for me from careful drawings." Henry ran a hand on the stern. "Oh, Adrian, the gold leaf is just the right touch for this boat. It brings out the name."

"I agree," Maggie chimed in.

"Ruff, ruff," added Jaxon.

"Well, then, shall we get the trailer down here? Or are you going to tow it back?"

Adrian listened to this exchange between the captain and Henry with some confusion.

Jimmy said, "We can tow it back right now, Mr. Henry, we have a bridle and a tow line. We'll go slow."

"Wait a second," Adrian interrupted the men, *"Dash* is going back to the yacht with you guys?" he asked with a total lack of understanding. "Why?"

"The boat was commissioned by your parents for you, Adrian, and the boat." The captain smiled. "Quite a surprise, right?"

"There's nowhere to put it." He asserted with the knowledge that the garage, as they called it, was full of jet skis, a limousine tender and a space for this v-hulled water jet tender tied to the dock just feet away.

"Dat would normally be true," Jimmy said with an impressed look on his face, "But your parents made an executive decision to send the limousine tender back to Ft. Lauderdale on a boat transporter because we don't use it right now and this made more sense for the family."

A flash of wonder entered Adrian's eyes as he realized *Dash* was going to be part of his family's water toy collection. "No. Way."

"Way, mon!" Jimmy said and put his knuckles forward to meet Adrian's in recognition of this moment.

"Henry, this is incredible!" He ran and threw his arms around Henry and hugged him for a long time. "You're just full of secrets!"

"You have no idea," Maggie shared with a laugh. "I'm so glad you love it. We know you will take good care of it, too."

"Yeah, Henry, you're just full of secrets." The captain smiled in his direction. "Maybe tonight over dinner you can unburden yourself of some of them." He threw a special wink in Adrian's direction and turned to Maggie. "What time shall we be at your place? I know the family are itching to see the lighthouse."

"Oh, any time after 5PM is perfectly fine." Maggie looked at her watch and gasped, "Gentlemen, we had best get a move on! It's going on to one o'clock."

"Henry, we've got it from here," the captain stated and gave him a big hug, "Or should I call you dad from now on?" He laughed as he left Henry in a little state of confusion. Henry waved good-bye and called Jaxon to him. Together they all walked to the gas station where the SUV and trailer were parked.

"Well, I must say, that was a lovely morning for a maiden voyage. Would you agree, Adrian?" Henry asked him as he closed his car door and put his seat belt on.

"Oh, I loved it!" he enthused. "How about you, Maggie? Did you enjoy your time here at the beach?"

"I did. Thank you for asking. By the way, I've got most of the dinner plans in my head, but would you be interested in helping me in the kitchen later, Adrian? I heard you love to cook."

"Sure!"

"Everyone have their seatbelt on?" Henry glanced over at his wife and back at Adrian. "OK, let's go north up the west side. We should be home in ninety minutes or so." He started the engine and inched the vehicle out into the street. "I meant to ask you, how are your hands, Adrian? Did they do okay? That was a lot of rowing."

He glanced down at his hands and noticed there were small calluses forming. "They're good, Henry. I think because I lift weights in our gym and do pull-ups on a bar, I already had some calluses formed. I have a feeling that if I hadn't been doing all that, my hands would be raw right now."

"I'm sure they would be. Good," Henry affirmed, "I'm glad your hands did well. You turned out to be an excellent rower. You might want to consider joining a rowing team when you return to regular school or join a club at university."

"I'd love that, and I'll let you know what I end up doing." Adrian felt a small pang of separation that he would be leaving tomorrow. The Wrights were like family now. "Maggie, I have your email address so I will keep in touch."

"We'd love that, Adrian. Thank you."

They fell into a comfortable silence as they wound their way up the coast. Adrian woke up with a start when Maggie touched his knee with her hand, which was icy cold from being in front of the air conditioner. "Wake up, Adrian, we're home."

The Abercrombies arrived just after five o'clock and Adrian led them on a tour of the woodshop and lighthouse. His mom suggested that they build one someday, as it was such a unique idea which he loved. The captain joined Adrian as his parents and sister were leaving, and pulling him aside said, "Show me where you found the papers."

Adrian began by rolling up the lid on the captain's desk and pulling out the trays, then the wooden grid that held the drawers. "Oh, wow. I never knew that came out." The captain reached in and pulled out the envelopes and gave a brief laugh when he saw his graduation announcement. Then became solemn while reading the letter and certificate. He sat down and took in every word and signature.

Adrian asked him, "Should I put the desk back together? Are you going to keep those out?"

"Thanks, Adrian, yes, please." The captain smiled, "I got what I wanted. I'm not sure if that is what Henry wanted, but we're going to find out!"

Oh, boy. This could be a conflict. He put the desk back together and pushed the leather chair in to create room for walking down the stairs. "I hope this isn't a problem for Henry."

"I know Henry well enough now that I don't believe it will be a problem for this to come to light after all these years." His confidence was enough for Adrian, who let out the breath he was holding from fear.

"OK, let's go downstairs," Adrian invited and indicated the captain should go first.

The captain strode across the lawn with the envelopes tucked under his arm. He marched right up alongside Henry's chair and said, "Excuse me. Mr. and Mrs. A, there's no problem, but I wish to speak with Henry for a moment." He turned to Henry, "May we please go somewhere private to talk?"

"Sure," he stood up and indicated that they ought to walk to the edge of the property around the corner of the house. The captain put an arm across Henry's shoulders as he walked with him and kept his voice low so that no one would be able to overhear the conversation. All eyes were eager to see the pair return around the corner from which they walked. No one spoke while they strained their ears for the men's voices.

"What do you think is going on, Adrian?" Grace asked with deep curiosity. "You know anything about what they're talking about?"

"Uh, yeah, but don't think I can tell you." He paused then

added, "I'm cautiously optimistic that we may all know in a few minutes."

"That's some mystery," Adrian's father commented. "Are you a part of it?"

"Indirectly. Mom might know something about it," he added.

"What? I don't know what's going on!" She knit her brows as she searched her memory. "Does this have anything to do with that email you sent me about secrets?"

"Yep!" he confirmed, "Everything. And by the way, I may not have handled things as well as I could have, but there are no secrets between me and the captain at this point. But there might be between me and Henry. I have to clear those."

"What's going on here? Where's Henry and Gunnar?" Maggie asked from the sliding glass door to the house.

"Oh," Adrian said with a knowing look, "I think they are having a long overdue father-son talk, so to speak." When she looked at him funny, he gave her an exaggerated wink.

"Father-son talk...?" she repeated, looking lost for words.

"Maybe you should join them, Maggie. I think you ought to be a part of the conversation," he urged.

They heard Maggie gasp from the area that Adrian had directed her to.

"Can we please go look?" Grace asked her parents.

"No!" said Adrian, mom, and dad in unison.

Pouting, Grace heatedly said, "You don't even know what you are saying no to!"

"I do, and mom and dad know enough to know that this is a private family matter...for now." Adrian said, "Look, Grace, I'll tell you more when I get a green light. For now, hold your horses."

"How was your time here, Adrian? Enjoy yourself?" his dad asked. "I missed you at breakfast. Chef stopped making chocolate croissants this week and we're now eating apple turnovers, which are my favorites."

"Seriously? I forgot about apple turnovers!" His eyes got big with the idea of sinking his teeth into the warm flakey buttery crust filled with spiced apples. "Wow, what else did I miss?"

"Well, Dad and I did a lot of diving on the reef this week and it was incredible! I'm logging hours of diving and keeping notes of everything I see. We got an amazing underwater camera that takes high resolution pictures, and I am photographing everything so I can research it later."

"Cool, Grace! I can't wait to see what you've got." He turned to his mom, "What did you do all week?"

"I spent quite a bit of time on the computer this week doing research, writing, reviewing proposals and grants for projects. It got so bad that your father and sister had to come and pull me away to get me to go for a dive, which I did. It was really beautiful. The reef here is protected, and it is rich with sea life and healthy corals."

"Dad? What about...Oh, never mind, they're coming back!" He stopped talking and all four Abercrombies turned their heads to see Gunnar walking back towards the patio with his arms around the shoulders of Henry and Maggie, who were beaming.

"Wow! This looks positive!" Adrian's mom shared, "What's the good news?"

"The good news is..." Henry paused to look up at Gunnar, "do you want to tell them or shall I?"

Gunnar looked at Adrian, "Maybe Adrian would like to tell the story?" He looked at Maggie and Henry for approval. They nodded and lifted a hand by way of invitation.

All eyes turned to Adrian, who was rooted to the spot shaking his head no, so Grace said in a very impatient, demanding voice, "Out with it! The suspense is killing me!"

Gunnar started with, "Adrian brought to light something that has been a secret in our family for decades. Yes, family. You see, I just found out through Adrian that Henry and Maggie had adopted me but never said anything because I was such a jerk back then."

"Oh, you weren't so bad," Henry said with a slight chuckle, "A little bruised around the edges, but otherwise a good apple. Anyone with half a heart could see that."

"But you had a whole heart, Henry, and you listened to your heart and filed for adoption because you knew it was the right thing to do. Only, he never told me because the last really big argument I gave him was that I didn't want it.

"But that wasn't true. I loved this family and wanted to be a part of it. I just didn't think I was good enough. Henry and Maggie, and their daughter Alice proved me wrong. They've all been my best friends since I met them."

There was silence from everyone. No one knew what to say at first, then Grace spoke up, "Why did you keep it a secret all these years, Henry? And I'm guessing that it was Adrian that discovered the secret?"

"Yes, it was Adrian," Gunnar confirmed. "Henry?"

"I didn't want to make a big deal out of the adoption because no one needs a piece of paper to inform them that they belong to a family. It was that simple. So, I placed the envelopes there in the desk for safe keeping, and mostly forgot about them." He looked at Adrian, "You've nothing to fear, Adrian. I'm not mad or anything. I'm glad all this came to light. There's been some healing today."

He let out the breath he was holding, and his mom reached over to squeeze his arm in a reassuring way. He looked at the captain and smirked, "So, how does it feel?"

"Oddly enough, I gotta say something lifted in me when you first told me. I do consider Henry the best father figure in my life. I'm grateful he and Maggie had faith and trust in me. I couldn't have asked for a better family to be a part of." He suddenly snapped his fingers and turned to Henry, "Hey! Does Alice know?"

"Alice?" Grace asked.

"Our daughter, and yes, she had a say in it, too. We all wanted you to be officially included as a Wright but without any pressure. Keep in mind that as I became your legal guardian through the foster care system, that piece of paper allowed me, by law, to be your steward for your teen years."

"Gunnar was determined to be his own person," Maggie laughed as she recalled the teenage version of him. "No one could tell him what to do. We learned early on to give him multiple choices that were all good choices, so he couldn't lose no matter what he chose. Henry would guide him to think about things while working on the lighthouse." She giggled and looked with love towards Henry, "That lighthouse was either going to make or break him. Henry bet on it, that it would give Gunnar something to focus on with his mind and hands, daily accomplishments, and it worked. He thought he was paying off some debt to be here with us, which wasn't true, but Henry was helping him learn his value in the world."

Gunnar laughed, "I didn't want to be a burden to anyone. I was so afraid of being controlled, owing someone, you know, all the fears of someone who is at odds with the world when they think they are a victim. Henry...?"

"Yes, Gunnar?" he asked with a loving light in his eyes.

"It gives me great pleasure to know by adoption you are my father...and Maggie, you are my mother. I'm sure my mom is looking down on us and smiling right now!"

"We couldn't have asked for a nicer son to raise," Maggie added with love radiating from her face, too.

"Here! Here!" All the Abercrombies raised their sparkling water drinks and toasted Henry, Maggie, and the captain. "To family!" Adrian's dad toasted. "And love!" Adrian's mom added. "And happy endings!" Grace cheered. "And lighthouses!" Adrian declared and they all laughed.

After dinner, the entire group walked up the street to the Joseph family house. David opened the door to the crowd outside and his brother Jayden yelled to his mom and dad that the Wrights and Abercrombie families had arrived. Jaxon kept barking his head off at the excitement of having all the people present. David pulled Adrian out to the driveway, and they played with Jaxon for a bit with Grace looking on.

"Will you send me pics of Jaxon from time to time?" Adrian asked his new friend while snuggling Jaxon for what might be the last time.

"Yeah, mon, will do." The boys pulled out their phones and traded numbers and emails.

"Take pics of Henry and Maggie for me, will you?"

"Sure, mon. No problem." David said. "Take one right now." Adrian posed with Jaxon and he sent it to Adrian's phone.

"Hey, Jaxon, you be a good boy, okay? You be good for David and Jayden, but especially for their dad. You got that?" He said in a serious tone, "We don't want any problems. You be your best!"

Jaxon stood on his hind legs and licked Adrian's ear with ferocity. "Jaxon, com' on dog, that's a bit much!" Adrian stood up and laughed. He put out his knuckles for David to touch as a sign of gratitude and goodbye. "I'm going to go back to the lighthouse. I don't really want to stay if that's OK. See ya, David. I'll be in touch."

"Gotcha. We're good. Thanks, Adrian. I'll keep you posted," David promised, and took the leash from Adrian.

Adrian didn't look back. He walked down the dark lane back to the well-lit house of the Wrights and slipped through to the lighthouse to start packing and be by himself. He found the linens to change the sheets and towels out in the morning and set them aside. He cleaned the mirror of toothpaste spots and looked around to see what else he could do. There wasn't much garbage, but he gathered what little there was into a small plastic shopping bag, ready to go out the next morning. There was dog hair everywhere he looked. He would ask Henry about a vacuum tomorrow morning.

It's going to be weird sleeping without Jaxon on my feet tonight. He wandered up to the top of the lighthouse and stood looking out at the lights of the harbor. He heard the door open below and footsteps on both staircases. He didn't really care who it was, he just wanted space to process his emotions and thoughts. It had been a long but good week. He kept silent as he stared out the window into the darkness.

"Adrian?" It was the captain.

"Up here." He continued the last few steps to the top with that invitation.

The captain took a window adjacent to Adrian and looked out at the same view. He allowed the silence to fill the space and minutes passed without words. Eventually, he spoke, "I used to stand up here for hours staring out at the world."

"And here I am thinking I've only been up here twice in one week, asking myself why I didn't come up here more often." Adrian sighed. "For one week I had a dog and my own space. It was heaven."

"I can imagine," he said with knowing. "I lived here once and had a dog, too. Maggie got me one to care for and he was a part of my life for four good years before I shipped off to the naval college.

I think I may have suffered separation anxiety back then. I almost didn't get to Dartmouth!" He gave a slight self-deprecating laugh as he recalled his anguish at having to leave his beloved pet.

"What happened to him?"

"He grew old with Maggie and Henry. Alice and I went off to college and never looked back. We got off the island and that was that. I think they knew we would leave the proverbial nest, you know? Just come back for holidays and visits."

"What's Alice like?"

"You'd like her. She's great. Big heart. Tons of fun. She's Bryce's mom. Oh, wow, I just put two and two together..."

"What?"

"She adopted Bryce and I bet she did that because she learned what it meant to me." The captain nodded his head with understanding. "She agreed to adopt me, too, remember? Henry took her perspective as well. And she saw how I was saved from a difficult life. I'll have to call her and hear her side of the story."

"Cool."

"Listen, I just came by to say that we'll come get you in the tender tomorrow morning at Marigot Bay after breakfast." He turned to go back down the stairs, then paused and said, "I hope you find the perspective you're looking for."

"I don't even know what I'm looking for, to be honest. I just wanted to..." he stopped as a dawning realization hit him, "Avoid showing my feelings to anyone."

"What are your feelings?" the captain asked.

"I was bummed to say goodbye to Jaxon and my new friends. I was feeling like I don't get to have what I want." He paused, then clarified, "I don't get to have a dog, and yeah, I know Jaxon was not the right dog for our family or boat, even though he is an awesome dog. I guess I was moving into a pity party, as my mom calls it of 'I didn't get what I want.'

"The funny thing is," he continued, "I'm not sure I know what I want anymore. I don't think I want a dog for the foreseeable future. I realized that it would be impossible on this trip and I was surprised that I came to that conclusion. Me of all people! Nope. No dog for me right now. Maybe later. It's like I am sad that I let go of a dream and don't have another dream to replace it. Is that weird?"

"No, not at all. I think what is important here is that you recognize that your wants and needs are changing as you grow and change. It happens all the time to people. We don't have to be fixed in our positions like a lighthouse on land. We can be fluid and dynamic like water and go with the flow. What's right for you today may not be right for you tomorrow, and a wise person will notice that and correct their course."

"Oh, dude you're back! You sound like the captain I know," Adrian laughed for the first time all evening. "You were in a time warp, I think, being back at your family home. I thought you had regressed or something! Hahaha!"

The captain grinned, "Hey! Good stuff happens on the observation deck! I could write a book about it."

"I'll bet," Adrian gave him a brief and comical salute. Straightening up, he said, "Thanks, Captain, I'll be at the dock around nine."

The captain gave him a sarcastic salute back and left without another word. Just before he left the building, he yelled up the stairs to Adrian, "Be sure you check what's behind the drawers under your bunk." And with that, he left.

What?!! The drawers under the bunk? Adrian took the stairs two at a time in his bare feet and knelt before the bed and pulled out the first drawer. Sticking his head under it, he saw nothing. He pulled out the second one and saw nothing. *Huh.* He pulled out his phone and turned on the flashlight to look in. He investigated every nook and cranny. *Nothing. What the heck is he referencing?* He turned on the selfie mode in the camera and carefully scanned the inside of the front face of the furniture to see if there was anything taped to the wood. *There's nothing there! What is this, a wild goose chase?*

He started to put back the drawers when he thought of looking at the backside of the drawer itself. A thick double wall. He slid the inside panel off the back of the drawer that was held on with a slot to hold the wood.

There was a signed cricket player card, an American baseball card, a postcard from a girl named Mary, and a yellowed newspaper cut out of Anna Mossberg Johnson's obituary. After reading his mother's notice and looking at the captain's childhood treasures, he carefully placed them all back the way he found them. There was nothing in the other drawer, although he checked the bottom, sides, and interior before putting them back in.

He lay back on his bed and placed his hands behind his head. *What a week.* He closed his eyes and thought about the captain's early years. *The captain is alright.*

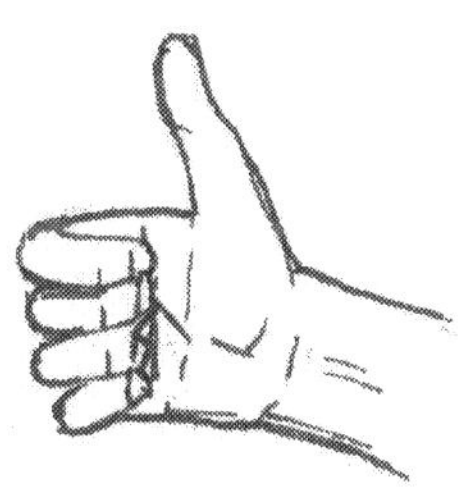

Chapter 11
Farewells

The next morning, Adrian got up early and stripped the bed linens and grabbed the towels and threw them down the stairs to go over the main house. He put fresh sheets on the bed and towels in the bathroom. He grabbed his duffle bag and backpack and, with a final look around to make sure that he hadn't left his phone or laptop charger, he said goodbye to the lighthouse. "I hope to see you again sometime." And walking down the staircase with care to not mar the walls with his duffle bag, he made it to the landing. Picking up the heap of laundry, he rolled it all into a bundle before he opened the door and awkwardly made his way out.

Dropping his bags at the door, he met Maggie in the kitchen and asked her where to dump the laundry. "Over by those double doors, dear."

"Would you like me to start a load of laundry, Maggie?" he asked, ready to lift the lid and put it in.

"No, sweetheart, I'll take care of it, thank you." She gave a wag of her head indicating that he should come into the kitchen and cease doing laundry.

"What's up?" he asked.

"Nothing, just relax. It's your last hour here for a while, so you should just enjoy it. Henry will be out of the shower in a moment." She handed him some plates and flatware. "Set the table for me, love, will you?"

"Sure."

"How are you really doing, Adrian?" she asked as she took fresh blueberry scones out of the oven.

"Surprisingly, Maggie, I'm fine." He moved around the end of the table closest to the kitchen with ease, putting a setting at each chair. "The captain was funny last night."

"How so?"

He chuckled a bit and then said, "He is so different when he is around you and Henry. It's hard to explain. But as soon as he went into helping me with my problems, he became the captain again. I had to laugh."

"He was worried about you after you left the Joseph's house. He really cares about you, Adrian."

"I know, Maggie." Adrian shared, "He's been nothing but nice to me and my sister the entire time. Now I understand where he gets it. From both of you!"

"Good morning, Adrian." Henry came out of nowhere and took a seat. "Did you sleep well?"

"Morning, Henry, I did, thank you." Adrian stood between the kitchen and the dining room. He turned to Maggie and pointed to the plate of scones. She picked them up and passed them to him to place on the table. "Wow, they look and smell amazing!"

"Adrian, I swear I am going to miss your YouTube-style critique and narration of my food when you're gone." Maggie laughed and passed him butter and jam to put on the table. Henry was pouring everyone a mug of tea.

She brought out plates of scrambled eggs, sausage, and potatoes. Both he and Henry piled their plates high with food.

"Maggie, you can come cook on our yacht any day! You could give Chef a run for his money. And I heard the food hasn't been the same since I left."

Henry and Maggie laughed, and she took her seat at the table. "Well, thank you, Adrian, that is a lovely compliment, but I think that would be a lot of work to cook for twenty odd people."

"I'm glad you stayed one more night," Henry started, "I relished our time together. It felt like old times with Gunnar here and working on a project together."

"I really enjoyed being here and thank you for everything." Adrian took a swig of burning hot tea to help move the lump in his throat that developed suddenly. "Sorry I disappeared last night. I, uh, I had a hard time saying goodbye to Jaxon. I hope my family wasn't upset."

Henry put his fork down and dabbed his mouth before speaking, "No, not at all. In fact, it was your mother who told everyone to leave you alone to process your thoughts and feelings. You have her to thank."

"Yeah, my mom knows I'm kinda sensitive about things. I don't want to be, but I feel the connection to people and animals...and sometimes weird stuff, like toys that have sentimental value." He tried to laugh it off but couldn't.

Maggie spoke up and said, "Adrian, we are all wired differently. It's who we are. Sometimes we are sensitive, sometimes we are logical, or have something that makes us unique. It's part of what makes you...you!"

"Yeah, sometimes it gets in the way. Like when I am around my guy friends. Adults are cool, you know, but kids don't always treat you nicely when you are moody or not feeling it. Whatever it is." He used his fork to poke at his eggs and consider his next words. "I leave when I am not sure if I am going to get all emotional."

Henry laughed, "Gunnar was a bit like that, too."

Adrian sat up straighter in his chair and looked at Henry, "No way! Yer jokin', right?"

"Oh, no, love, he was super sensitive. But he has better mastery over his emotions now as an adult." Maggie smiled with compassion. "He was a mess. A beautiful mess of emotions when we took him in. He didn't even know what he was feeling. I had to teach him basic emotional wisdom and get him to connect with his emotions so he could talk about them."

"No way," Adrian repeated. "The captain is such a cool dude with everyone. How is that even possible?"

"He was committed to his process," Henry stated, "Simple."

"What do you mean?" Adrian asked.

"Well," Henry began, "He decided that it was more important to know what emotions he was creating, what created them and if he didn't like them, he could choose something different."

"Let me get this straight," Adrian began, "If the captain didn't like being sad, he would figure out what was making him sad and then choose something like happy? How does that work?"

"No, wait a second, there's more to it than that," Maggie interjected. "He had to unlearn the same lie everyone is told. He believed that others and life were the source of his feelings. It's just not true. Thoughts create feelings, and feelings create emotions. He had to learn that he created every one of his emotions and feelings from his thoughts. If he didn't like the emotions he created, he could change it by changing what he believed was making him, for example, sad."

"It's like this, Adrian," Henry began, "Gunnar thought, like many young people, that the world was against him. He would get defensive and angry that others and life were controlling him. We would help him sort out if that was the truth or was it his belief that made the evidence before him appear real. For instance, he was angry that he was left without a mother and blamed the driver of the other car for his feelings. The driver of that car died, too, by the way, but he blamed that driver for his woundedness. Eventually, he came to understand that if you blame people, you also expect them to fix your feelings. Perhaps the best learning of all was that he knew a dead person couldn't fix his feelings, and that included his mom. So he worked to get clear and found the truth; He was creating his feelings. Now, instead of being powerless to others, he is more empowered. It's what makes him a good leader."

Maggie added. "Simply put, he was angry at everyone because he believed they were the source of his feelings and experience. When he came to realize that he was the creator of his feelings and experience, that was some wake-up call. He did not like that at all."

"I wouldn't like it either," Adrian shared, "there's no one to blame but yourself."

"Precisely our point," Henry agreed. "How can you live life fully if you don't take ownership of your life? You can't believe everyone is making your life terrible and not take ownership. It doesn't work that way. You take ownership for everything, not just the good stuff."

Adrian nibbled on his scone while he thought about that one. "I came here thinking Chef was not happy with me for interrupting him and causing him to make a mistake in the galley. I felt bad about it, and at first I blamed him for my feelings."

"And now?" Maggie asked.

"Um, I'm over it. I think I owned my part in the problem and that changed my thinking about Zak. I was then able to see how I had created a problem for him." He paused for a moment and then added, "I get it. Zak blamed me for his stress and errors. Then I blamed Zak for making me wrong for interrupting him. Then I acted all hurt, thinking no one liked me anymore. Don't ask me how I got to the conclusion that I did it all to myself, but I got there."

"Being able to process your feelings is a huge skill. It will help you get through life and stay healthy," Henry added, "I lived a very stressful life when I was practicing law. I got out and never looked back. I had to own that I created the stress I was living under and undo it. It wasn't easy, but I did it and probably added thirty years to my life, right darling?"

"No way, you? I can't believe you were a stressed-out dude!" Adrian was shocked hearing this about Henry. "I can't believe that. No. No way, no how."

Maggie laughed, "Oh, you have no idea! This guy was bringing his stress home. We were both going gray from stress."

"Stress creates gray hair?" Adrian asked with some confusion. "What?"

"Adrian," Henry began, "Stress is created from fear. It's simple. But don't worry, most people don't go gray from stress until later in life."

"Well, I don't want to go gray!" he asserted, "I don't like anxiety, or stress, or whatever."

"Then my suggestion to you is that you learn now how to manage your emotions by naming them and letting them go. Don't stuff them in your body. Got it?"

"I think so." He contemplated that for a second or two, "I've lived with stress for so long. I'm an anxious kid. What causes that?"

"Fear," Maggie said. "Plain and simple. You have to pay attention to your fears. They sound like judgments in your thoughts or speech."

"Or," Henry began, "They are the fears other people source to judge you with. Ever notice those?"

"All the time. I hate it." He confessed.

"You're not powerless to let all that go, you know." Henry

shared back. "You get to acknowledge it's there and let it go. You don't have to hold it in your body or mind, own it, agree with it, or anything else. Let it go."

"You mean I can just say, for example, I notice Zak's judgment on me that I am inconsiderate of others when they are working and I let it go?" He leaned forward on the table with interest. *Finally! Someone who may have an answer to my anxiety issues.*

"That works," Henry said, "Or you could say inside your heart, I acknowledge I have a conflict with being blamed for being inconsiderate and I let that go."

"As a lawyer, Henry worked in conflict resolution for years, Adrian. He was very good at it because he figured out people needed to acknowledge they had a conflict, or else it never really got solved. You can't beat around the bush, or the conflict never gets a place of importance front and center in your awareness."

"I can see that."

"Oh, my! Look at the time. We need to get out to the car and drop Adrian at the dock." Henry wiped his mouth with a napkin and pushed his chair back in a hurry. "Darling, we can clean up after we get back."

"I agree." Maggie stood up and collected her purse from the kitchen. "I'm ready."

Adrian retrieved his bags and reentered the house and slid the glass door shut and locked it behind him. "I'm good!"

They exited the front door and climbed into Henry's SUV. "Henry, I didn't have a chance to clean all the dog hair in the lighthouse. I'm sorry, but you will have to do it. And your car is also a mess of paw prints and hair."

"Adrian, we've lived with dogs all our lives. We get it. Not to worry." Maggie assured him that there was nothing wrong. "I'm curious what dog is going to come into our lives next."

"Keep me posted with pictures!" Adrian enthused.

At the harbor's guest dock, Jimmy and Francesco were waiting at the dock with the tender. Both wearing dark sunglasses, navy t-shirts with the *M/Y Arabella* logo on the front and back. They both had khaki-colored shorts and webbed belts. Neither wore shoes. *"Ciao, senora e senor! Ciao, Adriano!"*

"Ciao, Francesco! Ciao, Jimmy!" Adrian said in a happy and cheery voice. He was in fact very happy to see both guys. He slung his bags over the stern onto the seat then turned to give hugs to Maggie and Henry.

Maggie wrapped her arms around Adrian for a long hug, which he returned in kind. "Thanks for everything, Maggie," he whispered in her ear and kissed her soft wrinkled cheek. "Oh, you are so welcome, my love," she whispered in return. "I hope to see you again sometime. Be sure to write."

"I will. I promise," and he released her to turn to Henry.

"Come here, you!" Henry said in a gruff voice. Adrian put both arms around his waist and hugged him tight. "Thanks, Henry. I will never forget any part of this...or you or Maggie." He stood back from Henry and looked at him good and hard. "I hope I get to spend time with you again."

"Me, too, son." Henry put an arm around his shoulder and squeezed him to his side in a hug and Adrian felt him rest his cheek on the side of his head. "Go on, now! *Bon voyage!*"

"Bon voyage," Maggie shouted and waved until they rounded a boat and couldn't see them anymore.

"That young man is so much like Gunnar, I'm going to miss him." Henry confided to Maggie as the wake of the boat settled in the harbor.

"Me, too." Maggie took her husband's hand and walked back to the car. "I think we need to go to the animal shelter and look for a dog." For an answer, he smiled, shook his head in amazement and opened her car door for her to get in.

Adrian couldn't believe he was in the tender and flying fast across the water. The guys left him alone for the most part, but Francesco wanted to know how his visit was, and he responded by giving two thumbs up. He nodded and smiled in return. *"Molto bene!"*

After they tied up, he climbed aboard the stern swim platform and raced up the teak steps to the main deck aiming to drop off his bags in his cabin. Jane intercepted him and asked if she could take them from him. Relenting, he said, "Everything in the duffle needs to be washed. There's nothing in my backpack you need, just stick it on the floor by my bed, please."

He wandered upstairs to his parent's apartment and knocked on the door. He heard his dad say, "Enter," so he did. His mom jumped up and ran to greet him with a big hug. "Sweetie! You're back!"

"Hi, Dad!" He gave his dad a quick hug then sat down on a lounger on the deck where they were having a late morning coffee.

"Shall I call Grace up?" his mom asked.

"Um, not yet. I just want to see how you are all doing first. What's new?"

"Not a whole heck of a lot," his dad replied. "Although everyone has been out rowing on *Dash* since it arrived yesterday. It was a big hit with us and the crew!"

"Really?" he was amazed to hear that. It was the last thing he expected. "What else?"

"Well, we sent the limousine tender home since we're not using it, to make room for *Dash*," his dad added.

"Yep, I figured that out."

"We really just hung around the yacht. Your dad and Grace hiked the pitons and I stayed here."

"That's cool. Did you bring the drone, Dad?"

"We did! I'll show you those videos later."

"I was thinking I would head over to the bridge and see what the plans are, then check in with the crew. You were my first stop."

"OK, welcome back, Adrian, it's good to have you back home."

Home. He smiled, "I never thought I would say this, but it feels good to be home. See ya around."

He flew up the port staircase to the bridge deck and found the captain, Pete, and Jimmy in a conference over the chart table.

"Hey! Welcome back, stranger," Pete grinned when Adrian got close enough, and he put a wrestler's hold around his neck and dragged him into some sense of a man hug. Adrian laughed and got himself out of the stranglehold. "You wait until I'm big enough to take you down. You won't do that to me anymore."

"You're big enough now," the captain shared quietly.

"Hey, Jimmy." Adrian greeted him with a casual air. "Just checking in and wondering what the plan is."

"Well, we are heading to Barbados Island in an hour or so. We were trying to decide if we wanted to go from there to Grenada and come back up the Grenadines or go to Barbados to St. Vincent's then Grenada. Your parents are interested in eventually heading over to Mexico."

"Any chance we can stop in Aruba?" Adrian asked, bending over the charts. "It's in a straight line from Grenada."

"I don't see why not," the captain said, tracing the chart from Aruba to Jamaica, then to the Cayman's. "Yes, a definite possibility. I'll run it by your parents."

"Do we ever go to South America?" Adrian asked with curiosity.

"Right now, there is political unrest in many of those countries and insurance companies won't cover us if we go into waters where the yacht could be attacked by pirates or taken over by a crime lord."

"Whoa," he uttered with a bit of shock. "I didn't know it was so bad."

Pete tapped his shoulders and said, "Follow me." He spoke into his walkie-talkie to Gabriella to find Grace and meet him on the main deck.

"I heard you had a good time!" Pete shared, "I'm glad. And *Dash* is an incredible addition to the boat toys."

"I know! It's hard to call her a toy..." he mused, "She's more like a piece of art."

"Yes! Good description," he praised. "I'd be reluctant to take her out. I'd probably put her in my living room and sit in it to watch movies or something."

"OK, Pete," he laughed, "That's just weird! You'd be the last person who would be comfortable in something like that. Kids, maybe."

Pete looked deadpan serious and said, "No, I'd fit and be totally comfortable. I could probably watch all three Lord of the Rings sitting in it at one go."

All he could do was shake his head. Grace met them at the bar. "What's up?"

Pete reached around behind the bar and lifted a small but heavy plastic box and placed it between the teens. "I got some stuff for you."

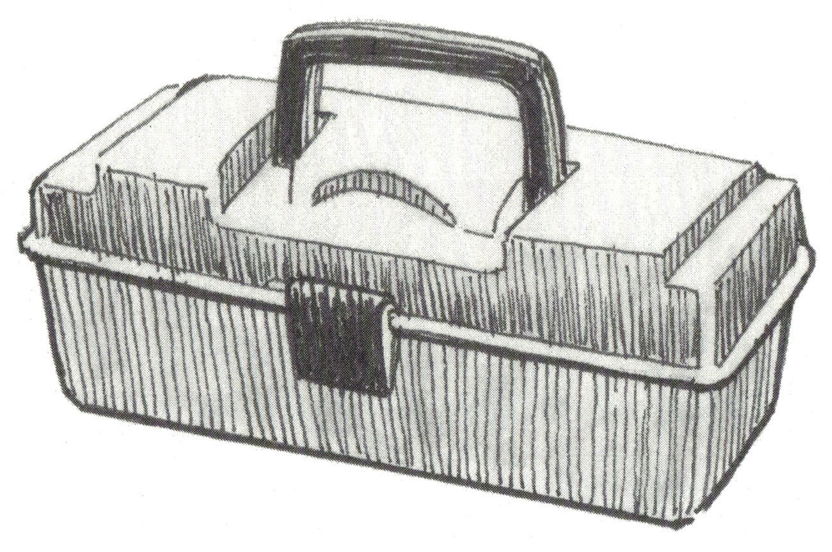

Grace rushed to open the box and was more confused than ever. Adrian looked and exclaimed, "Ha! I know exactly what this stuff is for! No way, Pete, these are awesome!" He took out a spool of thin strand polypropylene line, heavy fishing weights with swivels and slices of red neon pool noodles. He high-fived Pete who stood back and grinned.

"Will someone explain to me what I am looking at?"

"Grace," Adrian began with extreme patience, "You are looking at our future sail racing buoys for the pool. We can make them while we are underway today."

"Thanks, Pete! I knew you would come up with something awesome!"

"Oh," Grace said as she picked up a fishing weight. "Thanks, Pete." Turning to her brother she said, "We better get some practice in and create some match races with you-know-who."

"Yeah, I'm not going to let you-know-who win any more."

Pete grinned to himself as he took in the two discussing their recent loss to the first officer. Backing away, he said, "Let me know, guys, if you need anything else. Maybe I can act as Race Committee?"

"Yes!" said Grace emphatically, "That's a good idea, Pete! That might keep ole Jimmy from pulling a fast one on us."

"You got it! See ya round." Pete headed back to the bridge deck and disappeared from view.

"Can you figure out when Jimmy is busy so we can practice with the boats? I'd almost practice in mom's big bathtub just to be out of sight. Know what I mean?"

"Yeah, roger that." Grace said.

"You talkin' like a sailor now?" he teased her in good spirits.

"You know, bro', I thought I missed you this week, but I was wrong!" She punched his arm in a playful fashion, closed the box and asked, "We makin' these in your cabin or mine?"

The yacht hauled up its anchors off the coast of Sugar Beach under the Pitons and set a course for Barbados in the southeastern part of the Caribbean. Adrian let the crew do their thing and hung out with his sister making the floats. At one point, they snuck into the main salon and carefully placed one weight on the bottom of the pool, which was empty because they were underway. They measured the line length to where the pool water level maxed out and tied a knot on the pool noodle float material. They ran back to Adrian's cabin and made the other floats the same length.

"Cool. Phase one is complete."

"We're going to have to wait and practice in Barbados," Grace said with a hint of disappointment.

"It's okay. There's no rush. But we're ready." They high-fived each other and headed up to the owner's deck to hang out with their parents.

Chef Zak made Adrian's favorite Margarita pizza, Caesar salad and chocolate mousse pie with chocolate shortbread crust for dessert.

Zak came up to the owner's deck where the family was dining. "Hey, Adrian! Welcome back! We all missed you. I hope you enjoyed lunch today. "

"Thanks, Zak! I'm happy to be back." He meant it and was surprised that in a week he could have turned his feelings around. "Lunch was amazing. Thanks for making all my favorites."

"With pleasure. Jean-Marie and I put our heads together to figure out what would be your favorite dishes. But I regret to inform you that your chocolate croissants have been off the menu for a short time, as your father has insisted that we live on apple turnovers for a while, stating that you've had a good run and it's his turn now."

"It's all good. I love a good apple turnover, Zak. I'm sure Jean-Marie makes a mean turnover." He grinned at the thought of the sweet sous-chef being mean to pastry. "But I don't think she could look cross-eyed at pastry." He laughed at his wisecrack. "She puts so much love in her baking, as she likes to say."

"Is someone talking about *moi*?" Jean-Marie appeared beside him. She bent to kiss both his cheeks. "Welcome home, Master Adrian. I miss you so much, and so did Chef. You don't know this, but his food was sad with you gone."

"It was not!" Zak defended himself hotly, "You people complain too much."

"Ooh, he had big tears rolling into the soup," she pantomimed, and her delightful French laugh floated up into the air. "I say, 'Stop Zak, the soup will be too salty.' The crew were ready to throw him overboard. But I saved the day."

"Would you...stop! Not true!" Zak blustered and threw his

hands up in the air. Rather than keep Jean-Marie going, he bowed to the family and turned to leave with a smile. Turning to Adrian, he said, "It is nice to have you back home. Come visit the galley sometime, and we will make something together. I'll text you visiting hours."

Adrian gave him a short salute of recognition and smiled back at him. He leaned back in his seat and sighed a pleasant sigh of relief. His mom gave him a subtle wink. His smile grew into a grin. *It feels good to be back. New and fresh.*

All the crew were extra attentive. "Geez, Mom, I should leave more often. Everyone's being extra nice."

"Adrian, they were always this attentive."

"Really? It feels different." His face bore a faint trace of a frown. "Why does it seem different?"

"Maybe you are different?"

"Oh, I'm way different," he agreed, "In fact, I'm going to take a nap." He stood up and pushed his chair in. He put his arms around his mom's neck and kissed her cheek. "Thanks for your help through email."

"You're so welcome. Anytime." She grabbed one of his hands and kissed it. "See you later.

Chapter 12
Gotcha

St. Peter, Barbados
British Commonwealth
West Indies

They arrived at sunset to the Port of St. Charles. The captain backed the yacht's stern into the space the port authority directed him into. The family chose to stay on board for the evening and plan an excursion for tomorrow with Gabrielle's help.

Having taken a nap earlier, Adrian wasn't tired. When he found himself awake well past midnight, he sat at his desk with his laptop open and wrote a few short emails to friends old and new. Out of boredom, he started searching the web for Thor Sixten Johnson. He didn't get any hits, per se, so he tried different versions of the name with first initial, middle initial, and then began researching the Swedish Naval Academy, then naval records, and he got a hit on a seaman's database and archive. He bookmarked the page and digs into the name of a ship in the database referenced for T. Sixten Johnson. While he was not sure there was a connection to the captain, he read about the shipping company out of Malta that particular ship was registered with. Opening a word processing document, he entered all the leads and saved it.

On a hunch, he looked at agencies representing captains and

crew for hire and found it overwhelming. *I need to narrow my search. Maybe a Swedish company? Or crew agency?* Trying multiple keywords, Adrian navigated the web and found several companies that could represent captains for hire. Nothing brought him answers.

Switching to social media for relief, he tried variations of the name and found a group of British folks on vacation who had posted a photo and tagged everyone. They referenced a man with a receding gray hairline called Captain Thor Johnson in Cyprus. He was on the tall side with olive-gold weathered skin and almond-shaped eyes with loads of crinkles. He wore a navy blazer with brass buttons over a crisp white shirt open to the middle, revealing a gold chain around his neck. He wore jeans and deck shoes. He looked like the life of the party with his right arm around a pretty tourist and a glass of something in his left hand. *Wow, if this is him...* He downloaded the image and scanned some of the people's other vacation photos but didn't see anything else. The group appeared to be staying at the Lamissol marina on the island of Cyprus and there was a yacht sales sign in the photo in the background. He looked up the location on Google maps and found the company and clicked on the website for the yacht sales.

He scrolled through the website looking for clues and found none. He clicked the link on the "contact us" page and, without further thought, wrote a note to the yacht sales company.

Hi,

I'm writing to see if you know a captain named Thor S. Johnson from Sweden.

Thanks,

Adrian Abercrombie
M/Y Arabella

He hit the send button, then had a moment of paranoia land in his gut. *Shoot! What did I just do? I probably shouldn't have written. What if they know him? What do I do if I do reach him?* A new email entered his inbox.

Hi Adrian,

That would be me! How may I help you?

-TSJ

Adrian closed his laptop with a loud snap. *Oh, no! Oh, no! Oh, no, I didn't just go and find his father. That was too easy. It was supposed to be a longshot and I wasn't supposed to find anything. Shoot, shoot, shoot!!!* He got up and paced the floor of his cabin. He went into his bathroom and splashed cool water on his face and looked at himself in the mirror. *Adrian, you're an idiot! What the heck were you thinking! You weren't thinking!* His self-judgments mounted as his anxiety rose.

He walked back to his desk and stood over it. He opened his laptop back up. *What time is it in Cyprus?* He googled the time difference and saw that they were seven hours ahead. *It's the start of business over there. There's no way it's him. It's unlikely. Johnson is a common Swedish last name and Thor is common. Yeah, but Sixten is not.*

Another email in his inbox.

Hi Adrian,

I looked up your yacht on my ship finder app. She's a beauty! And it appears you are currently in Barbados. That's a wonderful island. One of my favorites. Let me know how I can assist you with your yachting needs. We represent talent in all positions and do yacht sales and chartering. Our offices are open every day except Monday. My contact info is as follows... TSJ

Oh, dang! I'm so glad mom and dad insisted we did not make a webpage for our yacht and post anything about the captain or crew to protect their privacy. Ship finder, huh? Shoot. I forgot about that.

He hit reply to the second email and sat at his desk agonizing.

Dear Captain Johnson,

Sorry to be vague, but I wrote to see if it was possible if you were related to a Gunnar Johnson. I recently learned of your name and thought I would try to find you. I'm a friend of his.

Regards,
Adrian

Within minutes, his inbox had a new email.

Dear Adrian,

I would be very interested in knowing if this Gunnar's middle name is Erik and if his mother's name is Anna.
Regards,
TJS

Oh...no. I'm dead meat. He covered his eyes with his right hand and cringed. He thought long and hard about his answer and decided to shut down the email conversation.

Dear Captain Johnson,

Yes, that's correct. I'm just the researcher. I'll pass your information on to him and if he wants to connect, he'll have your contact info.
Regards,
Adrian

OK, that should be fine. I'll pretend to have given the info to the captain, and never tell him about this discovery, and if Captain Johnson never hears from the captain he'll think this is where it ended. Adrian crossed his fingers and sent the email.

Harrison's Cave
St. Thomas Parish
Barbados

After a late breakfast, the Abercrombies set out from the marina in a taxi to the center of the island to see the famous Harrison Caves. Adrian's dad bought four tickets to enter the cave and ride the underground tram tour. They proceeded to walk through the interpretation center with scientific explanations, island history, large pictures, and diagrams of the cave features. They entered the glass elevators that took them down to the cave entrance where they put on hardhats to ride the electric tram.

The limestone cavern was over a mile and a half long and, as the explanation in the visitor center had shared, it was created by hundreds of thousands of years of acid rain created by carbon dioxide in the atmosphere that had melted the limestone, leaving behind the hollowed-out cavity filled structure under the earth.

They marveled at the various kinds of calcite deposits known as speleothems. They were everywhere in the cave. From sparkly white flow stones that grew rapidly on the walls, to the stalactites growing down from the ceiling and stalagmites growing up from the floor.

Their senses were heightened by the variety of sounds in the cave, which provided multiple layers of dimension and sensation. Adrian was in heaven. *This is so cool! It's a pirate's paradise!*

Every turn on the tram rail revealed running streams of water, emerald and crystal-clear pools of water, a forty-foot underground waterfall, the ancient gold colors of eroded limestone and creamy calcites. They enjoyed the cool and constant temperature in contrast to the blazing hot tropical sun outside.

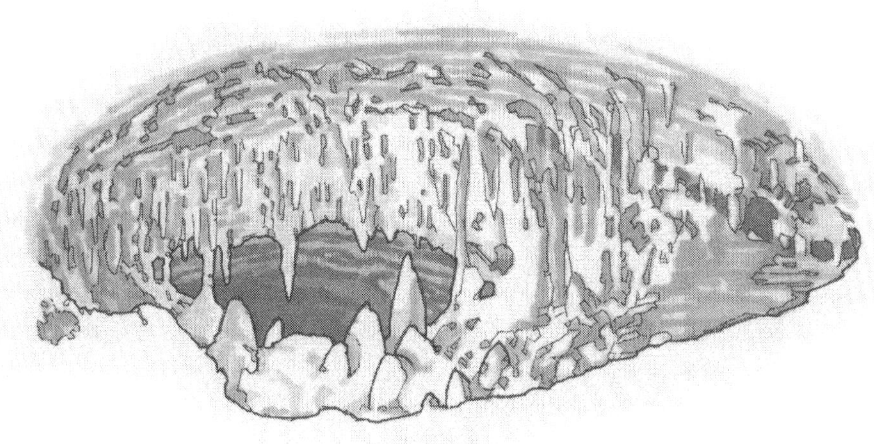

"Dad, how do they know the cave stones are eight-hundred-thousand years old? How can they tell? Do they use carbon dating?" Grace asked.

"Great question, Grace," He replied and mulled over his answer.

"I do believe it is hard to pinpoint the actual date of a cave. Especially one like this, which was created as a result of carbonic acid-bearing water that trickled from above.

"That being shared, I suspect researchers have looked at how long it takes to dissolve rocks. They now use a chalky mineral called alunite, that forms structures as rock dissolves and then crystalizes on cave walls. Alunite is created where ground water mixes with sulfuric acid, which eats limestone away from underneath. But this wouldn't apply here. This is all from the top down."

"Do they look at the speleothems like tree rings? Could they saw it open and look at the thickness and deposits inside it?" she asked.

"Hmm. The speleothems do record the CO2 records of the atmosphere from the time they were born, and scientists could look at the amount of carbonate from rock weathering, which is simply dead carbon that is in the speleothem, but it is difficult to calibrate. I would think radiocarbon dating for calibration can only go so far."

"I know they said these caves are a direct result of rainwater, but is there any chance they were created by sea water at one time?" Adrian asked. "I did read we are seven-hundred feet above sea level and on the Atlantic and Caribbean tectonic plates under this part of the sea. Both are pushing against each other in a volcanic region."

"Barbados is a coral reef island, which is limestone, so I suspect millions of years ago it was under the sea. These speleothems are created from acidic rainwater, so I doubt the sea created any of what we are seeing. There are still miles and miles of cave to be discovered on this island. We're only seeing about two miles of it."

"Well, that was definitely very interesting!" Adrian's mom declared when they came out into the bright sunlight and got blasted by the heat. "I say we go through the gardens on the shady side, see the gift shop, get something to eat and plan our next stop."

Due to the heat, they opted to return home to *M/Y Arabella* and find a beach to cool off in. Jean-Marie made slushy fruit drinks for them and placed a plate of sugar cookies shaped like hearts on the table. "De are in de shape of de hearts because we all love sugar, no?"

"*Merci, Jean-Marie! Tre bien!*" his mom said. "You know we all have a sweet tooth in this family."

"Just ask me about dental bills," his dad joked, taking a bite. "They're delicious. *Merci.*"

"So, Mom, catch me up on what's on our calendar," Adrian invited. "I haven't heard about any plans for future travel, but the captain said that you want to head over to Mexico after we finish with the Grenadines."

She wiped her fingers of sugar on a small napkin and started with, "Well, I guess you should know that we have some visitors coming to the yacht."

"Who?" Grace asked at the exact time that Adrian asked, "When?"

"Whoa! Slow down!" she laughed and leaned forward to rest

on her arms. "I've invited some friends of mine who are originally from Japan. Mr. and Mrs. Taka Kageyama. They have a son your age, Adrian. His name is Ryu. The mom's name is Natsu. They are bringing a friend named Mrs. Kayoko Sasaki, and she's bringing her son Sota and daughter Kanade. I believe Sota is about the same age as you and Ryu, and the girl is a year younger than Grace."

"Do they speak English, Mom?" Grace asked with concern.

"Oh, yeah," she waved her hand in the air to dismiss the concern. "These kids have all gone to British boarding schools and are fluent in English, Japanese and French."

"How do you know these people, Mom?" Adrian asked.

"Remember I told you I studied art history and fine art back in the day? Well, I met Natsu in my senior year of university and we sat next to each other for two semesters of Japanese sumi-e brush painting. Oh, how we giggled our butts off in that class. She is an international art dealer based in Los Angeles and Tokyo.

I've bought several pieces through her over the years. You remember the water lily paintings in the dining room with the bamboo gold frames? Well, those are two that I purchased from her last year."

"What does her husband do?" asked Grace.

"Excuse me," the captain interrupted, in his formal dress-whites, which were a tropical weight uniform for meeting and greeting new passengers. He crossed the main deck to where they sat in the air-conditioned shade ready to go to the beach after their snack. His captain's hat was tucked under his arm. "Just a quick question. What time are your guests arriving? I heard there were delays this morning at the airport coming in from Miami due to a storm. Any update?"

"Let me check my phone. Have a seat, Captain." His mom pulled her phone out of her beach tote and scrolled through her text messages. "Oh, they made it. Hang on, that was over an hour ago. And they got through immigration. They ought to be here any minute."

"So, what does Natsu's husband do?" Grace asked again to pry info out of her about the mysterious guests that were about to arrive. The captain leaned back in his seat to listen to the conversation.

"Taka is a high-level officer of the Organized Crime Department of the Criminal Affairs Bureau in Japan but working in Los Angeles. They put him on administrative leave after a very difficult case that he solved. It was the perfect time for them to take a holiday."

Adrian looked at the captain while he asked his mom, "So, let me get this straight: you have an art dealer and a detective who solves organized crime coming to stay on our yacht?" The captain gave him a blank stare with a micro shake of his head that said, "I had nothing to do with this," which Adrian returned with a narrowing of his eyes and twist of his lips. He caught his mother looking at him. She smiled innocently and said, "I have friends in high places, Adrian. I think you'll enjoy Mr. Kageyama and his family. His specialty is tracking and arresting art thieves."

The captain bit his lower lip to keep from laughing. His eyebrows rose high into his forehead and his eyes were bright with mischief as he pushed away from the table. He put his hands up in the air and declared, "I had nothing to do with this, Adrian! This is all your mom."

"And what about the girl and her mom?" Grace asked, "What are they like? Am I going to like them?"

"Oh, honey, they'll tell you all about themselves when they get here, which should be any minute. I suppose we should change and skip the beach."

"I'm going in the pool then," Grace declared.

"I'll join you," said Adrian.

"I'll go change," said their dad.

Left alone, the two teens got in the pool to hang out. "I did miss you, Adrian. It was fun diving with dad but when we do things with Jimmy, Brian, and the Italian guys, it's different. It's more fun. No offense to dad, but you know."

"Yeah, I know," he smiled. "The guys are younger than dad, but older than us and they probably remember better what it was like to be our age."

"I wonder what these new kids are going to be like," Grace mused. "Mom had me worried for a minute when she said they were from Japan. I thought, Oh, great, how are we going to talk with them?" she laughed at her fear. "Duh."

"Well, after mom has had foreign students that barely spoke English, stay with us for months in the guest house, I think we've learned not to trust her entirely!" They both laughed at that.

"I guess we should be proper and get dressed to meet them." Grace stepped out of the pool. "That quick dip was perfect."

"Yeah, I guess I will, too."

Fifteen minutes later, the entourage of their Japanese guests came down the dock pulling suitcases behind them. The male deckhands of the *Arabella*, dressed in summer whites, raced down the passerelle to meet them and take their luggage. Jane and Gabrielle were positioned at the end of the line of officers, who stood poised and ready to greet their guests, with cold finger towels and a tray of sparkling waters on ice. They wore navy and white matching dresses with their rank on their shoulders.

With their eyes wide open, the young teens made their way up the passerelle with curiosity, taking in the aqua blue pool with a clear glass wall built into the stern. "Wow! You've got a pool!" said the one in the white shirt. "Check out the size of those ropes, Sota!"

Once aboard, Jane passed a towel to each boy who spent no more than two seconds with it before passing it back and walking past each member of the crew saying, "Hi, hello, hi, hello, hi Captain," then stood by the pool checking out the glass wall. Adrian made his way over to them.

"Hi, guys, I'm Adrian." He stuck out his hand and the one in the white polo shirt stuck out his hand and said in a British accented voice, "Hi, I'm Ryu, this is my friend, Sota." Sota stuck his hand out, too, but only nodded and didn't say anything.

Ryu turned to wave the teenage girl over, "Kanade, this is Adrian."

"Hi, Kanade, nice to meet you." Adrian said, "Welcome aboard."

She, too, was reserved, "Hello."

Adrian went to meet the parents and be part of the receiving line. The crew was bringing up bags and everyone was busy talking and sharing airport stories. He saw Grace trying to talk to Kanade, and it didn't look like it was going very well. *She is either very shy, doesn't want to be here or...* He watched as Kanade turned and spoke to her brother in Japanese and they ignored Grace. Ryu came over to talk to Adrian. "How long have you been in Barbados?"

"We just got here last night," he said to the friendly guy in front of him. "We went to see the caves this morning and we were headed to the beach when we learned you all made the flight in. Crazy storm, huh?"

"Yeah, we were the last plane to get out before they shut the airport. The pilot was happy to tell us we made it. It was a bumpy ride, but we got above the storm and got down here in no time. Nice boat, by the way."

"Yeah," Adrian laughed, "I didn't like it at first. You know, I had to leave my friends at school, my teammates, etcetera."

"I would love this! Are you kidding me?" He said, "Anything to get out of boring school."

"Everyone gather round," his mom called out to the group

mingling with the captain, crew and new passengers. "We will have snacks out here in twenty minutes, and then the captain will lead the emergency drills. The crew will see you to your stateroom, or cabins, as we like to call them. We can go to the beach afterwards."

Grace and Adrian hung back on the stern while the guests went downstairs to their cabins. "What's up with that girl and her brother?" Grace asked, "They would hardly speak to me."

"I know, me neither." Adrian shared, "Maybe they take a while to warm up to people."

"Maybe." Grace chewed her lower lip, "Gosh, I hope they warm up sooner than later. A boat is not a good place to be strangers or be stuck in your ways. Did mom say how long they were staying here?"

"No," Adrian said, "Come to think of it, Mr. Kageyama is on administrative leave. Does that sound open-ended to you?"

"Kinda," Grace hedged. "Maybe they didn't want to come here. Let's at least show them a fun time. It's hard to feel mad or anti-social when you are snorkeling and seeing a million fishies."

"Right!"

Minutes later the galley crew placed platters of snacks on the tables and began making drinks at the bar. They got Grace and Adrian salted lime soda water, which they loved. The deck grew loud with chatter as everyone came out and enjoyed the food and cold drinks.

Jimmy and the Captain got everyone to sit down and listen to what to do in the event of an emergency. They covered fire, water, first aid, and man overboard drills. They were about to do a walking tour of the yacht beginning in the stern with pool safety, when Francesco came hurrying up the passerelle and said, *"Mi scusi, Capitano,* there is someone here asking for you specifically. He is insisting that he see you."

Everyone turned and looked over to the dock where a tallish man in a woven shade hat wearing a white linen short sleeve shirt, navy dress shorts and deck shoes waved like crazy from the dock. "Hallo! Gunnar! It's me, your father, Thor Johnson! I want to talk to you!"

Time stood still and no one moved or spoke. Adrian was having a heart attack and frozen to the spot. *No way.* He closed his eyes. When he opened them he saw the captain looking at him with stone cold pale blue eyes and he simply pointed a finger at Adrian. He felt the color drained out of his face, his stomach flip flop and a panic attack coming on. He felt Grace touch his arm and in a weirdly distant voice heard her say, "Adrian...?"

His mom and dad had followed the captain's accusatory finger and saw it land on their son. They looked at him in confusion. "What's going on?" His mom asked, a bit bewildered.

"Jimmy, please take over the tour and show our guests the rest of the yacht." The captain commanded in a neutral tone, as he turned his head slightly to look at the man on the dock. "It appears I have some personal business to attend to."

The man had also followed the captain's finger and turned to look at him. "Adrian? Is that you?" he asked with a bright smile. "I was in Antigua brokering a yacht sale when I got your email. I hopped a flight here as soon as I saw you had only just arrived on the island."

The captain waited until the guests had left. He said something quietly to Adrian's parents and then turned to Adrian. He changed his mind, which both increased Adrian's anxiety and offered relief. *I am so busted.* He watched the captain walk down the passerelle and walk briskly down the dock indicating that Captain Johnson follow him. He stopped when he was far enough away, made an abrupt turn, crossed his arms over his chest and kept his feet squarely planted under his hips. *Uh, oh. He is not happy. This is bad.*

"Sweetheart," his mom nudged him, "Please tell me and your dad what is going on. The captain shared that this man is his father, but he hadn't seen him in almost four decades. And he said his father could only be here because of you. Is this true?"

Adrian confessed the entire story to his parents and Grace. His parents looked at each other with a look of resignation. "Let's hear what the captain has to say." They all looked down the dock to see what was going on.

Captain Thor Johnson was fanning his face with his Panama hat. The captain was looking impatient and obstinate. The older guy bent his head in the heat and seemed to crump a bit, which was when his mom jumped up, ran down the passerelle and down the dock to get to his side. The rest of the family ran to the top of the stern steps to watch. The captain had his father by the elbow and his mom had his other arm. They began helping him back to the yacht. A conversation was going on over the old guy's head and the captain seemed to roll his eyes and head with disbelief.

They came up the passerelle slowly and let Captain Thor Johnson sit on the nearest lounger under the air conditioning in the shade. Neither the captain nor Adrian wanted to make eye contact with each other. Adrian hung his head and looked at the deck with deep uncertainty. His mom was barking orders to get mineral water or juice and snacks. And a cold cloth! Captain Johnson mumbled something about being fussed over and his mom raised her voice over his. "No, Thor, I don't care what you say, you are staying here as our guest, whether Captain Gunnar likes it or not," she insisted. "You're not well and in no shape to travel. You need to normalize your blood sugar and hydrate. You almost collapsed out there in the heat."

The captain stepped in front of Thor, "Hand me your passport. Tell me where you are staying. Any other health issues? You have a ticket to fly out of here? I need to add you to the passenger list and report you to the port authorities as a guest. You know the drill." The captain was impersonal with the man before him. He was almost treating him like a criminal.

"Captain, I understand this is a shock to you. Would you like to gather your thoughts and take a break?" his mom invited in a gentle tone. "I'll care for Thor. It's not a problem. You can send Jane up to help me." The captain nodded his thanks and took the portside staircase two at a time towards his office without a word or backwards glance.

Captain Johnson looked over at Adrian, "Adrian! Call me Thor. I'm a retired captain now."

No one spoke. All eyes were on Adrian. *Why does everyone have to look at me? I didn't know this was going to happen.* He jumped to his feet and glared at Thor. "OK...Thor! What the heck were you thinking? I just asked you if you knew him. I didn't invite you down here to ruin everything! Now, I'm in deep trouble with everybody and I just got through having a bad week with the chef and now I'm set up to have a bad year with the captain. Thanks a lot for nothing!" He stormed off towards his cabin to escape the tension, leaving his mom and dad looking speechless at each other and their newest guest.

"Hi, Thor! I'm Grace," she extended her hand with a mischievous smile, "Welcome aboard the *Arabella*. We're the Abercrombies!"

To be continued...

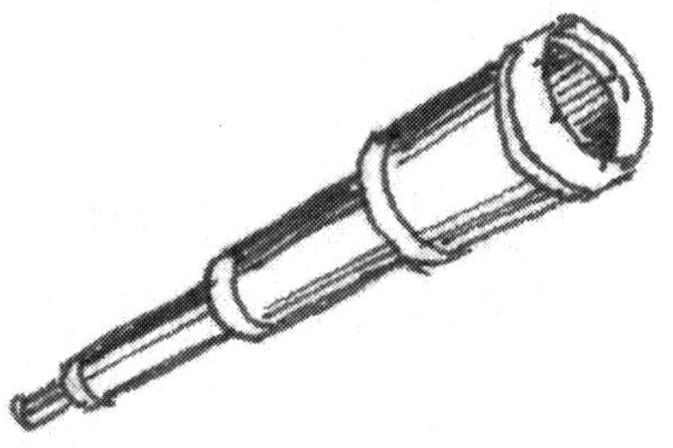

Glossary Of Nautical Terms

NOTE: This glossary is expanded from the first book in the series.

Aft – this word means at, near or towards the stern, or back of the ship.

Amidship – middle of the ship; or on the midline of the ship. Example, "I was amidship when the main boom swung over suddenly and almost swept me into the sea."

Anchor – a weighted object typically made of metal or concrete and attached to a chain or rope that is lowered to the floor of the sea or lakebed to hold your boat in place, so it does not drift away. There are many designs of anchors, and the most popular have "flukes" that can easily grab into mud, sand, even rocky bottoms to provide reliable strength to hold the boat in place. Anchors are usually stored in a locker and the anchor line is kept neatly coiled and ready to go overboard without getting tangled. On super yachts and ships, only a robust galvanized steel and carbon steel chain is trusted to hold a boat that big.

Antiquities – ancient items that are considered historical treasure.

Beam – this is the middle section of the boat. It is typically the widest part of the entire boat. The beam can be referred to as "port beam" or "starboard beam." For further clarification, and to increase your communication, you can use "forward of the port beam" or "aft the port beam."

Bow – this is the pointy end of the boat. It is the forward part. It's good to remember that not all bows are pointy. Check out a punt, hydroplaning flat boats, sled boats or blunt nose inflatable if you want to learn more.

Bow line – the rope or line attached to the pointy or front end of the boat that is used to secure it, so it doesn't drift away.

Bowline knot – A strong knot that never jams, even after being placed under extreme tension or pressure or from being wet. Pronounced bow-luhn, it's known as the King of Knots.

Bridge – the bridge on a large vessel is the area where the captain commands and controls the ship. The bridge is manned by an officer of the watch. Since the captain also needs to eat and sleep, a second or third in command may be appointed to take control of the vessel. Sometimes the bridge is referred to as the pilothouse or wheelhouse, which is the name for the housing around the helm or steering wheel.

Bulwark – side of a ship above the deck.

Captain – the captain of a vessel, no matter the size, is the ultimate authority onboard. His or her responsibility is to make sure all people aboard are safe, the vessel is safe, and the environment remains safe. All incidents involving the boat are the responsibility of the captain, whether or not the captain and crew were the source of the problem. Captains are very educated about the workings of vessels, engines, and electrical systems, navigating, maritime law, weather and have logged thousands of hours.

Collar – The inboard part of the oar that has a leather wrapping to prevent wear and tear on the wooden oar and provide a small amount of friction to keep the oar in the oarlock.

Compass Heading – the direction a boat is moving. All headings have a numerical value, and any one of the 32-points that are named can be used to describe the heading. Most people navigate by a numerical value. "Keep the boat pointed at 123 degrees or we will miss the channel marker."

Compass Rose - The compass rose, as it is called, is an ancient system for navigating around the earth. The rose refers to the evenly spaced marks around the face of the compass, which represent a unique direction. Each name has a numerical value.

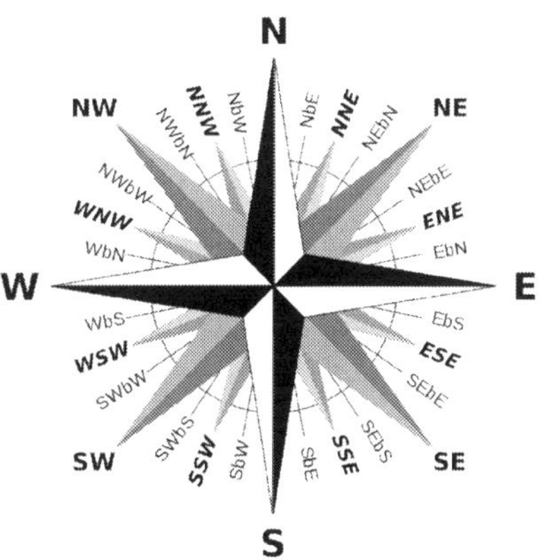

The cardinal points (4) are North, East, South and West. Each is 90-degrees apart.

The intercardinal points are (4) additional divisions of the four points, namely, Northeast, Southeast, Southwest, and Northwest. The cardinal and intercardinal are referred to as the 8 Winds or 8 Principle Winds (meaning the wind directions). Each is 45-degrees from each other.

Each of the named points below are separated by 11.25 degrees on the compass. These 32-points, multiplied by 11.25-degrees equal 360-degrees, which is the total number of degrees in a circle.

[32-point compass rose illustration courtesy of Wikipedia Commons, the free media repository; Brosen derivative work: Auanika (talk) - Brosen_windrose.svg]

N - North
NbE - North by East
NNE - North Northeast
NEbN - Northeast by North
NE - Northeast
NbE - Northeast by East
ENE - East Northeast
EbN - East by North
E - East
EbS - East by South
ESE - East Southeast
SEbE – Southeast by East
Southeast
SEbE - Southeast by South
ESE – East S
SbE – South by East
S - South

SbW - South by West
SSW - South Southwest
SWbS – Southwest by South
SW - Southwest
SWbS - Southwest by West
WSW - West Southwest
West by South
W - West
WbN - West by North
WNW - West Northwest
NWbW – Northwest by West
NW - Northwest
NWbN – Northwest by North
NNW – North Northwest
NbW - North by West
N – North (repeat)

Deck – on any boat, the flooring that you walk on is called the deck or decking. On super yachts, teak is the preferred wood for the floor due to its ease of maintenance. See teak definition below. When there are multiple floors or levels on a ship, each level is referred to as a deck. Here are some examples: The "upper deck" is the topmost deck unless it is topped by a "bridge deck" or an "observation deck." The "main deck" is where most of the ship's activity occurs. "Lower deck" has the vessel's engines and bilge pumps, water storage and other mechanical or electrical systems.

Deckhand – a person who serves as crew on a boat that works lines, anchors, sails (if any), fenders, the operation of small boats, maintenance to the boat itself, keeping the boat exterior clean, safe, and operational. There may be other job duties that are not listed here and that depend on the type of vessel, the captain, location, and skill level. Overall, these are men and women that help run the vessel.

Dinghy – any small boat (with or without a mast) that serves multiple needs, from traveling from shore to ship or between places, racing, or pleasure. These small boats can be constructed from wood, metal, rubber (inflatable) or fiberglass. They can be powered by wind (sails), outboard motors or by rowing.

Dinghy Dolly – A dolly is a lightweight metal trailer with two inflatable rubber wheels that transports a small rowboat to a launching site.

Displacement - the amount of water moved by the boat's hull or object placed directly in the water. Hull displacement describes the volume of water moved by the space it occupies.

Epaulette – Worn on the shoulder of a yacht crew or captain's uniform, the word comes from epaule, which is the word for shoulder in French. Hundreds of years ago, soldiers would tie ribbons to their shoulder to prevent their bayonet or sword belt from slipping. Traditionally, captains wore two, and lieutenants wore one. The uniform system has evolved in modern times and yachts use them to communicate rank aboard ship. Symbols and their colors on the epaulette or shoulder boards reveal your job aboard:

Anchor = Captain, First Officer, and Deckhands

Propellor = Engineers

Crescent moon = Stewardesses; the historic symbol of the moon refers to food, and it was used by Napoleon when he introduced crescent-shaped bread, also known as croissants, into the rations for the Grande Armée.

Four stripes = Captain or Chief Engineer

Three stripes = First Officer, First Engineer, Chief Stewardess or Chef

Two stripes = Bosun, Second Stewardess, Second Engineer

One stripe = Deckhand, Third Stewardess, Third Engineer

E.P.I.R.B. (Emergency Positioning Indicating Radio Beacon) – A personal safety device that activates upon entering the water or is manually turned on. It sends a signal which is picked up by satellites and sent to search and rescue teams. Alerts, locates, tracks, and recovers the individual or vessel.

Fenders – inflated plastic or rubber tubes that protect the boat when tied up alongside a dock or other boat. They are tied to the boat and hung over the side where the boat touches another object. They can be small, for a rowboat, or extra-large for a yacht. In ancient days, ropes would be woven intricately to protect a boat. In some scenarios, tugboats use recycled automotive tires to act as fenders.

Flemishing - To "flemish down a line" means that you coil the line on a flat surface, such as a deck or dock, by starting with the bitter end (the end part that is not being used) and lay it on the deck in successive circles of line in the manner of a clock spring with the bitter end at the center. It is important to know that right-laid line is laid down clockwise and left-laid line is laid down counter-clockwise. This helps the line lay flat, prevent unnecessary knots, trip hazards, and aids in drying the line.

Galley – the kitchen area on a boat where food and drinks are prepared. It can be very tiny and consist of a sink and cutting board on a small boat with a portable stove or BBQ for cooking off the side of the boat, or it can be a full-scale kitchen that could serve a small military on board a ship. Most super yachts have a full array of high-end professional restaurant grade equipment, multiple floor-to-ceiling or walk-in freezers and refrigerators, dishwashers, stacking convection ovens that can hold, for example, several trays of bread, and much more. The galley can be plumbed (piped) for natural gas (propane) or operate completely as an electricity-sourced power supply.

Gunnel - the top edge of the hull of a ship or boat. Originally, the structure was the "gunwale" on a sailing warship, a horizontal reinforcing band added at and above the level of a gun deck to off-set the stresses created by firing artillery (Wikipedia). The gunnel, now, has more functions on different boats. Sailboats have scupper holes to allow water to run off the decks built into the gunnel. Cleats can be mounted on the gunnel. Having a raised gunnel along a deck creates a place for a foot to brace one's body against the angle of the vessel when underway. Gunnels can also have padding on small boats to protect the edge. Oarlocks are often inserted into the gunnels or mounted just inside the gunnel.

Head – The toilet or bathroom on board a boat. In the olden days, the box for the toilet was built into the bow or "head" of the ship, typically one on port and starboard, and the biological waste matter would drop into the sea. It is believed that the water action from the bow wave would wash the side of the ship. Sailors used these boxes primarily to defecate, preferring to stand at the leeward rails to relieve themselves of urine on the side that the wind wouldn't blow it back on themselves.

Helm – the steering mechanism on a boat. It can be a wheel, which is typical on all powerboats, or it can be a tiller, which is a "long handle or rod" typically made of wood connected to the rudder which is steered by pulling or pushing it to port or starboard or simply keeping it amidships. On ultra-modern yachts, the helm may be a joystick attached to a computer system, much like a gaming console.

Hydronym – from the Greek hydro meaning water and nym meaning name. On nautical charts and maps, hydronyms label oceans, seas, rivers, lakes, ponds, and even waterfalls and springs.

Jet Ski – this is the brand name of a personal watercraft (PWC) manufactured by Kawasaki, a Japanese company. However, the term is generically used to denote any type of personal watercraft used for recreational play. It is a gas-powered water toy that one rides on, similar to a motorcycle. All PWC come with inherent risks of injury when used improperly or falling off one, since these PWC can reach speeds of 40-70 miles per hour. Falling off a jet ski and hitting the water at any speed is painful and can result in death or serious injury.

Knots – refers to both ropes and lines tied in a particular fashion, but also the speed across the water. "We were traveling at 2 knots per hour, and it seemed like we would never reach our destination." While it may seem like the phrase may have come from traveling "nautical miles"... and naut sounds like knot, read the knot meter explanation below, to further learn how knots in a line were used to measure a nautical mile, then decide.

Knot Meter – a meter that measures your speed across the water. In the olden days, a line on a spool would be thrown over the side and timed until it reached a certain length off the spool. This would tell the sailor how fast they were going. A simple device can be installed in the hull of a boat that consists of a tiny paddle wheel attached to a transducer. The transducer is hooked up to a simple meter that has a speedometer and a needle to point to the numerical speed. In modern times, a knot meter has a device inside it called a transmitter and a receiver. The transmitter sends a ping down to the ground or floor of the lake or sea and it bounces back up to the surface where it is received by a receiver. The computer translates the difference over the water into a meaningful number for the sailor.

Kraken - a legendary and mythological sea monster of gigantic size and cephalopod-like appearance in Scandinavian folklore. A popular phrase is "release the Kracken," meaning to wreak destruction and terror upon the enemy.

Latitude – the angular distance of a place north or south of the equator. It is expressed in degrees of latitude or minutes of latitude and parallels of latitude. The parallel lines to the equator go from the north pole to the south pole. San Francisco is roughly 38-degrees of latitude north of the equator on planet Earth. Here are the coordinates for San Francisco as obtained from Google: 37.7749° N, 122.4194° W. See longitude and coordinate definitions.

Lazarette – a storage compartment, under a seat on a boat. The heavy lid opens on a set of hinges and has a latch, if it is meant to be locked.

Leeward – the side protected from the wind.

Line – all rope and even the anchor rope and chain tied together is called a line (or rode) once it reaches the maritime environment. Lines are used to tie off a boat, become or are called sheets when attached to the sails, are used as halyards to hoist sails, shrouds, and stays to hold up the mast, and too many other terms to mention here. See the entry below for rope to learn when rope is called rope on a boat.

Longitude – the angular distance of a place east or west of the meridian in Greenwich, England. It is expressed in degrees and minutes. These lines are not parallel and begin at the north pole and end at the south pole. Longitude lines make the earth look like the segments of an orange, pointy at the top and bottom, wide in the middle.

Loom – The inboard part of an oar.

Marine – relates to the sea and the practice of sailing across the sea. Mar in Latin means sea. Here are a few examples of how the word is used: marine radio, marine chart, marine life, marine biology (study of sea life), marine painter (someone who paints seascapes or ships), marines (military that supports naval operations), mariner (to describe a sailor), mariscos (Spanish word for seafood), and maritime law (laws that govern the sea.)

Mast – any tall, vertical structure on a boat that has a light atop, or holds a sail, radio antenna or other device.

Midline – the centerline of any vessel that divides the boat in half for ease of referencing sides, direction, location, and steering. "Keep your helm midline to maintain your compass heading."

Nautical – anything that pertains or relates to ships, sailors, navigation, meaning maritime. Both Greek (nautikos, from nautēs meaning sailor) and Latin (nauticus) have a common root word: naus meaning ship.

Nautical Mile (NM) – nautical miles are used to measure the distance traveled through the water. A nautical mile is slightly longer than a mile on land. If you were to use land or statute miles, it would equal 1.1508 miles (1.85km). The nautical mile is based on the Earth's longitude and latitude coordinates, with one nautical mile equaling one minute of latitude. Degrees of latitude are approximately 60 nautical miles apart. Each minute of latitude is divided into 60-seconds. This makes navigation calculations somewhat easier. 60 x Distance = Speed x Time. The 60 refers to minutes in an hour used in all (T)ime calculations. An easy way to remember this formula is the address "60 D Street" or 60D=ST also written as (60)(D)=(S)(T), which is a simple algebraic equation. Also see Knots.

Oar – Traditionally made from Douglas fir, spruce, or ash, it is a long pole used to propel a boat through the water. Oars can have a spoon shape at the end or a rectangular blade. The oar is placed in a metal oarlock, which provides a leverage point (fulcrum) for maneuvering through the water.

Oarlock – The piece of metal hardware that holds an oar. Oarlocks typically have a small latch or clasp across the top that acts like a gate to keep the oar from popping up. The post part is called a tholepin and slips inside the gunnel where it acts like a fulcrum (leverage point) for pulling the boat through the water.

Passerelle - the single or double-telescoping type passerelle is a design that increases and enhances the stowed efficiency of the plank used to walk from a yacht's stern to the dock. By doubling the plank-sections, the ratio of stowed length to deployed length is increased. This allows the pocketing hydraulic passerelle to be used in a variety of boarding conditions and stowed in shorter spaces in the yacht.

Phonetic Alphabet Used By The American Military - When conditions are poor over a two-way radio or telephone, or there is a noisy background, spelling out important words or numbers is critical to avoid confusion. The letters B, D, and P often sound the same, so using a word to explain yourself is helpful. In this case, you would use "Bravo, Delta, Papa" to distinguish the differences.

A	Alpha		N	November
B	Bravo		O	Oscar
C	Charlie		P	Papa
D	Delta		Q	Quebec
E	Echo		R	Romeo
F	Foxtrot		S	Sierra
G	Golf		T	Tango
H	Hotel		U	Uniform
I	India		V	Victor
J	Juliet		W	Whiskey
K	Kilo		X	X-ray
L	Lima		Y	Yankee
M	Mike		Z	Zulu

Port – the left side of the boat as you face forward. This is also the side of the boat that historically would be clean and could be used to approach a dock, quay, or wharf for offloading goods. The starboard side is the right side, and back in the Viking days it was the side the sailors would use the bathroom. You can remember port is on the left because the words left and port both have four letters in it. (PS: Starboard and right have more letters; now you can't forget.)

Rope – is any group of natural (e.g., plant or animal), synthetic (e.g., polypropylene, nylon) or metal (e.g., steel, and other alloys made into cables) yarns, plies, fibers or stands that are twisted or braided together into larger, thicker or stronger form to increase tensile strength by distributing the load to different strands. Ropes are used for lifting, dragging, tying, and weaving primarily for, but not limited to, the maritime environment. On a boat, a rope is called a line. See the entry above for line to learn more.

The only time rope is called rope is when it is a bell rope, which your hand holds to bang the clapper to the sides of the bell to ring it; tow rope, which is used to tow a boat behind your boat and hopefully not the other way around; rope ladder, used for a swim ladder; bolt rope, which is attached to the luff edge and foot of a mainsail; tiller rope, which is used on a sailboat to tie off the tiller when not in use so it doesn't flop around the cockpit or to tie the tiller off on a course; foot rope, which tall ship sailors stood on to reef, furl and stow the top sails; and the man rope, which are the two ropes people can hold to assist with boarding and disembarking a vessel.

Rope Trivia – "Learning the ropes" is a term that goes all the way back to becoming a sailor on a tall ship. New recruits had to learn what all the ropes were used for, how to manipulate the ropes to move the ship and how to tie knots. "Teaching someone the ropes" was done by someone with tremendous experience and knowledge of the ropes...and one would hope, patience and good humor.

Rowboat – A small boat that is manually powered by oars, typically seating one to two people. Rowboats were built to bring people from shore to a larger boat at anchor and back. Rowboats come in all materials, shapes, and sizes. The person propelling the boat is called a rower, but if they are in the stern giving orders, they are called a coxswain. If they are steering the rowboat, they are the steersman.

Rowlock – Pronounced and often spelled rollock, it is the metal hardware that holds an oar on the gunnel of a small boat. The post part that goes inside the wall of the boat inside the gunnel is called a tholepin. See oarlock.

Sea Room – This is the space around a vessel for maneuvering. Either there is room to move or there is not. The helmsperson may call for sea room if another vessel is obstructing their ability to conduct the vessel safely.

Shakedown Cruise - is a nautical term in which the performance of a ship is tested near marine services whereby the ship can return if something goes wrong or needs to be adjusted after being worked on. Maiden Voyage is a ship's first trip of note. A shakedown cruise can occur after every haul-out where yard work may have been done on the hull, propeller, engines and other equipment are repaired or installed. The idea is to test the vessel (or a new crew that's been installed) before taking the vessel on an extended cruise so that if anything goes wrong, the ship can turn around and return to port to correct the problem(s).

Skeg – the fin underneath the rear of a surfboard. It can also be a tapered or projecting piece of the stern section of a vessel's keel, which protects the propeller or rudder. Kayak's may have skegs that are retractable. At the bottom of an outboard engine, there is a small skeg just before the propeller. The skeg "takes the hit" so the propeller doesn't have to. Skegs also provide directional stability, lateral resistance, and steering when the engine is not running. Skegg in Scandinavian means "beard." Next time you see a skeg, consider if it looks somewhat like a beard!

Sous-Chef – the top or highest assistant in a professional kitchen that supports the chef. This person is in charge of the production of the food. The head chef is the creative force, the boss and administrator of the kitchen, or galley.

Stern – the back of the boat. The stern can have three areas, if it is square and boxy. The port quarter, the starboard quarter and dead-astern.

Stern line – the rope or line attached to the back end of the boat that is used to secure it, so it doesn't drift away.

Steward/Stewardess – also known as a stew or stu, these are men and women who serve the owner or guests on board the yacht, meet their needs and are often "people pleasers," making sure everyone is enjoying their time aboard the boat. They cover all duties including food and beverage service, housekeeping, laundry, and concierge activities such as obtaining tickets to a movie or concert. They may be part of the support staff for the galley. On occasion, they are required without a moment's notice to serve as a deckhand when docking the vessel or anchoring.

Teak – teak is an oily, tropical hardwood used for centuries to build boats. It is super resilient to walking on and maintains itself in all marine conditions.

Tholepin – The part of an oarlock that sits inside the gunwale of the rowboat. It is the post that is held inside the rail of the boat and acts like a fulcrum for rowing.

Transom – the flat part of the stern that forms the back wall of the boat. This part of the yacht may have an extended swim platform or step on to go ashore. In smaller boats, an outboard engine may be hung from it.

True – When a boat is determined to be true, it is the fully realized or fulfilled dream of the boatbuilder.

VHF (VERY HIGH FREQUENCY) VOCABULARY IN LAYMAN'S TERMS

Affirmative – Yes. (When speaking on a radio, the words yes and no can be easily misunderstood.)

Break, Break – inzterruption to the transmission to communicate urgently. Sometimes, people listen in on conversations and have something valuable to add something to the transmission. Saying, "Break, break" allows the caller and receiver to stop talking to hear a 3rd party chime in.

Come In – Inviting someone to talk to you or acknowledge they can hear you.

Emergency/Emergency – use this only if you are in grave or imminent danger to life and immediate assistance is needed.

Figures – I'm about to say numbers. For example, "My depth here is, figures, one-five feet" --meaning 15 feet of water.)

Go Ahead – tells the other party you are ready to listen.

I Spell – I'm going to use the phonetic alphabet to spell out something that might be difficult to understand. Example, "I'm anchored at Mary Island. I spell, Mike, Alpha, Romeo, Yankee." Most radios have a sticker with the phonetic alphabet or find it in your radio's owner's manual. You may always post a copy of the list next to your radio.

Over – I've completed my message and am asking the other party to reply.

Over and Out – Combo of two phrases meaning, "I'm complete with my sending and expect no reply from you."

Out – I've finished my message and expect no further reply.

Negative – No. (When speaking on a radio, the words yes and no can be misunderstood.)

Read You Loud And Clear – informs the other party that their transmission is good

Roger/Roger That – I received and understood your message. 10-4 and Copy That are also used.

Roger So Far – confirms with the speaker that part of their message has been received, especially if it is a long message.

Say Again – please repeat your last message.

Stand By – Wait for a short period and I will get back to you

Wilco – OK. I not only understood your last transmission, but I will also comply. (This is a contraction of the two words will comply.)

Watch – every qualified person on board a yacht has a turn being "on watch," which means they are caring for some aspect of the boat in the capacity they are appointed to. Here are some examples: steering, repair, routine maintenance, security, or normal operations. On superyachts, crew on "night watch" often clean the windows, mop floors, straighten pillows on deck chairs, and other relatively quiet duties that do not disturb the guests who are sleeping. Day watch crew may include vessel operations, such as moving the boat from one location to another, housekeeping and laundry, engine operations and more. Sometimes a crew member may say, "I'm on galley duty" rather than "galley watch." Night and day watch responsibilities always include making sure that the people are safe, the boat is safe, and the environment is safe. Phrases: keeping watch, on watch, my watch is about to begin (or almost over), and even "can I swap watches with you?" –and they don't mean the timepiece on your wrist!

Here are the maritime "watch standards" for keeping watch:

Middle Watch	Midnight to 4 AM (0000 – 0400)
Morning Watch	4 AM to 8 AM (0400 – 0800)
Forenoon Watch	8 AM to Noon (0800 – 1200)
Afternoon Watch	Noon to 4 PM (1200 – 1600)
First Dog Watch	4 PM to 6 PM (1600 – 1800)
Second Dog Watch	6 PM to 8 PM (1800 – 2000)
First Watch	8 PM to Midnight (2000 – 0000)

Wheelhouse – the area or room that is enclosed on a boat that includes the wheel for steering the boat. On larger boats, it is also called the bridge. It could even be a platform that is constructed in such a way that the officer stands on it and commands the vessel from there.

Windward – the side the wind is approaching from.

LIST OF CHARACTERS for SEA DOG

Passenger List

Abercrombie Family

Mr. Abercrombie – American

Mrs. Abercrombie – American

Grace Abercrombie – American

Adrian Abercrombie – American

Kageyama Family

Mr. Taka Kageyama – Japanese, husband of Natsu, father of Ryu, bodyguard for Sasaki family, INTERPOL Tokyo

Mrs. Natsu Kageyama – Japanese, wife of Taka, mother of Ryu, art dealer in Tokyo and Los Angeles

Ryu Kageyama – Japanese, son of Taka and Natsu Kageyama, student

Sasaki Family

Mrs. Kayoko Sasaki – Japanese, mother of Kanade and Sota, resides in Tokyo

Kanade Sasaki – Japanese, daughter of Mrs. Sasaki, sister to Sota, student

Sota Sasaki – Japanese, son of Mrs. Sasaki, brother to Kanade, student

Thor S. Johnson - Swedish, retired captain, yacht broker, lives in Cyprus

SHIP'S MASTER and CREW LIST

Gunnar Johnson – Captain: Sweden; holds a 100-ton master captain's license

Jimmy Williams – First Officer: Jamaica; steward to Adrian on special assignment, holds a 100-ton master captain's license, certified in SCUBA, lifeguarding, small boats

Pete Ferguson – Chief Engineer: American; California Maritime Academy graduate

Bryce Fraser – Chief Electrical Engineer; American; computer expert, nephew to the captain

Brian Kelly – Deckhand and Bosun: Ireland, longtime friend of Jimmy

James Perkins – Deckhand: England; prefers night watch

Gabriella De Vries – Chief Stewardess: South Africa; personal stewardess to Grace

Jane Higgins – Stewardess: Australia; stewardess to Mr. and Mrs. Abercrombie

Zak Broussard – Chief Chef: American

Jean-Marie Fournier – Sous Chef: France; doubles as a bartender

Roberto Bonnano – Deckhand: Italy; doubles as bartender, occasional steward, likes night watch, cousin to Francesco

Francesco Demattei – Deckhand: Italy; cousin to Roberto

Raffaele "Raffa" Marino – Deckhand: Italy; occasional steward

Colophon

In publishing, a colophon is a brief statement containing information about the publication of a book such as the place of publication, the publisher, and the date of publication. A colophon may include the device of a printer or publisher. - Wikipedia

Kailash Black brings his deep expertise of prepress to The Adventures of Yacht Boy Series. Continuing the style from Shakedown Cruise, the text of Sea Dog is set in Marcia, licensed through the Adobe Font Library, which contains Font Bureau fonts, in the Adobe Creative Suite.

Font Bureau "Marcia" was designed by Victoria Rushton in 2015. It is a didone typeface (also referred to as Neoclassical and Modern typeface as it was born from Didot and Bondoni typefaces), which Wikipedia states is a genre of serif typeface that emerged in the late eighteenth century and was the standard style of general-purpose printing during the nineteenth century. This genre of fonts is characterized by extreme weight contrast between thicks and thins, vertical stress, and serifs with little or no bracketing. Marcia font has many quirks and curvy surprises, which you can observe in the title on the cover of the book.

Helvetica font was used for the name of the series. Helvetica is a mid-century font from the twentieth century and attributed to a typeface designers Max Miedinger and Eduard Hoffman at the Haas Foundry in Switzerland. His goal was to create a sans-serif typeface that was completely neutral and would not contribute any additional meaning. It has become one of the most popular fonts in the world. Helvetica is Latin for Swiss. Look for very definitive vertical and horizontal strokes in this font. Look for the teardrop shape inside the lowercase "a", which is a trademark of Helvetica.

Roboto is a Google font used for digital devices and we choose to highlight the many texts and emails our hero sends from his phone and computer. Roboto is sans serif meaning plain and this makes it easier to read on devices.

The handwriting font selected for Captain Gunnar Johnson is called Chalkduster. Kailash Black modified it slightly to give it a 17° rightward slant, to match the description in the book. This font is often pre-installed on all Macs, as it's owned by Apple.

Courier font is perhaps one of the most recognizable typefaces, possessing a certain plain uniformity, and is based on typewriters. Because it was used by many governments as their official font for decades, it is associated with bureaucracy and stability. If you are looking for consistency in spacing and height, this is a font that is predictable. A little known bit of trivia is that screenplays are written in this font since one page is equivalent to one minute of screen time.

Acknowledgements

This is my favorite part of the book, where I can be transparent and authentic about the gratitude I feel and share with the world around me.

Arigato gozaimasu to my dear friend Chinatsu Kato for helping me pick Japanese names for the new characters in the upcoming book "Mutiny." She is an amazing wife, mother and gourmet chef.

A second round of hat-tips to the most patient prepress hero ever...Kailash Black; and the incredible illustrator of our story, Jon Tocchini. Liza, my editor who shines light on the story and supports it staying on point. What a team!!

And to all my beloved readers who shared their experience with Shakedown Cruise, and desire to get reading this second book...I welcomed your words into my heart! It is a pleasure to write for you.

Finally, to my husband Anand, so steadfast and true. I would not be empowered to write without your loving attention on our family. You have my eternal love and gratitude. Salute!

Biographies

Anne Marie Peterson
Author

Annie Peterson is a third generation native San Franciscan. She spent her youth sail racing SF Bay and cruising the California coast and inland waterways as a sea scout and achieved the top rank of Quartermaster (Boy Scouts of America Sea Explorer Program). An avid traveler and adventure seeker, the world provides inspiration for the many oil paintings and stories she creates from exotic destinations. When she is not writing or helping others heal their consciousness for optimal experiences, she spends her time with her husband and two young children in Los Angeles. To learn more about her work, please visit www.LeapofConsciousness.com

Jon Tocchini
Artist/Illustrator

Jon Tocchini is an artist born and raised in San Francisco, California. He received his B.F.A. degree from the Academy of Art University, Fine Art School, San Francisco, CA, USA. He is a member of the California Art Club (CAC) and Associate Member of the Oil Painters of America (OPA). To see Jon's artwork, please visit www.FineArtByJon.com

**Thank you for reading
Sea Dog - The Adventures of Yacht Boy**

Please leave an honest review of this book on Amazon.
Your comments support others determining if this book
is something they would enjoy, find valuable, or helpful in
learning more about the world.

You may find us on multiple Social Media platforms
under Young Navigator Books.

Manufactured by Amazon.ca
Bolton, ON

34184430R00189